Minor Leagues,
Major Boom

Minor Leagues, Major Boom

Local Professional Baseball Revitalized

JON C. STOTT

for Doug Brunson
my friend & Telus Field
neighbor
— with all good wishes ,

[signature]

[illegible] April 24/04
Opening day 2004

McFarland & Company, Inc., Publishers
Jefferson, North Carolina, and London

To Mel Kowalchuk, Dennis Henke,
and Sophie Caroline
and to the memory of
Pat McKernan and Joe Buzas

LIBRARY OF CONGRESS CATALOGUING-IN-PUBLICATION DATA

Stott, Jon C.
  Minor leagues, minor boom : local professional baseball
revitalized / Jon C. Stott.
      p.   cm.
  Includes bibliographical references and index.

  ISBN 0-7864-1759-5 (softcover : 50# alkaline paper) ♾

  1. Minor league baseball—Economic aspects—United
States. I. Title.
  GV880.S86   2004
  796.357'64—dc22   2004002814

British Library cataloguing data are available

Front cover photograph ©2004 Corbis Images

Manufactured in the United States of America

McFarland & Company, Inc., Publishers
  Box 611, Jefferson, North Carolina 28640
    www.mcfarlandpub.com

Table of Contents

Preface. Rediscovering the Minor Leagues

TYEES FOLD! BASEBALL CLUB BANKRUPT

It was August 2, 1954. I stared in shock at the banner headline of the afternoon paper my father had put on the kitchen counter. Late this morning, the lead paragraph stated, the Victoria Professional Baseball Club had announced that it was financially unable to continue operations. I didn't know until 30 years later that Victoria was just one of 18 minor-league teams that did not complete their seasons in 1954.[1] All I understood was that the center of my summers, the Tyees of the Single-A Western International League, no longer existed. During three summers, my sister and I had spent our Saturday afternoons in the knothole gang section of the left field bleachers of Victoria's Royal Athletic Park cheering for our heroes, Cece Garriott, Granny Gladstone, Don Pries, and Bob Moniz. They would play amateur ball at Royal Athletic Park for several years after 1954, but I never visited the stadium again.

My father, who didn't like watching baseball—five innings, he used to grumble, were more than enough—did appreciate my sense of loss. A week later, on a family vacation in Vancouver, he took me to a game at Capilano Stadium, home of the Tyees' hated rivals, the Caps, who, I again learned later, had had more than once purchased former Victoria players, helping themselves while keeping the financially struggling Tyees solvent. But I couldn't muster any enthusiasm for the game. By the next summer, Elvis Presley, Little Richard, and Barbara Bowen (a cute redhead who lived two blocks over on Quimper Street) had driven baseball from my mind. Over the next 25 years, I doubt if I watched more than a dozen minor league games. Summer jobs in the forests of western Canada, followed by graduate school, then a career in university teaching, and a growing family commanded my time and energy and gave me my greatest joy.

In 1981, Edmonton, Alberta, where I was then teaching, joined the Pacific Coast League, and, once or twice a year, my family and I made the mile walk through the park to John Ducey Field to watch the Trappers. But looking at the blanks in the score cards I've saved from those visits and the fact that the columns for the eighth and ninth innings were seldom completed, I realize that I spent as much time taking the kids to the bathroom and waiting in concession lines as I did watching the games. And sitting for nine innings on the splintery wooden bleacher seats of aging John Ducey Field was as impossible for the children as it would have been for my father.

My waning and gradually reviving interest in minor-league baseball, I now realize, paralleled that of fans in general. In 1952, when I first sat in the left field bleachers, clapping as outfielder Bob Moniz entertained us with headstands during pitching changes, 312 teams played in 44 minor leagues. Four years later, when Elvis, Little Richard, and Barbara entered my life, the numbers had shrunk to 240 teams in 33 leagues. By 1970, 140 teams played in 20 leagues. While adolescent passions accounted for my initial loss of interest, historians blamed the expansion of major-league telecasts into minor-league markets and the joys of spending hot summer nights in air-conditioned homes or at lakeside cottages.

I also didn't realize that, just when I began attending occasional Trapper games, minor-league baseball had started its gradual comeback. In 1981, over 500,000 fans watched Denver Bear games in the American Association and 13 teams topped 200,000 in attendance. In 1988 the movie *Bull Durham* convinced people across the country that going to minor-league games could be fun, and, in the final year of the decade, Buffalo topped the million mark for the second of six consecutive seasons, while 14 other teams attracted over 300,000 fans. Even Eugene, Oregon, playing just over 40 home dates, drew 141,000 spectators. Minor-league baseball was on the way back.

However, until August 1994, baseball, for me, was still a sometime thing. Then I discovered that my love of the minor leagues, which I thought had died at Capilano Stadium in 1954, was not dead, just dormant. My grown son and I were helping my daughter to move to Knoxville, to continue her studies at the University of Tennessee. As our route would take us through Cincinnati, he suggested that we stop to see the Reds. Even my daughter—who had inherited her grandfather's low tolerance for sitting at ballparks—agreed. But, just before our arrival, the major league strike began, and we drove straight through the Queen City, only slowing down slightly to glance to our left at vacant Riverfront Stadium.

Two days later, my son handed me the front page of the *Knoxville Sentinel*. "Look," he said, pointing to a picture of the general manager of the Smokies draping a huge banner over the entrance to Bill Meyer Stadium. "We're not on strike," the five-foot-high letters exclaimed. "Baseball tonight!" And so we went to a professional game, but not the major-league one we'd originally planned.

The park, my daughter noted as we drove into the free parking lot, looked like a set from *Bull Durham*. In an industrial area northeast of the city center, it was constructed of cinder blocks, a well-weathered wooden roof covered the grandstand, three tiers of signs lined the outfield walls, the Marlboro Man loomed above the fence in right-center, and beyond left field, a 100-foot length of 29-foot-high netting protected the windows of the neighboring factory.

We had fun: we watched kids collect autographs from players younger

Built in 1955, Bill Meyer Stadium, home of the Knoxville Smokies of the Southern League, was typical of the type of park that was fast-disappearing in the 1990s. In 2002, the team moved to a new park and promptly set a franchise attendance record of 256,141.

than my son and daughter, bought coffee mugs at the souvenir counter, ate tasteless hot dogs and drank flat beer and enjoyed both, shook hands with a mascot dressed as some kind of bird, watched dozens of bats swoop across the outfield harvesting mosquitoes, and tried in vain to cheer the home team Smokies to a victory. On the way out, my son bought me a navy blue hat with a white "S" (for Smokies) on the front. "They'll think it stands for Stott, when we get home," he insisted. I still wear it when I go to games.

For me, the high point of the evening came in the third inning. The man sitting in the row in front of us, who had been explaining to his eager son and less enthusiastic daughter and wife the intricacies of keeping score, turned to ask whether I'd call the close play at first a hit or an error on the shortstop, who'd had trouble coming up cleanly with a sharp grounder to his right. We discussed the variables, agreed it was an infield single, and muttered in derision when the scoreboard flashed an "E" (for error) sign.

"Do you come to the games often?" he asked, and when I explained that we were from out of town and that it was our first Smokies game, he replied that it was the first time for his family. He lived four miles from Chicago's Wrigley Field; but, he told me, he'd become tired of the traffic, the parking problems, the ticket prices, and particularly the attitudes and salaries of the players. Two years ago, he began taking day and later week-end trips to nearby cities in the Midwest League. "The kids like the hotel pools, my wife and daughter go the the mall in the afternoon, and we all have dinner at the ballpark. It doesn't cost much more than if we all went to Wrigley Field."

He used to play baseball; his son played; and his wife—an Australian— was beginning to understand the rules. The little girl, five years old, was happy if the concessions stocked cotton candy and if she could shake hands with the mascot, buy a pennant, and fall asleeep in her mother's lap. This was their first extended minor-league road trip; it had gone well, and they were planning to head to the Texas League in 1995. I would later learn that, except for the fact they had come from so far away, this family represented the target audience of the people who now operated teams in the minor leagues.

"What a great idea that family had—traveling to see minor-league games," I said to my family as we drove back to my daughter's apartment.

"Not for us, Dad," my son replied. "But why don't you do it? Your summers at the university are flexible; you're not tied down by us; and we can look after the house while you're away."

It wasn't quite so easy as that: there were more summer duties at the university than I had thought about, and, with their mother having recently passed away, my adult kids liked having me at home more than they let on. But I did attend lots of games in Edmonton, more each year than I'd gone to in all the preceding 40 years.

I also began to plan the times and routes of my academic research travels, my May and August trips to Tennessee to accompany my daughter home for summer jobs and back to school, and vacation visits to old friends so that I passed through towns and cities that had now become magical to me because they had minor-league ball clubs. When the team was in town, I stopped for the night; if not, I took pictures of the stadium and moved on. And I chatted with whatever front-office people I could buttonhole, asking questions about running minor-league teams. In Edmonton, the Trappers moved into their new stadium in 1995, and I spent many summer evenings in my favorite seat—last row of the grandstand, just to the left of home plate. After Labor Day, which signaled the end of the season and the beginning of the university year, I read the growing number of books on minor-league ball, and watched my mailbox for the biweekly arrival of *Baseball America*. In January, when the Trappers released the coming season's schedule, I began counting down the days until Opening Day.

David Lamb's *Stolen Season*[2] and Ernest J. Green's *The Diamonds of Dixie*,[3] the first minor-league books I read, increased my urge to travel to distant baseball cities. Lamb, a foreign correspondent for the *Los Angeles Times*, and Green, a university professor, were both my age, had loved baseball as boys and had then drifted away from it. In 1989, Lamb had taken an unpaid leave from the paper and made a circular journey from and back to California, visiting fifteen minor-league cities and rediscovering an America and a sports enthusiasm he'd lost in his years abroad. Green took the summer of 1993 off from his college near the Washington, D.C. area and traveled through the South, going to games in 30 cities and chronicling the changes in the parts of the country he'd known in his youth.

I shared my enthusiasm for the books with my son, who, after reading them told me, "You should write one, too!" Then he added, "And more people would be interested in it than that freshman textbook you're doing." I explained to him the importance of professional duties and obligations. However, I did write a few pieces about my baseball travels for the Edmonton Trappers' Yearbook and a couple of articles for *Nine*, a baseball journal. And, in 1999 and 2000, I visited and wrote about the independent leagues that had sprung up in the 1990s.[4] However, the idea of doing a book about the affiliated minor leagues, the member organizations of the National Association of Professional Leagues, remained dormant until the fall of 2001. As the year's first snows fell on Edmonton, Alberta, and the land and most of the animals moved into a five-month period of dormancy, the idea came back into my consciousness. With all my writing obligations fulfilled and having retired from university teaching, I realized that I could devote the upcoming winter, the spring and summer of 2002, and the fall and winter of the next year reading and thinking about, then watching, and finally writing about minor-league baseball.

My focus would be on the 2002 season, the 101st in the National Association's long history. I'd spend time visiting one club from each of the minor league classifications from advanced rookie to Triple-A, examining the two main aspects of minor-league baseball: that taking place on the field, involving players, coaches, and managers, all of them controlled by major-league organizations, and that taking place in the stands, in the front offices, and the communities, the facet controlled by team owners, general managers and their staffs.

But first, I would examine the historical background, the period since 1990, against which the 2002 season would be played. As the snowbanks along the sidewalk rose and the temperatures dropped, I reread the over 50 books that had been written about the minors, my six years of bound copies of *Baseball America*, and a foot-high stack of reporter's notebooks I'd been keeping since 1995, which were filled with observations and quotes from the conversations with on-field and off-field baseball people. The results of my "Hot Stove League" reading, thinking, and writing form the basis of this book's introduction: "1991–2001: The Coming of Age of the 'New' Minors."

On March 21, 2002, the official beginning of spring, the northern Alberta snow still lay deep, not only in my front yard, but also on the diamond of Edmonton's Telus Field, five miles distant. However, that morning, the mailman delivered my copy of the *Baseball America Directory 2002*. It contained schedules for all minor-league teams, and, as I studied them, planning my itinerary, I realized that the real beginning of spring— Opening Day—was only two weeks away. During the next five months, I watched baseball games in Edmonton; Rancho Cucamonga, California; Billings, Montana; El Paso, Texas; Lansing, Michigan; and Mahoning Valley, Ohio. I talked with players—first-round draft choices and players who hadn't been selected; managers and coaches—some who'd played in the majors and others who'd never made the show and begun their coaching careers at colleges; umpires—from around the country and from Japan. I visited with scouts, broadcasters, newspaper reporters; learned about the intricacies of front-office management from owners, general managers, and community relations directors; and discovered the anxieties experienced by mothers, fathers, wives, and girlfriends. My encounters and observations make up the main portion of the book. (Unless otherwise noted, all quotations are from personal interviews.) Finally, after I had spent much of the fall and winter after the 2002 season writing about my experiences, I contemplated the state of flux and change that is the essential nature of the off-season in the minor leagues.

During the research and writing of this book, I have been assisted by a great number of people. The baseball people whose names and conversations are recorded on the following pages gave freely of their time to talk about the game for which they hold so much respect and love. I must especially thank Gary Tater and Denyse Conroy of the Edmonton Trappers, two extremely knowledgeable and deeply committed baseball people, for their ongoing help and encouragement. Denyse generously supplied some of the photos accompanying the chapter on the Edmonton Trappers. The many people who had written about minor-league baseball before I began my project have provided information and insights which have guided my explorations.

Finally, I must comment on the five names appearing on the dedication page. The late Joe Buzas and Pat McKernan represent the many people who kept minor-league baseball alive during the very lean years between 1955 and 1975. Buzas, who purchased his first team in 1957, always ran a small and tight-fisted organization. But, at a time when bankrupt clubs often folded in mid-season and and disappeared in the dead of night, he had a reputation of always paying his bills on time and even making a small yearly profit. Pat McKernan, who began working for Buzas in the 1960s, went on to become the president of the Eastern League and for two decades president and general manager of the Albuquerque Dukes of the Pacific Coast League. Between 1974 and 1981, he worked tirelessly to keep the Eastern League afloat, securing franchises in such unlikely cities as Thetford Mines, Quebec, and Holyoke, Massachusetts. In the last season of his leadership, the league drew 620,893 people, the second-highest attendance in over two decades.

Mel Kowalchuk and Dennis Henke are two Canadians whose careers embody the incredibly hard work, dedication, and creative thinking that have characterized the leaders of the successful clubs of the minor league renaissance of the final two decades of the 20th century. Kowalchuk, who served as general manager of the Edmonton Trappers from 1981 to 2001, was instrumental in pro baseball's northernmost city securing a Pacific Coast League franchise. With Dennis Henke, who joined him in 1983 and is still the club's assistant general manager, Kowalchuk built one of the most stable and respected minor-league organizations of the 1980s and 1990s. Operating out of a very old and small park, fighting frequently bad early spring weather, and living under the shadow of the city's hugely popular National Hockey League and Canadian Football League clubs, the Trappers regularly attracted an average of 250,000 fans, a figure that increased 70 percent when they moved into their new park in 1995. Henke and Kowalchuk, along with such other minor-league executives as Salem, Virginia's Sam Lazzaro, Providence, Rhode Island's Ben Mondor and Mike Tamburro, and Little Rock, Arkansas's Bill Valentine, laid the foundations that made possible the minor-league boom of the last decade of the 20th century.

Finally, Sophie Caroline—my very young first grandchild—symbolizes the debt I owe to my family, which has provided so much support in my academic and baseball ventures. I look forward to the not-too-distant seasons, when she can accompany me to the ballpark and learn the pleasures and intricacies of keeping score.

Introduction.
1991–2001: The Coming of Age of the "New" Minors

Between the close of the 1990 season and the start of the 2002 season, the size, structure, and purpose of the National Association of Professional Baseball Leagues—the umbrella organization of the minor leagues—remained essentially unchanged. The number of leagues dropped by one to 16 after the 1997 season when the teams of the American Association were absorbed into the Pacific Coast and International Leagues. The number of clubs increased slightly, from 170 to 181, in order to supply farm teams for the four major-league expansion franchises: Florida, Colorado, Tampa Bay, and Arizona.

Each league maintained its classification in a seven-tier system dating from 1963 that indicated both the level of experience of the players and the size of the host cities. At the bottom, the rookie leagues—Gulf Coast and Arizona—played in the spring training complexes of the major-league clubs. The advanced rookie leagues—the Appalachian and Pioneer—fielded clubs in smaller cities in the southeastern and northwestern mountains respectively. The short-season Single-A leagues—the New York–Pennsylvania and Northwest—were bicoastal, in both the United States and Canada. The low and high Single-A leagues—the Midwest and South Atlantic and the California, Carolina, and Florida State respectively—played full-season schedules in medium sized cities of the geographical areas indicated by their names.[1] The Double-A leagues—Eastern, Southern, and Texas—played in larger cities, while the Triple-A Pacific Coast and International Leagues located in cities which generally had populations of half a million or more.

9

As this classification system implicitly indicates, the main baseball purpose of the minor leagues has been to develop players, moving them up the ranks as their experience increases and abilities improve. The ultimate goal was to provide players of sufficient skill to join major-league clubs. Beginning with the 1963 season, when the major leagues implemented a player development plan that has remained essentially unchanged four decades later, nearly every athlete to play for a National Association team has been under contract to a major-league organization. In 1990, only five teams, three in the high Single-A leagues, one in a short-season Single-A, and one in an advanced rookie league, signed and owned the contracts of their own players. By 1996, there were none. Each year close to 1,200 recently drafted college and high school athletes, along with a lesser number of non-drafted players, were signed by major-league organizations and assigned to minor-league teams where they began the process of development and advancement. Of course, although many were chosen in the draft, few were finally called to the major leagues. Highly rated prospects were given the most opportunities to develop; the others were there to assist in that developmental process by providing a full complement of players for the select few to play with or against.

If the size, structure, and purpose of minor-league baseball changed little with regard to the teams and athletes, the geography and landscape changed enormously, as did the attendance figures and the non-baseball activities in each minor-league park. In the 11-year period following the 1990 season, 71 franchises shifted to new locations. Although in some cases, new National Association teams, in the same or other leagues, replaced the recently departed clubs, 50 cities were left without National Association clubs. During the same period, new stadiums were built in 81 cities, either to keep existing teams from leaving or to lure teams to new locations.

Although the rules and the way the game was played on the field remained unchanged, the names of the clubs and the logos on their uniforms gave a new look to the old game. In 1990, 75 clubs bore the nicknames of their major-league parent clubs; in 2002, the number had dropped to 40. The Jamestown Expos became the Jammers; the Savannah Cardinals, the Sand Gnats; the Quad City Angels, the River Bandits. When the London Tigers moved to Trenton, New Jersey, in 1994, they didn't keep the name of the parent Detroit team; they became the Trenton Thunder. A new name, logo, and uniforms gave a team a distinct, unique, local look and identity, one which didn't have to be altered if the club were to become affiliated with another major-league club.

In the stands, there was also a great change. Each year, there were fewer and fewer empty seats. In 1990, just over 25 million fans attended minor-league games. The numbers rose in nine of the next 11 seasons to nearly 39 million in 2001, an increase of over 50 percent and the largest total attendance since 1949.[2]

As attendance rose, so, too, did the value of minor-league franchises. During the 1970s, most clubs could be purchased for a small fee and the assumption of existing debts. "There used to be a joke," Dennis Henke, the assistant general-manager of the Edmonton Trappers, once remarked, "that the only qualification for owning a minor-league team was the ability to pass the mirror test. They held a mirror under your nose, and if moisture formed it meant you were alive and you qualified." While the story is make-believe, the almost unbelievable escalation of minor-league franchise values is not. In 1978, Joe Buzas, who owned the Eastern League's Bristol, Connecticut, team, was asked by the league to take over the shaky Reading franchise. He bought the team for a dollar, turned it around and, in 1987 sold the club for a handsome profit of one million dollars. He insisted that the bill of sale be for one million *and one* dollars so that he could tell his friends about the earning power of a one-buck investment.

The money he made from the sale of the Reading purchase indirectly helped Buzas purchase what would become his most valuable asset, Salt Lake City of the Pacific Coast League. "The Coast League approached me about buying and running their Portland team, which had been losing money for several years. Along with Hollywood agent Tino Barzie and actress Pia Zadora, we bought the team. Then, with the Reading money, I bought them out." In 1994, he moved the franchise to Salt Lake City, where the local government had built a multimillion dollar stadium. The baseball team was an instant success, and, after the 2001 season, when Buzas was in failing health, offers reported to be around 14 million dollars were made by investors who wanted to purchase the club.

In 1968, when minor-league attendance reached its post–World War II low, under 10 million people went to games. Nine full-season clubs drew less than 25,000; another 30, under 50,000. Only 20 attracted more than 100,000 spectators. The most successful franchise, the Hawaii Islanders attracted 255,000. It is highly likely that the largest number of people who attended the games were die-hard fans, knowledgeable spectators who watched the action on the diamond with a critical, evaluative eye. The number of die-hard fans had probably not increased much by the 1990s; what had increased was the number of casual fans—college buddies, couples, business associates, and families—who came to the park for an evening's or weekend afternoon's summer entertainment. They cheered when the home team scored, although they might have had little awareness of who the players were, where the team was in the standings, what league it was in, or who its major-league affiliate was.

But there was plenty of other entertainment for them when there wasn't action on the field—or even when there was. Entering the park, fans might receive a gift—anything from a magnetic schedule, to a T-shirt bearing the team's and sponsor's logos, to a bobble-head doll representing a popular major leaguer who'd played with the minor-league team. They might arrive on a special theme night—Hawaiian Day, Elvis Lives, Christmas in July—when front-office and game-day staff dressed accordingly, the music was appropriate, and patrons who wore theme-related attire received discounted admission.

Entertainment would be laid on between innings and during such delays as pitching changes. Then a mascot—a giant baseball, a crawdad, or a hoot owl—would dance on the dugout roofs. Sometimes it might even be the San Diego Chicken, who appeared at over 100 minor-league parks each year. There might be some other traveling entertainer or group, such as the Blues Brothers of Lacrosse, Wisconsin, who entered the park in a beat-up car and then lip-synched songs from the popular movie

The Blues Brothers, one of the many groups that tour minor-league parks each year, entertain fans between innings at Toledo's Ned Skeldon Stadium.

between innings. In most parks, there were between-inning contests on the field as fans raced the mascot or couples tried to break as many balloons as possible by pressing against, sitting on, or even lying on top of each other. After the game there might be a fireworks display or a concert by a group like the Beach Boys.

Seating options were no longer limited to box seats consisting of folding aluminum chairs, grandstand reserved seats that were benches with backs, or general admission backless bleacher seats. Corporate big-wigs and schmoozers took out season-long leases on luxury suites that were air-conditioned or heated as the weather demanded. The less affluent enjoyed club seats where attractive young female attendants took food orders. Groups could sit at party decks taking in the action after enjoying an all-you-can-eat pregame buffet. And good-old-boys could cheer on their heroes from open-air sports bars situated behind the outfield walls. In a few places, patrons could rent a hot tub for their group and really get steamed up when they saw the home team losing. And in Reading, Pennsylvania, a small swimming pool beyond center field helped people keep cool even when the home team's bats were hot or the starting pitcher's deliveries were smoking.

Going to baseball games also provided fans with the opportunity to buy apparel and souvenirs ranging from keychains to autographed, game-worn jerseys. T-shirts and hats were the biggest sellers; but coffee cups, shot glasses, and, for a while in Portland, Maine, pasta in the shape of the team mascot, were also available. Everything was prominently stamped with the club's logo, so that purchasers could identify with the home team, while at the same time advertising it. And if young people brought the baby or toddler along, they could start indoctrinating the child on the glories of the local nine by purchasing infant wear. No family outing to the park could be considered complete without spending time at the walk-in gift store. And when parents wanted a break from the kids, they could send the youngsters to the supervised playground behind the bleachers or to the games area conveniently situated next to the concessions stands.

And there was food—not just hot dogs and peanuts, soda and beer, but full-course meals served in restaurants overlooking the field. A person could eat crab cakes in Frederick, Maryland, or tuck into a steak or salmon dinner in Lansing, Michigan. Suite holders could order platters of shrimp for their guests. And adults could wash down their food with beer, not just from the mega-breweries, but also from local micros.

"For the price of a $7 ticket," one slightly cynical grandparent was heard to remark, "you sure get a lot of chances to spend money."

What caused the tremendous changes that occurred in minor-league

The gift shop at Fifth Third Field of Dayton, Ohio, stocks a complete range of Dragons clothing, along with pennants, coffee mugs, and other novelty items.

baseball during the 1990s—the franchise shifts, new stadiums, new nicknames, new ballpark activities, constantly increasing attendance, and soaring franchise values? The reasons are complex and are both baseball and business related. One fact is certain: they didn't happen overnight; they marked the increasing growth of forces that had begun gradually in the 1970s. *Baseball America*, in several articles printed in the 1990s, pointed to earlier signs of the gradually developing minor-league renaissance.[3] In the early 1970s, Jim Paul, owner of the El Paso Diablos, introduced the concept of non-baseball activities as an important part of the family entertainment package and spread his ideas through the minor leagues with an annual seminar. In Columbus, Ohio, a community organization purchased the Charleston, West Virginia, International League team for $25,000 and then spent $5 million renovating Franklin County Stadium. In 1977, their first year in the International League, the Clippers drew 457,251 fans, 110,000 more than any other minor league club. In each of ten seasons between 1978 and 1990, over half a million fans turned out to the renovated park to watch the team.

Fans at the Harry Grove Stadium in Frederick, Maryland, enjoy a full-course buffet supper before a Carolina League game. In addition to concession stands and picnic areas, many new parks feature baanquet rooms and full-service restaurants.

In the winter of 1979–80 Miles Wolff payed a few thousand dollars to purchase an expansion team in the Carolina League. It its first season, the Durham Bulls attracted 175,000 fans to aging Durham Athletic Park to enjoy summer evenings' fun. The club led the league in attendance for nine of ten years during the 1980s, and in 1988, the year the movie based on the team was released, and in 1989, drew 271,000 and 272,000 fans respectively. The movie not only made sales of Bulls' merchandise skyrocket, it also made thousands of people in the United States and Canada consider minor-league ballparks good places in which to spend their entertainment dollars. During the 1980s, the half million season's attendance mark was reached by clubs 23 times. Three times, in Louisville in 1983 and Buffalo in 1988 and 1989, over one million fans attended a team's games in a season.

During the 1980s, over three dozen new parks were constructed. Many were of the steel and aluminum variety, and by the late 1990s many were deemed inadequate, both as revenue producers and in terms of facilities standards established by professional baseball. However, five were har-

bingers of the types of parks to be built in the 1990s. Three International
League stadiums—Richmond's The Diamond, opened in 1985; Buffalo's
Pilot Field, in 1988; and Scranton/Wilkes-Barre's Lackawanna County
Stadium, in 1989—had a combined seating capacity of 44,000. All had lux-
ury boxes, walk-in gift shops, and banquet or restaurant facilities. So did
South Bend's Stanley Coveleski Stadium, the 5,000-seat home of the low
Single A Midwest League's Silver Hawks, which opened in 1988, and Harry
Grove Stadium the 5,400-seat home of the advanced Class A Carolina
League's Keys, built for the 1990 season. Among them, the five teams
attracted 2.6 million fans in 1990. Ten percent of the minor leagues' total
attendance had come from just over three percent of the total number of
teams.

With increasing interest and growing attendance, improved facilities
and good business practices, many minor-league franchises began to show
profits in the 1980s. And, because there was a fixed number of franchises,
many less than there were prospective buyers, franchises rose quickly in

Originally built to attract a major-league franchise, Buffalo's baseball stadium drew
over a million fans a year between 1988 and 1993. The park has had three different
names—Pilot Field, North AmeriCare Park, and Dunn Tire Park—as different businesses have purchased naming rights over the years.

value. During the later 1980s, more than one entrepreneur made considerable profit through flipping franchises, buying a club low, fixing up the business operations, and then, after a couple of good seasons, selling at a very healthy mark-up.

These changes of the 1980s did not pass unnoticed by the Lords of Baseball, the owners of the big-league clubs. During the 1960s and 1970s, for reasons of self-interest, the major-league teams had subsidized minor league teams and, in some cases, owned them. Without National Association teams, they would have had difficulty in developing players. But by 1990, two things became obvious to them: on the one hand, some franchises were worth a lot of money and making a lot; on the other, some of their minor leaguers were playing in substandard facilities that made the risk of serious injury a real possibility. If the minor leagues were making money, the majors didn't want to continue their subsidies, and they wanted a share of the new-found wealth. And they wanted no facilities that were inferior. In the minor leagues, at least, the Lords of Baseball wanted to make sure that it was a level field for all teams—literally, as well as figuratively.

Matters came to a head in 1990 as the major and minor leagues began to negotiate terms for the renewal of the Professional Baseball Agreement, the document that spelled out the relationships between the two levels of professional baseball and established regulations involving minor-league ballpark standards and operating procedures. Negotiations were difficult and hostile; at one point, the major leaguers threatened to stop sending players to the minor leagues and to begin developing all their talent in their Arizona and Florida spring training complexes.

An agreement was reached in time for the 1991 season, but it was one in which conditions imposed by the major leagues made running minor league franchises much more expensive. The major leagues would no longer pay subsidies that had ranged from $5,500 per team at the short-season level to $25,000 at Triple-A. On the other hand, the minor leagues would have to pay the major leagues a fee or tax beginning at $750,000 in 1991, increasing to $2 million by 1994. The money would be raised through teams contributing a portion of their ticket revenues. Over the same period, minor-league clubs would gradually assume the entire travel costs of a total of 30 team members—coaches, a manager and trainer, and players. The Professional Baseball Agreement also imposed a series of facility standards which all minor-league parks had to meet by April 1995. The attachments to Rule 58 consisted of 70 items arranged under such categories as playing field, team facilities, media facilities, seating, parking, and public comfort stations. Virtually all of the stadiums built before the 1980s were deficient in some and usually a large number of categories.

The Professional Baseball Agreement of 1991 played a large role in accelerating the changes that had begun in the 1980s. Many smaller-market cities with older parks could afford neither the added expenses nor upgraded or new facilities. Jerry Klinkowitz, a member of the large ownership group of the Waterloo Diamonds of the Midwest League, cynically remarked that the PBA was "engineered [by the major leagues] to drive out the little folks."[4] Be that as it may, many clubs did move to cities that promised revenue-generating, standards-compliant new parks. Others were able to convince their host cities to finance all or the largest part of building a new park or extensively renovating the existing one.

All of this became very expensive. In addition to the baseball taxes and the initial cost of purchasing a franchise, clubs had to sign much more expensive leases on the new or improved parks and faced constantly increasing operating expenses. The money of the die-hard fans who had been the source of much of the revenue during the lean years would not be anywhere near sufficient a source of ticket revenue. There weren't that many of them and, moreover, beyond the price of their tickets—usually

(*Above and facing page*) Built in 1983, Albany, New York's Heritage Park had become outmoded by 1995. In that year, the Albany-Colonie Yankees of the Eastern League became the Norwich (Connecticut) Navigators, playing in Senator Thomas J. Dodd Memorial Stadium, a brand new park that had been built especially for them.

in the general admission sections—they didn't spend much money at the park. Sales staffs were hired to pursue new markets: businesses; church, service, and social organizations; and family groups. Brought to the park, given an entertaining two or three hours, they would spend money and, in all likelihood, return to the park later in the season or during the next one.This is where the nicknames, logos, contests, and fireworks displays came in. They enhanced the experience and created those repeat customers.

The customers' dollars also augmented other revenue streams. Larger crowds meant that scoreboard, fence, and yearbook advertising became more appealing to potential sponsors. The fans bought merchandise sporting the team's logo and displaying its nickname. Between 1991 and 1994, annual retail sails of minor league merchandise increased from $2.5 million to $60 million.[5] A particularly cute or catchy logo or nickname would enhance sales. The Piedmont Boll Weevils were more salable than the Piedmont Phillies, and when the club was bought by a group that included race car driver Dale Earnhardt, Jr., who was killed shortly after, hats and shirts of the renamed Kannapolis Intimidators became even more popular. In many instances, nicknames and logos were created specifically because of their revenue-producing potential—how else could the exis-

Harry Grove Stadium offered a children's playground complete with carousel.

tence of the Muckdogs (Batavia), Warthogs (Winston-Salem), BlueClaws (Lakewood), or 51s—the number given an area supposed to be housing the remains of aliens (Las Vegas)—be explained?

As the National Association of Minor Leagues (or the Minor Leagues as it was officially re-named in 1999) began its second century of operations in 2002, the game between the lines remained basically the same as it had during the first hundred years. But outside the lines—in the stands, the luxury boxes, stadium restaurants, children's play areas, gift shops, and front-office meeting rooms, it was, to use a baseball cliché, a brand new ballgame. Born in the late 1970s, making their first tentative steps in the early 1980s, and developing rapidly in the 1990s, by 2002 the "New Minors" had come of age.

1—Minor League Baseball's Winter of Discontent

Fans and players joyfully anticipated April 4, the opening of the 2002 minor-league baseball season. On that day, the long winter would be over, the days would be getting warmer and the evenings longer. The athletes hoped that the day would begin a career year that would move them a step or two closer to fulfilling their dreams of becoming major leaguers. Fans, happy to be outdoors again, hoped that this year's version of the home team would win the pennant. But in 2002, the happiest people might well have been the officials of the minor leagues. They were overjoyed to see the last of what had been the most unsettling off-season in over a decade. The period from September 2001 to March 2001 had truly been the minor leagues' winter of discontent.

After Labor Day, with the regular seasons finished, the minor leagues had completed a hugely successful 100th anniversary year. Over 38.8 million people attended games, the most since 1949 and a 1.2 million increase over 2000. New parks in Brooklyn; Staten Island; Lakewood, New Jersey; and Lexington attracted nearly 1.5 million fans. Four leagues and 29 clubs set attendance records. As the playoffs began, front-office personnel from Portland, Oregon, to Portland, Maine, from El Paso, Texas, to Edmonton, Canada, began to plan for Opening Day 2002. However, the early September euphoria was short-lived. As Minor League Vice-President Pat O'Connor remarked at the 2001 Winter Meetings: "Baseball's 2001 playing season left us satisfied and fulfilled as fans. So far the off-season has taken the sizzle out of our game."[1]

The mood changed abruptly on September 11, 2001, with the terrorist attacks on the World Trade Center and the Pentagon. All playoff games were immediately postponed and, a few days later, Minor League Baseball canceled all ongoing series. Co-champions were declared in the four leagues that had not begun the finals and in two leagues in which the championship round was tied. The leaders of four other series were awarded pennants. The September 16th decision was, of course, the correct one and was accepted by all teams concerned. Although it was a disappointing ending to a highly successful year, O'Connor noted that the tragedies could have long-lasting effects on Minor League Baseball: "We are looking at a wartime recessionary economy for the 2002 season.... Things might cost more as a result of this new age. The discretionary income of our fans may be reduced. Sponsors may play it closer to the vest."[2]

If the cancellation of the playoffs was a disappointment, two sets of actions taken by Major League Baseball proved enormously unsettling to the minor leagues. In early November, baseball commissioner Bud Selig announced that the major leagues planned to eliminate two of their franchises over the winter. Although no clubs were named, the strongest rumors pointed to Minnesota and Montreal. Because of the terms of the Professional Baseball Agreement, contraction would not extend to the minor leagues; but it meant that at least eight minor league teams, two at each of the top four levels, could become co-op teams. That is, they would be stocked by a hodgepodge group of players, non-prospect roster-fillers. While watching a winning team is only part of the attraction of going to minor league games, losing teams can be detrimental to attendance. Eleven of the fifteen co-op teams that performed between 1992 and 1996 (the last year of the co-op system) finished in last place. Significantly, nearly all co-op clubs were among the poorest-drawing franchises in their leagues.

By the time it appeared that contraction plans would not be executed in 2002 and that the most-mentioned clubs, Montreal and Minnesota, would be fielding farm teams for the upcoming season, the two clubs had lost valuable time in which to sign six-year free agents, veteran minor leaguers who play important roles in Triple-A franchises. Many experienced players had joined other organizations, and so Triple-A teams like Edmonton and Ottawa, the Minnesota and Montreal affiliates, might find themselves with less competitive teams.

The second action of Major League Baseball that impacted on the minors related to the sale of the Florida Marlins to Jeffrey Loria and his sale of the Montreal Expos to Major League Baseball just weeks before the beginning of spring training. As soon as the sales had been completed, Loria fired the majority of the Marlins' minor-league personnel—scouts, managers, coaches, and trainers—and offered financial enticements to Montreal's baseball staff to join the Marlins. Only four did not take up the offer, two of whom, Tom Lapier and Randy St. Claire, chose to remain with the Ottawa Lynx. However, both the Harrisburg Senators and Portland (Maine) Sea Dogs found themselves with last-minute managerial changes. Dave Huppert, who'd been named the Sea Dogs' skipper in January, became Harrisburg's manager in early March; while Ernie Fox, whom the Expos had assigned to Harrisburg in December, followed Loria from Montreal and wound up managing Portland. The final shuffle was not over until March 12, just a few days before minor-league camps opened. Although managerial shifts are frequent in the minors, the prospect of an entire changeover of minor-league operations just a few weeks before Opening Day must have been unsettling for players and a publicity nightmare for the minor league teams affected.

Other problems the minor leagues faced over the winter came from within. In spite of the attendance records of 2001, the financial picture was not completely positive. At the 2001 meetings, Mike Moore, president of Minor League Baseball, warned:

> Our first 100 years produced many positive milestones—but we must be ever vigilant to subtle signs of potential problems—such as baseball leaving small communities.... I have a list of some 30 teams, which I constantly monitor because of problems. Debt on stadiums, leases, and operating costs already have a couple of teams on the brink of disaster.[3]

Pat O'Connor warned about escalating costs:

> While we see gross revenues growing annually at 13 plus percent, operating costs have been rising at the same rate. Specifically, park and game expenses are up nearly 23 percent over the last three years, administrative expenses are up 11 percent and debt service costs, the cost of borrowed money is up a staggering 51 percent over the last three fiscal years.... Long-term high-priced leases are straining profit and loss statements at alarming rates and with troublesome intensity.[4]

Both Moore and O'Connor expressed worry about small- and large-market teams. In the 1990s, Waterton, New York; St. Catharines, Ontario; and Wausau, Wisconsin, had lost clubs to the metropolitan areas of New York and Chicago. Cities like Clinton and Burlington, Iowa, playing in aging ballparks, do not have the income to provide the amenities to induce more fans to attend or club houses and field conditions to acquire working agreements with "attractive" major league clubs. In 2002, the minor leagues would have to deal with facility and attendance problems in such markets as Medicine Hat, Alberta; Visalia, California; Wichita, Kansas; New Haven, Connecticut; Tacoma, Washington; and Battle Creek, Michigan.

Moving to greener pastures—to larger markets and new facilities—did not always provide solutions. In 2001, the Portland Beavers, who had moved from Albuquerque, New Mexico, at a cost of over $30 million—for the purchase of the franchise and extensive renovations to Portland Civic Stadium—lost over $7 million. The Wilmington, North Carolina, Waves, an expansion franchise in the South Atlantic League, lost $1 million in its first year. New stadiums were not cure-alls. When Ottawa joined the International League in 1993, it attracted 663,000 fans to its state-of-the-art facility. However, attendance fell in each of the next seven years, reaching a low of 135,000 in 2000.

In the year before a club relocates, it acquires lame-duck status in its old city, often drawing even more poorly than it had before. In 2002, teams spending their final seasons in Columbus and Macon, Georgia; Calgary, Alberta; and Shreveport, Louisiana, might well perform poorly at the gate. Baseball experts have recently asked whether the minor leagues are running out of good relocation markets and beginning a program of recycling, returning to cities they had left, often fairly recently. Thus, the Pittsfield Mets would move to Troy, New York, a suburb of Albany which the Eastern League had abandoned after the 1994 season; and the Wilmington Waves would move to Albany, Georgia, which the South Atlantic League left in 1995. The biggest recycling operation has occurred in the Pacific Coast League. In 1986, Salt Lake City moved to Calgary; in 1994 Portland moved to Salt Lake; in 2001, Albuquerque moved to Portland, and in 2003, Calgary would head to Albuquerque, completing the cycle.

On April 4, when umpires would call "Play Ball" and the first pitches would be thrown at 53 minor-league parks, winter would be over. Minor League Baseball would be hoping for another record year. With nine new stadiums opening and three clubs moving to new cities, that seemed highly likely. However, although spring would have come to the playing fields of Minor League Baseball, only a great deal of hard thinking and careful planning, along with a little luck, would enable the leagues to solve the problems they confronted during their long winter of discontent.

2—The Great White North: The Edmonton Trappers of the Pacific Coast League

The Edmonton (Alberta) Trappers joined the Pacific Coast League in January 1981 when Peter Pocklington, the flamboyant owner of the Edmonton Oilers of the National Hockey League, purchased the struggling Ogden A's for $200,000 and the assumption of $200,000 in debts. He turned the running of the team, newly named the Trappers after the fur trappers of pioneer days and a first baseman's glove, over to Mel Kowalchuk, an area advertising executive. For 21 years, Kowalchuk guided the fortunes of professional baseball's most northerly team. One of his biggest challenges was securing affiliations with major-league clubs, as many big-league executives viewed the international boundary, the early spring weather, and the city's distance from major-league centers—the nearest club, the Seattle Mariners, was 800 miles away—as obstacles.

The Trappers played at Renfrew Park, later renamed John Ducey Field in honor of a local player and executive. Although the wooden structure, which had been constructed in the 1930s, was inferior to most Triple-A parks, the club prospered, drawing an average of 250,000 fans a year. Meanwhile, four of the eight clubs that had been in the league in 1981 had relocated.

However, during the 1990s, two crises put the franchise's future in Edmonton in doubt. After the passage of the Professional Baseball Agreement of 1991, the park was deemed substandard in most categories and, when funding for a new stadium did not appear to be forthcoming, Pocklington entertained offers from Americans who planned to move the team. However, with the aid of the Canadian federal government, Telus Field was built between the close of the 1994 season and the opening of the 1995 campaign.

Edmonton's Telus Field, home of the Trappers, was built in nine months on the site of its predecessor John Ducey Field. Located five minutes from downtown, near the banks of the North Saskatchewan River, it is part of a 10-mile stretch of recreational facilities, parks, and woodland trails that cuts through the heart of the city.

Then, in 1999, Pocklington, whose many businesses were in severe financial jeopardy, was forced to surrender his two sports franchises: the baseball Trappers and the hockey Oilers. When no local owner could be found, the Trappers again looked south. On the final day for tendering offers to purchase the franchise, the Edmonton Eskimos of the Canadian Football League presented an acceptable offer.

After the 2001 season, Mel Kowalchuk, the only general manager the Trappers had known, announced his resignation. Three months later, he accepted a similar position with the PCL team that would begin play in Albuquerque, New Mexico, in 2003.

Thursday, April 4

The Edmonton Trappers opened their 2002 Pacific Coast League season in Tucson, Arizona. And that was a good thing. On the morning of April 4, the temperature in Edmonton hovered around 10 degrees, snow was forecast during the day, and the remains of a recent spring snowfall still covered Telus Field. For the Trappers, playing baseball at home in April had always been an "iffy" proposition. Since the club's arrival in the northern Canadian city in 1981, three home openers had been lost to snow or cold, including in 1985, when all April games were postponed and one series transferred to Tucson. In 2000, the Trappers managed to get in their opener and one more game before an April blizzard dumped eight inches of snow, wiping out four contests.

Because of the April weather, many baseball people considered Edmonton a poor baseball city. In 1992, Whitey Herzog of the California Angels was quoted as saying: "Four times this month they were snowed out in Edmonton.... We don't need to be in goddamned *Edmonton!*"[1] That fall he terminated his club's ten-year working agreement with the Trappers. But, as long-time Trapper general manager Mel Kowalchuk emphatically stated: "We don't have the worst weather in the PCL. It can be bad; but it can be worse in Calgary, and even more dreadful in Colorado Springs. And in Tacoma, and Vancouver (when they were in the league), damp, foggy, rainy April weather is a killer."

Assistant general manager Dennis Henke added: "April can be wonderful here. We opened against Calgary one year and the temperature hit 75 degrees. Another time, when Phoenix came here in April, the Firebirds' players told us that it was warmer in Edmonton than it had been a week earlier at their park." In addition to the cities Kowalchuk mentioned, teams in New England, the Great Lakes, and the upper Midwest faced brutal early spring weather. The Portland Sea Dogs' Hadlock Field was only a mile from the Atlantic Ocean; the Erie SeaWolves' Jerry Uht Stadium, equally close to Lake Erie; and Fox Cities Stadium, home of the Wisconsin Timber Rattlers, often had to deal with Green Bay Packers' football-type weather.

Edmonton's favorite winter sport, not its winter weather, has been a greater influence on early-season home attendance at Trappers' games. "Hockey is king," said community relations director Karen Gurba. Although the National Hockey League's Edmonton Oilers are no longer the dominant team that they were in the 1980s, their appearances in the playoffs have kept fans from the ballpark, making the relatively small April crowds even smaller. And when the Stanley Cup hockey championships are on television in June, many people stay home to watch, no matter how warm and sunny it might be at Telus Field. This year, however, the Oilers would probably not be as great an April problem for the Trappers. They would play at nearby Skyreach Center only once during the baseball team's eight-game opening home stand. Should they make the playoffs, their first two or three home games would probably take place while the Trappers were on a 13-day road trip.

Worry about the weather and the hockey playoffs did not seem to be a concern inside the Trappers' offices on April 4. Although there was snow on the sidewalks and on the diamond, the mood inside was spring. Over seven months of hard work preparing for 2002 were nearing a close. The next nine days would be busy and sometimes hectic, but the groundwork had been laid.

"I remember my first opening game," remarked Henke, a former banker and real estate broker who joined the Trappers in 1983. "I was very excited and inexperienced. As April 10 got closer, I got behind on a lot of tasks. I was a sales rep; but then as now, everyone helped everyone else out. I didn't know the most efficient way to get things done, but it got easier as the years went by." However, experience was only of some help when the club moved into its new stadium, Telus Field, in 1995. "We tore the old place down and built the new one in the same spot in just under nine months. During the last 72 hours, we all kept asking, 'Will we ever make it?' We knew we would, but we sometimes felt overwhelmed. Most of us had no sleep. But it was exciting to see that first fan come through the gate. When I shook his hand, he was all smiles—it made it all worthwhile." He remembered that the team had to open the season with 21 straight road games. "This included some in which we were designated the home team. A couple were in Phoenix and there were only six of us in the stands. But we had to get them played because the new park wasn't going to be ready until May 2. Then when we did have our opener, the place was jammed; over 9,200 showed up. It was wonderful!"

As Henke sat in his office, answering phone calls, tending to last-minute details, and talking with staff who popped in and out, he noted that, busy though the nine days leading to the season would be, the hardest work had been done during the fall and winter, after the players had all left for their homes and the fans' attentions turned to football and hockey. "People are always asking me what we do in the winter. Many of them think that we close everything down from mid–September to mid–March. They're very surprised when I tell them that our nine-to-five days are busier in the winter than in the summer."

Henke explained that renovation and major cleanups and repairs could only be done in the off-season. Finding people to fill the seats and promotions to entertain them must be in place by Opening Day. "We have two-thirds of all the tickets that we're going to sell sold by Opening Day," he explained, continuing that it took time to contact season ticket holders, sign renewals, and to book picnic groups and company outings. And, because a good 20 percent of the team's revenue comes from stadium and program advertising, this also had to be sold in the winter so that fences could be painted and programs printed before the season started. In addition, the front office had to plan for the team's travel to such distant towns as New Orleans and Nashville—no easy task because there are no direct flights from Edmonton. "We get the next year's schedule by October and start to work. Long before Christmas, we've settled the details for a road trip that will be coming up in August, nine months away.

Henke disagreed with the oft-made statement that two-thirds of a front office's year's work must be done by Opening Day. "I'd say it's closer to 90 percent. Game days are so busy that if anything unforeseen occurred and we hadn't done that 90 percent, we'd have real difficulty coping. We need lots of lead time. Last year our home schedule ended a week early and this spring we start a week later. That was really welcome. But we always feel we'll run out of time. We always wish that there was another week."

When asked if he was worried that the weather might be poor for Opening Day, Henke smiled and recalled another favorite baseball statement: "There's an old general manager's saying, 'I can't control the players or the weather; everything else I'll make as good as I can.' Right now, I want to make sure that we've done all we can to give our fans a good time. And, you know, I'm excited—just as excited as I was the first time in 1983."

For many of the fans who would be coming to Telus Field in 2002, the non-baseball events taking place would be as important as the games themselves. That was because the Edmonton Trappers, like most other minor league teams, were in the summer entertainment business, where family groups, including young children more interested in cotton candy than in earned run averages, were more important than die-hard fans. On this cold, snowy April morning, Karen Gurba spoke enthusiastically about her winter preparations for the families who'd be coming to Telus Field.

Coordinating promotions for a baseball team is not easy in Edmonton where the Oilers of the NHL rule from October to late April, and the Eskimos of the Canadian Football League do from July to the start of the hockey season. "It's a lot different here than in the United States," Gurba explained. "Many of the American clubs have a contest or activity every half-inning and a giveaway or traveling entertainer every game. For them, baseball is like hockey is in Canada, almost a religion, and there are businesses anxious to sponsor almost any baseball-related promotion you can imagine. We've got some excellent and very loyal sponsors, but not as many. The advertising money is spread among the Trappers, the Oilers, and the Eskimos, and with only so much to go around, we're often third in line."

When Karen planned her promotions, the focus was on weekend events and kids. "That's when the families are here. We don't really use the promotions to lure people into the park—although we're glad if a promotion helps attendance. We want the folks who are here to have a good time. That way there's a good chance they'll be repeat customers." Many of the giveaways are for children only: posters, baseball whammers (inflatable noisemakers), baseballs, and Homer dolls (small replicas of the team mascot, an oversized baseball). So too are the Scout sleepover, when kids camp out on the outfield grass; Homer's birthday party, complete with cake; and Education Day matinees, when the Trappers treat over 5,000 area school children to a ballgame, sodas, and hotdogs.

When she described the promotions she'd been working on, Karen saved discussion of her favorite to the last. "May 5 is going to be Spider-Man Sunday," she announced, glee in her voice. "A lot of American clubs have theme nights—Christmas in July, Elvis Lives—that sort of thing. We think this will be different. One day in the winter, [baseball information manager] Gary Tater and I were talking about the Spider-Man movie that's coming in the spring. I loved Spider-Man comics when I was a kid, and when Gary showed me the movie trailers on the Internet, I knew right away that we had to do this promotion!"

She and the rest of the Trapper staff, who found her enthusiasm contagious, started batting ideas around, a sort of promotional pepper game. "We talked about decorating the park with spider webs, having a guy from the military base dress in a Spider-Man costume and rappel down the side of the stadium to deliver the game ball. People came up with all sorts of neat ideas. Maybe we can have a face painter to do mask decorations for the kids." Then came the hard work, choreographing the event and contacting potential sponsors. Gurba got in touch with the film's distributors, a local comic book store, the military base, a costume shop, as well as the local "kids" radio station. "Everyone's been very supportive," she reported. "We're not getting money, but people are going to donate services and product. That way we're going to be able to provide great family entertainment and keep our costs down." But before it was time for Peter Parker's alter-ego to visit Telus Field, Karen would have other work to do, including coordinating the first giveaway, free toques to the first 1,500 fans through the gates on Opening Day. If the weather continued the way it was on April 4, the knitted pullover caps might be the most popular giveaway of the season.

While Karen Gurba checked on the toque order, fellow Spider-Man aficionado Gary Tater stood in the main office contemplating a piece of paper he was about to feed into the fax machine. "This is really something," he said, a tone of appreciation in his voice, "the best I've seen in a long time." The paper concerned the element of the Trappers' operation over which the front office had no control: the makeup of the team's

Opening Day roster. One of Tater's preseason jobs was to prepare press releases describing the various players the Minnesota Twins had assigned to the Trappers. Over the last three seasons, the club had finished third, third, and fourth in the four-team North Division of the PCL. In the first two years, the Anaheim Angels, generally regarded as operating one of the poorer farm systems in the big leagues, sent weak clubs to Edmonton. In 2001, callups to the new parent team, the Twins, and a large number of injuries decimated the Trappers.

Young, talented, and—paradoxically—experienced. These three words described the twenty-four athletes listened on the sheet being faxed to Arizona, where the Trappers would open in seven hours. The Twins, in spite of a limited budget, and, in comparison to most other major league clubs, a small scouting staff, had developed a strong farm system. Going into the 2002 season, both *Baseball America* and *Baseball Weekly,* the leading national publications, ranked the Twins' organization fifth of the 30 major-league teams.

At a time when the average age of Triple-A rosters was rising— *Baseball America* reported in 2001 that the average was 27.1 years[2]—the Trappers were a surprisingly young 25.5 years of age. The youngest, Adam Johnson, was 22 on Opening Day; the oldest, Doug Bochtler, 31. Nine were under 25.

But they were talented. Six players had been selected in the first three rounds of the major leagues' annual draft, including first-round choices Matt LeCroy (1997), Michael Cuddyer (1997), and Adam Johnson (2000). Six players—Johnson and Cuddyer, along with Matt Kinney, Michael Restovich, Juan Rincon, and Brad Thomas—made the preseason top prospect lists of all the important baseball publications.

Johnson, who had signed his first pro contract on June 19 of 2000, moved with meteoric speed through the ranks. He played his first year in Fort Myers in the high Single-A Florida State League and started 2001 in Double-A New Britain. On June 16, less than a year after he signed with the Twins and with only 31 professional games under his belt, he made his major-league debut. He was then sent to Edmonton for further seasoning and struck out an average of 8.86 batters per nine innings, a feat which earned him another major-league stint after the close of the PCL season.

In addition to Johnson, 13 members of the Trappers had played in the majors. Although many of these had made brief September appearances when major-league clubs expanded their rosters from 25 to 40, pitchers Doug Bochtler (with 220 games) and Travis Miller (with 198) and catcher Javier Valentin (with 137) had logged considerable major-league playing time. Not only would their experience be valuable to younger players, but also their hunger to get back to the "Show" would inspire them to greater levels of performance. Sixteen players, two-thirds of the Opening Day roster had previously played at the Triple-A level.

A long infield throw from the front office, stadium operations manager Don Benson stood on the warning track surveying the snow-covered playing field in front of him. When he'd left Edmonton in September—a week earlier than usual because of the early close of the Trappers' home season—he'd done everything that needed to be done for the 2002 home opener nearly seven months away.

"After the team has left each fall, we power-wash the stands. It took us a week just to do the mezzanine—you'd be amazed how much gum people spit out. We've got to do the cleaning in September because it might be too cold in April, and the water could freeze. Now all we'll have to do is dust and mop just before April 13th." His crew also worked on the field, topping up the dirt areas cut out of the artificial turf around the bases and rebuilding the mound. "The biggest job on the diamond was reattaching the artificial turf to the ground," he stated, explaining that the constant running, starting and stopping loosened the material from the six-by-six timbers that run around the edge of the infield.

His job done, Don headed to Mexico's Baja Peninsula for the winter, and when he returned on the last Saturday of March he immediately visited Telus Field "All the winter snow had either been removed or had melted. The outfield was bone dry; everything was ready to go. But by Sunday afternoon, I wasn't very joyful." He was referring to the four inches of heavy, wet snow that came down on Easter Sunday. Now he'd have more than sweeping and dusting to worry about before Opening Day, and he was grateful for the extra week this year's schedule had made possible.

"On Saturday, I'd thought we'd be spending Monday and Tuesday power sweeping the outfield. During the last cutting in the fall, we leave a heavy layer of clippings on the ground to protect the grass. Now we're in a bind. We can't take a bobcat out on the field because the ground has thawed a couple of inches and the machinery would damage the roots. And we can't put any heavy machinery on the artificial turf for fear of ripping it." As he spoke, two members of the groundscrew were carefully putting snow into a small trailer, shovelful by shovelful.

Removing the snow from the infield would essentially make that part of the park ready for play. But the melting snow in the outfield would create a very soggy mess. Not only would it make playing conditions sloppy, if not dangerous, but also it would put the newly rejuvenated grass at risk, as players ran or skidded across it. "But," Benson stated, "we'll have hot air heaters going 24 hours a day in the outfield to dry it if we have to. A

The grounds crew removes the last of an April snowfall from Telus Field. Surprisingly, the April weather is less of a deterrent to attendance than the presence of hockey playoffs on television.

few warm days would be best." Benson was philosophical. "If we have no more snow and it warms up, we'll be fine. It's a way of life; every year, it's a crap shoot with the weather. But I certainly am glad that the team is on the road; I'll bet they are too. The weather's wonderful in Arizona at this time of year."

The weather in Tucson was wonderful—in the mid–70s when the game started that evening. Unfortunately the Trappers' bats didn't warm up until the seventh inning, when Michael Cuddyer lived up to his advance billing with a three-run homer. But by that time, the Sidewinders had built up a nine-run lead and went on to an 11 to 3 victory.

The weather for minor-league openers was not good in New England, the Great Lakes and the upper Midwest. Although all the games were played, a dozen of them took place in temperatures that began in the mid to upper 30s and then began to drop. Snow and flurries fell intermittently in Syracuse and Battle Creek, and in South Bend it was so cold that less than 600 fans turned out. The next day, snow and freezing temperatures led to the cancellation of three games. Only the headline writers appeared to be enjoying the situation as they worked to be witty: "Play (Snow) Ball!," "Snowball Affects Pitching," "Mother Nature Prevails in Midwest Opener," "Snow Fun for Lynx."

Saturday, April 13

By the weekend of April 6–7, Don Benson's crew had made good progress on clearing the infield. The fact that the weather had remained below freezing meant that the shovel brigade had been able to get to the snow before it had melted and run into the outfield. Then, on Sunday April 7, it began to snow again. "We were out there shoveling it off as fast as it came down," Dennis Henke remarked about himself and the other members of the front office who'd been pressed into duty. As the week began, the weather turned mild, reaching the low 50s by Wednesday. The sun and warmth, aided by heaters in the shaded part of the outfield and a couple of shovels, got rid of all the snow, and Telus Field, even if a little soggy around the edges, was ready for the Trappers to come home.

The baseball team, meanwhile, was alternately as hot as the southwest weather and as cold as Edmonton's lingering winter. After their 11–3 Opening Day loss to Tucson, they beat the Sidewinders 9–6 and 12–9 before losing 11–2. In Las Vegas, they dropped another two: 8–5 and 6–5. Their bats came alive in the third game against the 51s, and they triumphed 8–3. They closed off their eight-game road trip on the short end of a 4–3 score. Trapper batters had belted 13 home runs on the road; but their pitchers had given up a league-high 18 homers and an average of 6.55 earned runs a game.

On Friday, April 12, the team headed home, many of the players coming to Edmonton for the first time. And they would be staying in temporary homes. All would sleep the first four nights at the Sheraton Grande, with the Trappers paying the bill, as was specified in the team's agreement with the Twins. Because the players would be leaving in just over a week for a 13-day road trip that would take them from Colorado Springs to Oklahoma City and finally to New Orleans, most of them planned to stay at the hotel, looking for places they would move to on their return to Edmonton on May 3. By that time, those members of the Trappers who had reported to the Twins' major-league training camp in late February would have been living out of suitcases for close to 11 weeks.

On Opening Day, the free toques given to the fans weren't necessary; the weather was sunny to partly cloudy; the temperature, in the mid 50s. Many fans wore shorts and a few ladies even donned colorful summer dresses for the occasion. The fans applauded politely for the introductions of the visiting Tucson Sidewinders, and some cheered loudly when public address announcer Ron Rimer asked them to welcome "You-u-r-r-r 2002 Edmonton Trappers." In fact, they seemed as interested in enjoying the first warm weather of the year as in watching a ballgame.

Many fans were perhaps tired. The night before, the Edmonton Oilers, in their last home game, had played before a capacity crowd of 17,000, had lost and been eliminated from hockey playoff contention. The front page of the *Edmonton Journal* sports section was filled with hockey stories and pictures, as was the third page. Page two focused on the Masters' golf tournament, and page four on the World Curling Championship, where Canada's "Men with Brooms" were the front-runners. A short piece on Casey Blake, Trapper third baseman, appeared on page five. If the fans were somewhat restrained because they were tired and a little down after the Oilers' losing hockey game, they may have been relatively quiet because most of them didn't know much about "their" 2002 Trappers.

Although the team that Rimer announced had just assumed existence for the people at Telus Field, it had, in fact, been seven months in the making. Just as the Trapper front office had been working since the previous September, the player development department of the Minnesota Twins had spent an incredibly busy fall, winter, and earlier spring, preparing for the presentation of an on-field product that the Edmonton fans had began to think about only on this sunny mid–April afternoon. "In mid–September, we get all our minor-league staff—managers, scouts, coaches, and head-office people—together," explained Twins' minor league director Jim Rantz. "We look very carefully at the performance of every player in our system. We grade their season and ask whether or not they've reached the levels of achievement we expected of them. Then we consider which club they should be assigned to for the next season."

For some, as with such members of this year's Trappers as Michael Restovich, Juan Rincon, and Michael Cuddyer, it meant moving up to Triple-A. For others, such as B.J. Garbe, the Twins' top 1999 draft choice— who had not lived up to his early promise—it meant starting the season with the same club, high Class-A Fort Myers, with which he had finished 2001. A few were simply let go—their baseball dreams over, or at least on hold.

Some of the players no longer in the Twins system were what are termed six-year free agents. That is, they were players who, after six professional seasons, had not been named to the 40-man protected roster of the major-league club. They were automatically granted free agency and could either re-sign with the old club, should it wish to sign them, or seek employment in another organization. Although it is unlikely that Minnesota would have re-signed all of the six-year free agents, the fact that the Twins' very existence was threatened by the rumored contraction made signing any free agents difficult. As it was, the Twins did sign four from other clubs. That is how David Lamb, David Lee, Warren Morris, and Alejandro Prieto became a part of the Trappers' Opening-Day roster.

"Coming into spring training," Rantz continued, "rosters are pretty flexible. We move people around a lot, trying them at different levels. There are some really pleasant surprises; sometimes a young player will show he's ready for a higher level of competition than we thought; others disappoint us." All the minor-league staff meet regularly to discuss players, and gradually rosters that meet the developmental needs of individuals and the competition levels of specific leagues take shape. "For Triple-A, we're looking at a very good player, perhaps someone who has been around for a while, or who has been up and down from the majors. We also look for a player who's had a really good year at Double-A. What we want are people who can help the major-league club during the year and young players who are just on the verge of making it to the big leagues."

Rantz explained that the Trappers were a young club for Triple-A because the Twins chose to develop their own talent rather than seek expensive major-league free agents for the big club. Their farm teams were younger throughout the minors. "We draft a lot of players out of high school," he explained, noting that 12 of the top 15 picks they'd signed in the last three years had come out of high school. "So they'll be young by the time the get to Edmonton. And the group we have here this year has developed very quickly."

During March, the Trappers' Opening-Day roster gradually took shape. Several members of the Twins' 40-man roster who attended the major-league camp were reassigned to the Triple-A squad, the last of whom Matt Kinney and Matt LeCroy, joined the Trappers a week before Opening Day. Young players from New Britain proved they were ready to move up. But the roster that so pleased Gary Tater when he faxed it to Tucson on Opening Day would not be the same one announced to fans at Telus Field nine days later.

The adage that "at Triple-A, the majors are only a phone call away" had already been verified three times. On April 6th, Bobby Kielty and LeCroy, the kinds of players Rantz had said could be called on to help when needed, took a plane to Toronto to join the Twins in their games against the Blue Jays. To make up for their absence, infielder Joe Dillon reported to Edmonton from Double-A New Britain. Then on April 12, the Twins announced that two veteran players had switched teams. Pitcher Tony Fiore moved up to the Minnesota Twins, while infielder Warren Morris moved from the Twins to Edmonton. And, if what happened in 2001 was any indication, these could be just the first batch of a very large number of roster changes. The Trappers were involved in 64 transactions, as players were moved up, down, or, in a few cases, simply out.

As the Trappers players took the field after the playing of the national anthems, one fan remarked to another: "These guys sure have a good life; they're doing what they like to do, they makes bucketsful of money, and they get nearly six months off each year." The fan was only partly correct in his assumptions. Certainly, all the athletes on both teams were doing what they liked and getting paid for it. Only a few, like Adam Johnson, whose signing bonus had made him an instant millionaire two years ago, were earning bucketsful. And none of them took six month vacations between seasons. To have reached this level of competition, each player had had to make a year-round commitment to baseball. In fact, not unlike the surfers in the 1960s movie *Endless Summer,* who traveled the world through the year looking for the perfect wave, most baseball players leave the cold weather areas of Canada and the United States at the end of the summer to find places where the weather enables them to continue playing and to progress in their development.

After the 2001 minor-league season had ended, five members of this year's Trapper squad were called up to Minnesota. Two of these, LeCroy and Cuddyer, along with Grant Balfour, Michael Restovich, and Kevin Frederick spent October and November playing in the Arizona Fall League. Bobby Kielty played in the Dominican Republic, while Michael Ryan traveled to Venezuela to play with and against teammates Juan Rincon, Johan Santana, and Ruben Salazar, who combined a trip home with winter baseball. Javier Valentin played in his home country of Puerto Rico. By the time the various Latin American leagues had finished their seasons in mid–January, the players had little more than a month's off-time before they reported for spring training.

For Cuddyer, the fall months had been incredibly busy. After the end of the regular Eastern League season, the 22-year-old native of Norfolk, Virginia, was disappointed. Even though his team, the New Britain Rock Cats of the Eastern League, had finished in first place in the Northern Division and were about to enter the playoffs, he had hoped to be called up by the Minnesota Twins to play out the rest of the American League season as a member of their expanded 40-man roster. After bypassing rookie ball, he'd moved quickly up the ranks, spending his first pro season in 1998 at Fort Wayne in the low Single-A Midwest League and then the next year at high Single-A Fort Myers.

But he'd stalled at Double-A. "I knew, after 2000, that I hadn't conquered the league," he said, referring to his .263 average with the Rock Cats. "I had a decent year, but both the Twins and I felt I still had some thing to prove. I was determined to do that the next year. I wasn't going to go back for a third year." He did prove what he had to, bringing his average up to .301 and finding his power, blasting 30 home runs, a career high. His performance earned him a spot on the Eastern League All-Star team and on the *Baseball* America's Double-A All-Star team. But it didn't earn him a ticket to Minnesota, just a one-hour bus ride to Norwich, Connecticut, home of the Rock Cats' semi-final opponents, the Navigators.

New Britain defeated Norwich and was about to face the Reading Phillies when the terrorist attacks of September 11 halted the playoffs. Five days later, the final series was canceled, and New Britain manager Stan Cliburn called Cuddyer into his office with important news: Michael had been called up by the Twins and was to report as quickly as possible. "The planes weren't flying yet, so I threw a few clothes in a suitcase, jumped in my car, and started driving west," he recalled. The trip took him through Connecticut, Massachusetts, New York, Pennsylvania, Ohio, Indiana, Illinois, Wisconsin, and Minnesota. Twenty-three hours after pulling out of the parking lot of New Britain Stadium, he pulled up in front of the Metrodome in Minneapolis. He was about to fulfill a dream he'd first had when he was five years old: playing in the major leagues.

"When we were kids playing in the back yard, I'd always pretend I was Don Mattingly of the Yankees, even though he was left-handed and I'm right. It was always the bottom of the ninth, with two men in scoring position in the seventh game of the World Series. Of course, we were behind by two and the count was three and two. I never struck out. I must have hit a thousand World Series' home runs in my back yard." His arrival at Minneapolis wasn't quite so dramatic, but the reality was equally as thrilling. "It was so cool when I walked into the clubhouse to see my name above a locker and on the back of a uniform jersey."

Cuddyer played in his first major-league game on September 23, as a designated hitter against the Cleveland Indians. In his first at-bat, he worked the count to 3 and 2 against Cleveland's Chuck Finley. "The next pitch was a split-finger fastball that just missed, and I headed to first. The next at-bat, I hit a double to right field against Finley." Cuddyer was happy, but admits he didn't have time to take it all in. There were men on base, and he had a job to do. "I guess it really hit me when we went to Cleveland. It was my first start in the outfield and Jacobs Field was full. I just looked around me and thought, 'Wow, this is awesome!'"

When the Twins' season ended on October 7, Michael found himself on the road again, not back to Virginia's Tidewater country or to his Gulf Coast winter home of Fort Myers, but to the deserts of southern Arizona. Here he reported to the Grand Canyon Rafters in Scottsdale, Arizona. The Rafters are a member of the six-club Arizona Fall League, which was founded in 1992 as a high-powered training circuit for the top 180 prospects in Double and Triple-A. Every major-league club sends six players, so that each Arizona team is an amalgam of talented athletes from five major-league organizations. The 2001 fall season was Cuddyer's second with Grand Canyon. He'd attended in 1997, shortly after signing his first professional contract. This time, he hit .336 and was named by the managers to the league's All-Prospect team. "It was," he said, "a real help for me in getting ready for Triple-A ball. All of the pitchers were really good—every at-bat was a real test."

The Rafters made the playoffs, finishing first in their division, but lost to Phoenix in the finals. And just before Thanksgiving, Cuddyer headed for Norfolk, Virginia, and then on to Fort Myers, where he would be able to train at the Twins' Florida facilities. "I used to play baseball all year at home when I was a kid. I was in other sports, but after a game or practice was over, I'd find some place to work on baseball. Now it's my 12-month job."

The Trappers' home opener was doubly successful. Not only did they win—10–3—but they won well. Matt Kinney, who came into the game with one loss and a 20.25 earned run average, faced 26 batters over 6.2 innings, struck out eight, including the last two men he faced, and allowed three earned runs to take the win. Of the Trappers' 11 hits, six were doubles and two triples. Catcher Javier Valentin's three hits, all doubles, drove in four runs. The only disappointment of the afternoon was the size of the crowd. A respectable 7,307, it was the first time since the Trappers had moved into their new stadium in 1995 that they hadn't opened before a capacity house of 9,200. "The bad weather really kept our advance sales down," Dennis Henke explained. "It wasn't until Wednesday, when things warmed up that ticket sales picked up. But with today's beautiful day and a great game, things are looking up for tomorrow's double-header and next week's games."

Sunday, April 14, and Monday, April 15

The Trappers' victory didn't make the front page of the *Edmonton Journal*'s expanded 10-page Sunday sports section. That was reserved for post-mortems on the hockey team's failure to make the playoffs and another account of the curling team, which would go on to win the world championship. Pages two and three contained only hockey stories, while page four was devoted to the Masters' golf tournament. The Trappers were relegated to the bottom half of the back page.

"It was as if someone flicked a switch and suddenly it was spring," read Collin Gallant's lead.[3] Ironically, the baseball story was under the weather—it was placed beneath the detailed meteorological summary and

the entire page bore the heading "Baseball/Weather." But Sunday's forecast was for snow or rain showers with a high in the mid to upper 30s. It
certainly wasn't baseball weather. Dark clouds rolled in as the morning
progressed; by 10 o'clock rain began to fall; and shortly after noon the
wind rose while the temperature dropped to 34 degrees. It was the right
weather for wearing the toques given out the day before, but not for sitting at the ballpark. The afternoon's double-header was canceled and a
twin bill, scheduled for Monday. As this would be the last meeting between
the clubs this season, there would be no chance for the Trappers to make
up the lost home date and its revenue.

There was no baseball story in Monday morning's paper. If there had
been, it might have begun: "It was as if someone flicked a switch and suddenly it was winter." Telus Field was literally under the weather—six inches
of heavy wet snow had fallen on the diamond. It continued through the
morning, dumping another four inches. Monday's double-header, another
irrecoverable home date, was lost. But the news was worse: because of the
amount of snow and the still-fragile condition of the outfield, no equipment could get on the field and all home games for the remainder of the
week would be canceled.

The Trapper front office arranged for the team to hold an indoor
workout at Kinsman Field House, located just across the North Saskatchewan River from the ballpark. But officials of the Minnesota Twins
and Chicago Cubs, parent club of the Iowa team, didn't want their best
prospects to go four days without baseball. Many calls were placed between
Edmonton, Chicago, Minnesota, Des Moines, and the Pacific Coast League
offices in Colorado Springs. Before the players had crossed the bridge leading to the field house, the announcement was made that the upcoming
four-game series would be transferred to Iowa, with double-headers on
Wednesday and Thursday. The Iowa Cubs would be the home team and
would keep whatever profits might be made on the hastily scheduled
games. The Trappers had now lost six of their first seven home dates, nearly
10 percent of their seventy-game home schedule.

After the indoor practice, two of the Trappers stood in the parking
lot, ankle-deep in snow, and tossed baseball-sized snowballs at each other.
When one scored a direct hit, he laughed delightedly, like a schoolboy at
recess. The two wouldn't have tried to hit each other from the mound, for
both were pitchers. However, their present glee was understandable. Brad
Thomas and Michael Nakamura were Australians—two of three on the
Trappers' roster (the other was Grant Balfour)—and this was the first time
they'd seen snow during the baseball season. "We were disappointed at not
being able to play for the second day in a row," Nakamura explained, "but

it was exciting just to stand there watching the flakes come down and the snow getting deeper and deeper on the ground."

Thomas and Nakamura are two examples of an important fact about contemporary baseball: the great American game is becoming more and more international. Just as North American hockey teams are turning to northern European countries for players, so, too, major-league baseball teams are searching warm-weather countries for talent with which to stock their minor-league systems. A recent press release from the offices of Minor League Baseball announced that 2,865 athletes from outside of America have been signed to professional contracts.[4] That is almost 50 percent of the players.

Not surprisingly, the Dominican Republic, with 1,536 players; Venezuela, with 738, and Puerto Rico, with 123, are the top three "foreign" producers of minor leaguers. These countries have long been a rich source of baseball talent. Mexico is fourth, with a surprisingly low 91, and Canada is fifth with 88. The big surprise is that Australia is sixth with 64 minor leaguers (along with major-league pitchers Graeme Lloyd of Montreal, Damian Moss of Atlanta, and Luke Prokopec of Toronto). The Minnesota Twins have a scout, Howie Norsetter, who spends four months in Australia during the North American winter. He's one of the reasons the Twins now have 16 Australians playing in their minor-league system, the most of any major-league organization.

But Australia? Really? Isn't it supposed to be noted for world-class cricket, Australian rules football, shrimp on the barbe, and *Waltzing Matilda*? These things may be more important than baseball to most Australians, but baseball has been played downunder for nearly 150 years. The country has a very large youth and club program and it is starting to give cricket a run for the money as Australia's most popular summer sport.

Americans brought baseball to Australia in the 1850s.[5] Sailors and other travelers played when they came ashore, and local cricketers soon dabbled in the game. The sport got a huge shot in the arm in the late 19th century when Albert Spalding—the sporting goods giant—took two clubs of professionals, including Hall-of-Famer Cap Anson, on an around-the-world tour. Stops in Sydney, Melbourne, and Adelaide attracted crowds as large as 10,000. As a result of the interest generated, teams began to spring up throughout Australia. From 1934 to 1989, the Claxton Shield tournament was held, in which clubs from around the country competed for the national championship.

But baseball was essentially a winter sport, and teams were allowed to use cricket grounds only when these had been "abandoned" as the cooler weather set in. It was considered a keep-fit off-season activity for cricketers who opposed attempts made to move baseball into the Australian summer. However, when the switch in seasons finally occurred in the 1960s, the sport experienced major growth. It meant that games no longer had to be played in cold, damp, windy weather, on muddy fields. More important, because games were now being played during the American winter, scouts from the United States began to arrive searching for talent and, finding good players, began signing them in time for America's spring and summer minor-league seasons.

In 1967, Sid Thompson was signed to play in the Philadelphia minor-league system, and, in 1986, Craig Shipley became the first Australian major leaguer when he appeared with the Los Angeles Dodgers. When the Australian Baseball League was founded in 1989, it helped future major leaguers David Nilsson, along with Prokopec and Lloyd attract notice. In addition, Americans Homer Bush, John Jaha, Kevin Milwood and other major leaguers played winter ball in the league.

The high point in Australian baseball to date occurred in 1999, when the Australian national team, led by David Nilssen and fellow major leaguer Shayne Bennett, won the Intercontinental Cup, finishing in first place in the round-robin tournament and defeating Cuba 4–3 in a thrilling 11-inning final game.

Unlike their American counterparts, Thomas and Nakamura neither started with baseball nor enjoyed childhood fantasies of performing seventh-game World Series' heroics. They stumbled, as it were, onto the sport. "I was practicing with my soccer mates when I was seven or eight, and one of them suggested that we all try out for T ball. We did, and by the time I was nine years old," Thomas reported, "I'd made the commitment to concentrate on baseball." For Nakamura, baseball began after a father's exasperation on a shopping trip. "I was acting up in the car and, when we passed some athletic fields, my father said that, if I behaved, he'd buy me a mitt like the ones the kids on the field were using. I did and he did. Later that afternoon, he was playing catch with me and a couple of neighborhood kids joined in. We all decided to join a club and play baseball."

Both players revealed their baseball talents early; but they were playing a sport that was secondary in Australia. "We couldn't learn from watching major-league games on TV, because there weren't any until World Series time," Nakamura remembered. "Then I'd get up at three in the morning to watch. My dad, who used to be pretty strict about schooling, was lenient when the games were on and we couldn't wake up in time for school."

Both agreed that they really began to learn about baseball when they came to the United States. Nakamura attended the University of South

Alabama on a baseball scholarship. When he was not selected in the 1997 draft, he returned to Australia and contemplated an opportunity to play professionally in Japan. However, he signed an offer with the Twins the day before Christmas and began the 1998 season with Fort Wayne of the Midwest League. Here he became a teammate with Thomas, whom he'd known in Australia. "He was older than I was, and back home we looked up to Michael," Thomas noted. Brad had signed with the Los Angeles Dodgers and played with the Great Falls Dodgers of the advanced rookie Pioneer League before being let go. "It was the best thing that happened to me in baseball; it was such a huge organization," he remembered. He was quickly signed by the Twins, who had been interested in him earlier but had lost him to the Dodgers. "The Twins gave me the best coaching I'd ever had." He spent 1997 in Elizabethton, playing in the Appalachian League, the other advanced rookie circuit. He joined Nakamura in Fort Wayne the next year.

The two moved through the ranks together, although Thomas appeared in five major-league games with the Twins in 2001. "Two were pretty good and two were pretty bad. But I've had that first-time experience. I'm glad it's over; now I know what I have to do to get back to the majors to stay." The teammates became roommates and, according to Nakamura, are like brothers: "We argue like brothers and help each other like brothers. And I look up to him. I may be a year older, but I'm only 5-10; he's 6-4. And I really respect what he's done as a player."

Nakamura reached down, grabbed a handful of snow, shaped it into a sphere and aimed a beanball at his teammate and friend. Then they headed back to the Sheraton Grande. The players were no longer thinking about seeking more permanent lodging; they set about doing enough laundry to get them through the first part of their suddenly extended road trip. Instead of being an eight-game homestand, their stay in Edmonton had become a brief intermission in what had now become a 24-game road trip. Back at the Trappers' offices at Telus Field, the mood was somber. There was, as Dennis Henke had said earlier, nothing they could do about the weather. Unfortunately, there was also nothing they could do about the unforeseen travel expenses of the trip to Des Moines or about the loss of the estimated $150,000 in revenue that would have come from an expected total April attendance of over 25,000.

Saturday, May 4

"This is like a rehearsal for the Grey Cup Game," muttered Doug Brinson as he pulled up the parka of his down-filled winter jacket over his Edmonton Trappers' cap and tucked his stadium blanket more snugly around his legs. He was referring to the Canadian Football League championship to be held in Edmonton in late November. The problem was that November was nearly seven months away and he'd come to Telus Field to watch a baseball game, only the second home contest Edmonton's team would play during the first four and a half weeks of the PCL season.

It was noon, starting time of the first game of a double-header. The Trappers had been scheduled to play on Friday night, but their bad luck had continued. After completing a 16-game road trip in which two games had been postponed—one by snow and one by rain—and in which they had played four double-headers in ten days, they had been stuck for six hours in the New Orleans airport. Their Northwest flight was finally canceled and they arrived home close to midnight on a later flight. It was a tired group of athletes who tossed balls lazily back and forth on the still straw-colored outfield grass.

Beyond the outfield wall, at the top of the hill sloping back from the south banks of Edmonton's Saskatchewan River valley, a few dark spruce trees poked like black claws into the lowering gray sky. Birch, aspen, and poplar, which by now should have been mantled with the pale lime-green sheen of newly budded leaves, stood a sepulchral white against the dark earth of the hillside. The greenest parts of the northern Alberta landscape were the batter's eye in dead center, the artificial turf of the infield, and the grandstand seats. Only three or four hundred of these were occupied, and, like Doug, their occupants were all die-hards, baseball fans who had felt deprived when the Trappers had had to depart suddenly nearly three weeks ago. They smiled from beneath their giveaway toques and muttered through chattering teeth Ernie Banks' famous refrain: "Let's play two."

Doug clicked off his cell phone. "I was just talking to the wife and she said there were snow flurries out west around our place. She wanted to know if I would be coming home early. And I told her, 'Heck, no!' I've been waiting eight months for baseball. She told me that was great; she even suggested that after the game I visit my mother-in-law on the way home. It's my birthday, and I think she's cooking up something special."

"We'll play," Dennis Henke told reporters clustered around him near the Trappers' dugout, all of them standing close to the heaters that had been placed there. "The cold won't stop us, but," he hesitated as he glanced at the clouds advancing from the west, "the snow might." And, indeed it did. Thirty minutes into the game, in the top of the second, with the count two and two on Portland Beaver batter Ken Barker, the home plate umpire called time and waved the players off the field. They took no time sprinting toward the dugouts, through them, and into the heated clubhouses.

What in the first inning had been occasional wispy stray snowflakes turned into increasingly more frequent and increasingly bigger flakes. They weren't sticking on the ground, but they were becoming so thick that players couldn't pick out the ball against the swirling white background.

When the game resumed two hours later, Barker took another ball, fouled off a pitch, and then singled to left, setting the table for Scott Morgan, who blasted a home run to give Portland a 2–1 lead. As the ball disappeared over the left field fence, a fan sitting alone in the bleachers, one of the couple of hundred who had waited out the delay, sprinted down the stairs and out the gate by the left field foul pole. A few minutes later, he was back in his seat, holding a baseball in his hand and explaining to a visitor what he'd been doing.

One of the Trapper regulars, who could always be seen sitting in the first seat of the first row of the first section of the bleachers, Ken McKinstry had retrieved the ball for Scott Morgan. "When he was a member of the Trappers in 2000," Ken explained, "Scott's mother came to visit and he hit a home run. I retrieved it and gave it to her. She was really thrilled because she'd never been given one of her son's home run balls. But this one," he said, as he held up the ball, "is for Scott's wife; I'm going to give it to him to take to her after the game." Collecting home run balls is Ken's hobby. At first he used to stand in the public parking lot beyond right field shagging balls hit there during batting practice and return them in exchange for free admission. Now he does the same duty in the sealed-off area beyond left. "I come to the park early, gather the baseballs, and help out with any small chores that might need doing. Then I take my seat. It's unreserved, but I'm always right here. The Trappers treat me right; but I wish they'd turn the heat up. This is the coldest I've ever been at Telus Field."

By the time the second inning ended, the Beavers had scored five runs; they added two more in the third and one in the top of the final inning of the seven-inning game. As the Trappers came to bat, Portland was ahead nine to six. When Michael Restovich grounded to short, more of the dwindling number of fans moved to the exit. They shouldn't have, because they missed what Trappers' coach Phil Roof called "one of the most amazing things I've seen in my 43 years in professional baseball." Trapper catcher Javier Valentin sent a ball over the right field fence to narrow the gap to two; Will Morris singled and Chad Green, recently called up from New Britain, hit another one over the right-center field wall to tie the game. Angel Prieto walked and Mike Ryan produced the inning's third home run, what in sportswriting cliches is called "a moon shot," an even longer and higher blast over the right-center field wall, to give the Trappers the victory, 11 to 9.

When the game ended at close to five o'clock, there was another considerable thinning of the announced crowd of 6,225. Ken, having delivered Morgan's home run ball to the visitor's club house, decided to head home, remarking that the cold was too much for his aging knees. Doug phoned his wife, and when she heard that the second game might not be over until nearly seven, she suggested that he skip the visit to his mother-in-law and leave around six. "I'd better act surprised when I get home; now I'm really certain she's got something planned." The Trappers took the second contest 6 to 1.

In the press box, one self-styled humorist, noting the constant exodus of fans during the second game, remarked that there'd soon only be the "sound of one fan clapping" and, still enthusiastic about Mike Ryan's home run, quipped that today had been the second time in six months that the left fielder had played winter baseball for the first time. He was referring not just to the wintry conditions of today's contest, but to Ryan's time, from October to January, in the Venezuelan League.

Sunday, May 5

At 1:30 P.M., in the season's most eagerly anticipated and meticulously planned promotion, Spider-Man was scheduled to descend from the roof of the stadium, proceed to the field, and deliver the game ball to the mound. But in the predawn hours, twenty mile an hour winds came down from the north, sending the wind-chill factor several degrees below freezing. At eleven in the morning, the Edmonton Trappers' reluctantly canceled the game. Not only did the front office anticipate that the weather would so limit attendance as to make opening the gates a money-losing proposition, but they feared that the wind-chill could cause serious injuries to the players' muscles.

In the warm Trapper clubhouse, the players, suddenly finding themselves with an unexpected free Sunday afternoon, lounged or milled about, conferring about what to do with the rest of the day. Mike Ryan, sitting on a folding chair in front of his locker, commented that today was even colder than yesterday. "And that," he continued, "was the most frigid weather I'd ever played in." When told the humorist's line about his two winter ball debuts, he laughed and then related the Venezuelan one to the strong start he'd enjoyed during April, when he hit seven home runs in 28 games, a pace that, if continued, would lead to his knocking out 30 in the season, by far the most in his seven-year career.

A native of the western Pennsylvania town of Indiana, Ryan had been picked by the Minnesota Twins in the fifth round of the 1996 draft. He'd

Trappers baseball information manager Gary Tater (right) presents Mike Ryan the April 2002 Player-of-the-Month award. (Photograph by Denyse Conroy)

advanced a level a year, until 2000, when he started in Double-A and finished in Triple-A. His numbers, while not exceptional, were more than acceptable. He'd topped the .300 mark twice and in his last two years had developed more power, hitting 11 home runs for New Britain in 2000 and 18 with the Trappers last year. He was dedicated athlete who possessed, as the cliche goes, "a real work ethic," and who, to use another cliche, "came to play every day." His steady rise, however, had been overshadowed by the careers of his more celebrated and more highly drafted teammates. His name had never appeared in the various top prospects lists; he'd never been on an All-Star team; and he never appeared in *Baseball America*'s league-by-league best tools lists.

Then, in August 2001, when his agent informed him that a Venezuelan League team need a left-handed hitting outfielder, he saw an opportunity to extend his baseball season and work on areas of his game that need to be improved if he were to realize his childhood dream of playing in the majors. "I thought it would be a great opportunity and really interesting. The Twins gave me the go-ahead." And so, on October 16, 2001, Mike Ryan took the field wearing the uniform of the Aragua Tigers of Maracay, Venezuela and began his first experience of winter ball.

It was both a cultural and athletic learning experience. Sitting in the security of the Telus Field clubhouse, Ryan recalled his on- and off-field life in South America. "When I got there, I knew only three or four words of Spanish. By the end of the week I could order a Whopper meal at Burger King, and at the end of my time there, I could converse—sort of. In the clubhouse, people mainly spoke English to me—a lot of the guys had played in the United States. And I've always been a sort of quiet person, so I didn't mind just listening."

How frightening was it, he was asked by a person who knew Venezuela only through lurid news reports of ferocious jungle bandits and murdering drug lords. "It was scary sometimes," he replied. "The club put the Americans up in a deluxe hotel with lots of security. But if I wanted to go out at night to get something to eat, a security guard would go along. I'd have been in trouble if I went alone." The ballpark could be an adventure as well. "To the fans, baseball was almost a religion. I saw some bad fights in the stands between people cheering for different teams, and if you were a Venezuelan player and made a mistake in the game—a key error or strikeout with men on—the fans would threaten you. The Americans were treated differently, as if we were above the rest. The only time I felt uneasy was when I'd come out after the game and people would be very aggressive asking for autographs, pushing and grabbing at your clothes."

Mike found the caliber of play very high. "There were a lot of players who, like me, had reached the Triple-A level, and some Hispanic players with major-league experience. Over the year people like Andres Galarraga have played there. Last winter, Philadelphia's Bob Abreu and [former Trapper/Oakland A] Andrew Lorraine were there." Mike felt that he had become a smarter hitter because of his winter work, "because I faced a lot of guys who'd had major-league experience. I learned greater patience, to be more selective about which pitches I swung at. You'd only get one good pitch per at bat. If you missed it, they'd eat you up, just like in Triple-A. And I played regularly in left field. Last summer I had quite a few games in the infield. This was a real opportunity to work on my outfield skills."

Overall, playing winter ball was a good experience; but it did have a down side. "I didn't have much of a break between the end of their season and the beginning of spring training. I'd been invited to the Twins' major-league camp, so I had to report near the end of February. At first, the adrenaline kept me pumped up, but now I'm beginning to feel a little tired, like it's the end of June instead of early May." He thought about the weather outside and added, "If it really is May."

By 1:30, the clubhouse was deserted of players. Clubhouse manager James Rosnau set about cleaning up the remains of what was supposed to have been a pregame meal and began what, because the game uniforms hadn't been used, was a light laundry load. Outside the stadium, a couple

Theme days are becoming extremely popular at minor-league parks. Here, Spider-Man takes a practice "drop" in preparation for Spider-Man Day, when he would deliver the game ball to the mound.

Dennis Henke holds the Pacific Coast League championship trophy after the season. Ironically, none of the members of the winning team would be around the next year to admire the trophy as the Minnesota Twins moved their Triple-A affiliate to Rochester, N.Y.

After each game Trappers manager John Russell prepares reports on each player for the Minnesota Twins' Player Development Office. (Photograph by Denyse Conroy)

of hardy people turned disappointedly away from the ticket window. In the grandstand, there was a brief flurry of activity. Team photographer Denyse Conroy and another person aimed cameras at the overhanging roof of the grandstand while in the last row of seats a well-bundled fan waited for a friend to come from the press box. Spider-Man, having arrived to perform, decided to make a practice drop. He began his slow, head-first descent. From the last row of seats came the sound of one fan clapping.

Postseason Postscript

As the spring advanced, the Trappers' bats continued to be hot and their pitching arms as well. They moved up steadily in the standings and on July 3 took over and never relinquished first place in the North Division. They finished the season ten-and-a-half games ahead of second place Portland and in the playoffs went on to defeat first Las Vegas and then Salt Lake City for the PCL championship. Mike Ryan finished the season with 31 home runs. In all the club hit 202 round-trippers. Ryan also made his major-league debut with the Twins after the Trappers' playoff victory. Three other Trappers— Michael Restovich, Kevin Frederick, and Todd Sears— also played their first big-league games. In all, twenty players wore both Trappers' and Twins' uniforms during the season. John Russell, who was named minor-league manager-of-the-year by Baseball America *accepted a position as third base coach of the Pittsburgh Pirates. In late August, the Twins announced that they would not be renewing their affiliation with the Trappers, and in late September the Edmonton club signed a two-year agreement with the Montreal Expos. The Trappers' season attendance dropped 32,000 from the previous year to just over 340,000; however, the club made a profit of just under $20,000 dollars, Canadian.*

3—At the Epicenter of Baseball: The Rancho Cucamonga Quakes of the California League

Comedian Jack Benny gave the town of Cucamonga, California, national fame on his radio program of the 1940s and '50s. It was one of the destinations, along with Anaheim and Azuza, called out by the conductor of a train departing from the central Los Angeles station. To people living outside the greater Los Angeles area, the town's name faded along with memories of the radio program. Then, in the mid 1990s, the town—with a modified name—came into prominence in the baseball world. The Rancho Cucamonga Quakes, playing in a stadium named the Epicenter, were breaking attendance records, not only in the high Single-A California League in which they played, but throughout the lower ranks of minor-league baseball. Playing in a city that had been formed in 1977 from the amalgamation of Alta Loma, Cucamonga, and Etiwanda, they annually attracted over 300,000 fans to a park located in what had once been one of the largest, most prosperous grape-growing and wine-making areas of southern California. Big box stores and chain restaurants surrounded the ball park, located just south of Route 66, the famous "Mother Road," now an eight-lane wide highway taking commuters, many of them Quakes' fans, to their comfortable, middle-class homes.

The Epicenter, located at the corner of Rochester Avenue and Jack Benny Way, was built by Rancho Cucamonga for the purpose of attracting a minor-league team as a tenant, a business that would turn the edge of this bedroom community into an entertainment destination, enhance the quality of life for the residents, and publicize the relatively new and rapidly expanding area beyond the immediate greater Los Angeles area. The project attracted the attention of Hank Stickney, owner of the nearby San Bernardino Spirit, who

The Epicenter, home of the Rancho Cucamonga Quakes, was specifically built by the city to attract a minor-league franchise to the rapidly expanding suburban community. In 1993, the first year the stadium was opened, the Quakes drew 331,005 fans, a California League record.

moved his team fifteen miles west to the new park. The Epicenter and the team have realized the town's objectives beginning with the first game, played on April 8, 1993. In a 10th anniversary supplement, The Ontario Daily Bulletin *called the event "The Move that changed a city." Columnist Louis Brewster wrote: "Rancho Cucamonga had stepped out on its own, out from underneath the shadow of Ontario and San Bernardino. The city that could had thrust itself on the map with a minor-league team and would never be the same."[1]* The Inland Valley Times *declared: "Since the first tremor in 1993, the baseball vision of a city and a few innovative owners has been realized by phenomenal players, a strong fan base and a creative support staff, combining for a decade of aftershock."[2]*

Thursday, May 9

Walking along Route 66 beside one of the few remaining small fields of grapes, past the big box stores and the chain restaurants, through a plaza displaying plaques celebrating the now nearly vanished wine industry, up the palm-lined promenade leading to the park, the baseball fan who'd forgotten about Cucamonga after he'd quit listening to the Benny show comes full circle. At the entrance to the Epicenter stands a life-sized

Comedian Jack Benny made the name Cucamonga famous in his old radio program. A statue of him stands at the main entrance to the Epicenter. Behind is the Quakes' very profitable gift shop.

bronze statue of Jack Benny, chin cupped in hand, violin tucked under an arm, looking bemused as he gazes down the promenade along which, in an hour, the night's fans would walk.

The transformation of the San Bernardino Spirit into the Rancho Cucamonga Quakes and their move from Fiscalini Field to the Epicenter was the second of five franchise shifts that, in the 1990s, altered the geography and character of the California League, a high Single-A circuit that had begun operations in 1942. In 1990, only three of the ten clubs were

Before Hank Stickney moved the team to Rancho Cucamonga, the club played at San Bernardino's Fiscalini Field, which had formerly been used mainly by American Legion teams. In 1993, the city of San Bernardino acquired another California League team and, in 1996, a new stadium.

located in southern California: San Bernardino, Riverside, and Palm Springs. Only three of the league's teams, led by Stickney's Spirit with 190,890, drew over 100,000 spectators. Two clubs, Reno and Salinas, operated without major-league affiliation. Only two of the stadiums had been built in the 1980s, and both were of the aluminum bleachers and molded seats variety. None of the parks had the club seats, picnic pavilions, and luxury boxes so important for generating revenue.

In 1991, the Riverside Red Wave moved to a new stadium in Adelanto to become the High Desert Mavericks, who quickly set a league attendance record of 204, 438. Featuring a cafe and grassy berms for family seating, the Mavericks eclipsed their Riverside attendance record by over 110,000. In 1993, San Bernardino became the Quakes, and Salinas moved to the just-vacated San Bernardino where a new park would be built in time for the 1996 season. Palm Springs moved to the brand new "Diamond" in Lake Elsinore in 1994; and Reno spent three years as the Riverside Pilots before becoming, in 1996, the Lancaster JetHawks, who also played in a new park. Within five years, the Southern Division, which was briefly called the Freeway Division, had been radically altered. In each of the five new parks, attendance records were set. The Southern Division became a "commuters' league." Like the people who came to watch, visiting teams returned to their own home bases after each game.

At this time, the California League also became an organization of haves and have nots, with the northern teams playing before much smaller crowds in older, outmoded parks. But as the decade advanced, southern division clubs began to experience attendance drops. From a high of 218,000 fans, High Desert dropped to 137,000; Rancho Cucamonga from 446,000 to 292,000 ; Lake Elsinore from 388,000 to 223,000; Lancaster from 315,000 to 173,000 and San Bernardino from 273,000 to 151,000. These figures still placed the southern franchises above all but San Jose in the north; however, they represented a loss of revenue that had team officials, who had to deal with the high expenses of newer parks, worried. The Quakes, who had seen six consecutive years of attendance decline beginning in 1996, were one of these. Using the slogan "Ten Years of Hometown Baseball," they made plans designed to reverse the trend in 2002.

The Quakes' plans included designating each night a special occasion at the ballpark and making the lower-drawing week-nights more appealing. On Monday, $10 bought two club seats, two hot dogs, two sodas, and two boxes of Cracker Jacks. On Wednesdays, hot dogs were just $1. Tonight was labeled "Thirsty Thursday." All twelve-ounce beverages (including beer) were only $1.

Inside the park, a few minutes before game time, on-field public address announcer Jeff Wymer strode energetically back and forth across the infield, and informed the smallish crowd wandering into the stands: "You are about to be shaken in your seats." At that moment, Tremor, the oversized mascot, burst from the first base dugout, waving to people, dancing to the blaring music, and, as he-it neared home plate, hugging the umpires. He was described in the team's yearbook as a Rallysaurus who had been buried in an earthquake millions of years ago and been rescued when construction of the ballpark began in 1992. He, along, with Aftershock, a kind of me-too companion mascot, were part of the earthquake theme seen throughout the park and all during the game.

There was never a dull moment, as events seemed to occur spontaneously whenever baseball wasn't being played. Tremor clapped with exaggerated swings of his arms as the Quakes' players were announced and ran to their positions, each accompanied by a child from a local Little League team. In the "dead" time between innings, things got livelier. Wymer, striding intensely on the dugout roofs, exhorted: "You've got to be wild, you've got to be crazy." And fans shrieked, hoping to win T-shirts and pizzas. Tremor gyrated to *All Shook Up* and, during the fifth inning, joined the

Quakes mascot Tremor cools down an excited Sunday afternoon crowd.

ground crew dragging the infield. An old print house dress covered his uniform: he had become Rancho Cucamonga's unofficial drag queen. At another time, he raced a small child around the bases, and lost—as he had during every game that had been played at the Epicenter. And when the Rallysaurus wasn't entertaining, the Trash Family was. Local dancers, they performed between innings on the dugout tops and, midway through the game, circulated through the stands carrying large garbage bags into which fans tossed drink cups, Cracker Jack boxes and other ballpark debris.

Spontaneous as these non-baseball episodes appeared, they were as meticulously choreographed as a fight scene in a western movie. In fact, before each game, front office employees Heather Williams and Kristen Streit met with Tremor, Wymer, and the part-time game-day staff to go over a detailed script. It included a list of the 14 pregame events and precise times that these events and announcements took place before the scheduled first pitch at 7:15 P.M. The script also included directions for the between-innings activities, along with a list of where each event would occur, which staff members would supervise it, and what music would be played.

If these apparently effortless, but really carefully planned, events were fun for the fans, they were good business for the Quakes. Not only did they make coming to the park more appealing to casual family groups, they put money into the Quakes' bank account. Each daily event was sold to a sponsor for a season's price of $5,000. "Every Quakes' game is an event.… We can tailor an entertainment on-field or game-action contest that will make your company a part of the action at the Epicenter," read the promotional kit sent out to prospective sponsors. The fees were an important part of the advertising revenue that would make up one-third of the Quakes' annual revenue.

Early in the game, one of the spectators, a person who had attended very few baseball games at the Epicenter, asked his companion, "Which one is the home team?" His question was, perhaps, more apt than he realized, as the two clubs had only last year switched their affiliations with major-league teams. For the first eight years, Rancho Cucamonga had been a farm team of the San Diego Padres, while the visiting Lake Elsinore Storm had a working agreement with the Anaheim Angels. In 2001, both Lake Elsinore and Rancho, having become disenchanted with their player development contracts and believing that working with a major-league team closer to home would be beneficial, traded big-league partners. Affiliation switches between two clubs are not uncommon in the minor leagues and, for the first year or two, fans in each town are like Thursday night's novice, wondering which team to root for. The old home team was now wearing the uniforms of the visiting team. Should you cheer for or boo the fellow you applauded enthusiastically a season or two earlier? Thursday's fans at the Epicenter faced that dilemma, as five men wearing the scarlet caps of Lake Elsinore, had, just two seasons ago, worn Rancho's blue caps.

This game was the season's first of twenty-one games of what the publicity departments of both clubs had dubbed the I-5 rivalry: apprentice Angels against apprentice Padres, playing for the two cities that annually battled it out for the California League's attendance championship. The nine innings that followed Wymer's introduction of "Y-0-U-U-R-R R-R-ANCHO C-U-U-U-C-A-A-M-O-O-N-G-A Q-U-A-A-K-E-S" was a good complement—or perhaps supplement—to the contests, dancers, mascots, and dollar drinks. Fans who focused their attention of the field saw a fast, well-played game. The Quakes scored four runs in the third inning to take a lead they never surrendered. The final score was 4–2. Rancho Cucamonga's starting pitcher Brandon O'Neal scattered six hits over seven innings to earn the win.

An interesting aspect of the game involved the Storm's use of Wikki Gonzales as its designated hitter. Gonzales had been a member of the Quakes during the 1997 and 1998 seasons and, since 1999, a catcher for the San Diego Padres. Last year, he missed 35 games because of injuries and his bad luck had carried into the beginning of the current season. In the Padres' fourth game, he fractured his wrist. Sent to Lake Elsinore for a six-day rehabilitation stint, he had a walk and was hit by a pitch in four trips to the plate. On Friday, he would catch five innings; on Saturday, he would catch another five, and on Sunday, he would be the designated hitter. By the end of the following week he was scheduled to be back with the parent club.

One of the most entertaining events of the evening took place not on the field or in the stands, but within the cramped confines of the Epicenter's press box. Four reporters, the scoreboard operator, and the official scorer smiled and sometimes laughed out loud as they listened to the on- and off-air by-play between the play-by-play announcers Rob Brender of the Quakes and Sean McCall of the Storm. Not only was this the season's first on-field encounter of the I-15 rivals, it was also the first meeting of their two radio guys.

Brender, in his first year at Rancho Cucamonga and only his second broadcasting professional baseball, was the more formal and restrained of the two, frequently turning off his mike as he called over to his colleague, sitting five seats away. McCall was less inhibited, sharing his dialogue with the radio listeners, carrying on informal conversations with various press-box visitors, and mock-complaining about the excessive noise coming from next door—the luxury suite of Quakes' owner Hank Stickney.

Ken Scully, son of the famous Dodger announcer Vin Scully, once called McCall "slightly irreverent," and, over the four-game series, the Storm's play-by-play man would provide many examples of how he earned that reputation. On Thursday, after the paid attendance had been announced at 2,153, he commented to listeners: "There certainly were 153 people here, but the other 2000 seems to be stretching it." About a player who'd attended university, he cynically remarked. "He went to—university for his education, it that's what you call it." After one of the umpires had called a player out on a close play at first, he offered the opinion: "It was questionable. But the game's been pretty long. Maybe

Sean McCall, the witty and frequently irreverent radio announcer for Lake Elsinore, checks over his notes before beginning his play-by-play of the Storms' game against Rancho Cucamonga.

the ump had a movie he wanted to catch back at the motel." And when a notoriously lead-footed outfielder made a good running catch, he feigned surprise: "It's his uniform number; but I wonder if someone else is wearing his shirt?"

McCall, now in his eighth year with the Storm, began his career in Boise, Idaho, in 1991. His mother, who lived there, had heard they needed someone for the summer; he contacted the Hawks of the Northwest League, and was invited to head north. But upon arrival, he discovered that the job wasn't available and that they'd forgotten to notify him. As a consolation, they offered Sean a short segment on the pregame snow—but with no pay. During the season, he asked the general manager if he could do color during the broadcasts of road games. "I'd never done that before, and when he asked to listen to my tapes, I said they'd been lost or delayed in my move. He sent me on a first road trip—for free—and after that gave me $25 a game."

After the game between the Quakes and Lake Elsinore was over and he'd completed his wrap-up, Sean McCall offered the press box occupants a treat from the grocery bag full of Tootsie Pops and Rolls that he'd brought with him, covered his broadcasting equipment with a large beach towel, and sat down to await the departure of the team bus for Lake Elsinore. As he chewed on one of the candies he'd extracted from his sack, he talked about his style and philosophy of broadcasting.

"Basketball was my first passion," he commented, "but now it's baseball. I'm like a fan. I enjoy watching the players and then seeing them move up to higher levels. But I'm also a reporter; I try to convey the uniqueness of the game. A baseball broadcast should be multiple entertainment: there's the game itself that I describe; there's my enthusiasm; there's my humor— it's not rehearsed, it's improvisation. You have to be honest about the game, but remember that it's only a game, and so you have to have fun and encourage the listeners to have fun. I used to listen to Vin Scully a lot, but not to copy him. I'm not a traditionalist, and I know my style might not go over in some places. It would be nice to be in the major leagues. But as long as I'm working where people care about the game, I'm happy. That's the way it is in Lake Elsinore. What a place to call home."

At this point, Sean noticed several ballplayers heading across the parking lot to the idling bus. He picked up his goody bag, offered people in the press box a final treat, and headed toward home.

Friday May 10

By 9:30 the next morning, all of the Quakes' 16 front-office employees were back at the Epicenter beginning their preparations for Friday night's game. As it was to include the second of eight fireworks displays scheduled for the 2002 season, a large family crowd was expected. One of the first to arrive at work was also one of the last to have departed the previous evening: Pat Filippone, the general manager. "I've loved baseball all my life," he remarked when asked if the long hours spent at the park didn't get him down. "Ever since I was a little kid, I've loved baseball; but by sixth grade, I knew I really didn't have any kind of future on the field." And so, while some of his friends would fantasize about performing World Series heroics on the field, he'd sit in the bleachers of minor league parks in northern Virginia imagining ways of running the off-field business differently. "I inquired about jobs after high school and found that I'd be welcome in a lot of places if I would work for free."

Instead, Filippone attended university, earned a degree in business, and, to use his phrase, "worked a normal job" in order to save enough money to be able to afford a low-paying entry-level job in the minor leagues. The Prince William (Virginia) Cannons of the Carolina League offered him a sales position in 1991. He quickly worked his way into the position of general manager. "It was a challenge putting on a game there," he remembered, referring to the fact that G. Richard Pfitzner Stadium was a difficult place to get to and often an uncomfortable one in which to watch a game. With its aluminum bleachers and uncovered grandstands, afternoon games were sweltering experiences. "We worked hard, but we had fun. We took a grassroots approach and appealed to families. In a couple of years, we had doubled our attendance." But after the 1998 season, the Cannons' best year at the gate, Filippone discovered the challenge had disappeared. "Everything was running very smoothly, and I needed something new. The Quakes contacted me, and I accepted their proposal."

The owners had been looking for someone who could run a profitable organization, because, even though the club continued to lead the California League in attendance, it was starting to lose money. Deadwood needed to be cut away, budgets tightened, and outreach into the community increased. Although the attendance dropped in each of the first three years of Filippone's tenure, the general manager believed that his reorganization had successfully met the challenges. The staff he described as "leaner, younger, more efficient, and better trained." The Quakes began to sponsor programs that keep the club involved in the community during the fall, winter, and early spring months, as well as during the season.

One of the changes the Quakes had made was to recognize that they are no longer the only show in town. "In 1996, I visited here for the Carolina-California Leagues All-Star Game," Filippone recalled. "You could see the park for miles; it was visible to people driving along I-10 and I-15. That was a great advertisement. Now it's surrounded by other buildings. Not only can't people see us, there are malls and restaurants that weren't even here when I took this job. They can spend their money there instead of at the Epicenter." And so, in addition to community outreach programs, the Quakes' management worked to make people aware that coming to a ballgame was a great entertainment option. "We realized that most of our potential customers weren't really interested in season tickets. They wanted to come to specific games. So we focus on trying to achieve sell-outs for certain dates. The weekends are the best ones, so we're really trying to go beyond the eight weekend sell-outs we had last year." With only three exceptions—one of which was a fireworks display scheduled for Thursday, July 4, and the other, Fan Appreciation Day, on Thursday, August 29, the final home date—all of the promotions have been scheduled for weekends. "Our product and our pricing is directed at families," he emphasized.

Filippone discussed the significance of the product on the field: the baseball team. Although families attended the games for the total entertainment package, a good team was important. "This market wants a winner," he said, referring not only to Rancho Cucamonga, but also to the greater Los Angeles area, where the Angels and Dodgers are within an hour's drive. "The press emphasizes winning and we want a winner. Hank Stickney was upset in 2000 when the team San Diego sent us was very weak and said that we didn't want to be affiliated with them any longer." At the time, the Anaheim Angels wanted a new high Single-A affiliate and, recognizing the marketing value of a link with their closest Southern California major-league baseball neighbors, the Quakes quickly signed an agreement. Now in its second year, the relationship was rumored to be going through a rocky period. Filippone quickly denied this. "The press has exaggerated some of the difficulties we have had. We can and are doing some really interesting marketing things with them. And because this is Single-A ball, they don't make a lot of roster changes. Our fans will have a whole season to get to know most of the players and to see them develop."

At 10:30 A.M., over eight hours before game time, one of the men responsible for the development of the Angels' prospects had already arrived in the cramped Rancho Cucamonga clubhouse. Blake "Zeke" Zimmerman, the pitching coach, sat in the small, glass-walled office he shared with manager Bobby Meacham and hitting coach Damon Berryhill. "I'm renting an apartment with the trainer. I have a bed and a lamp," Zeke remarked. "I'd get bored sitting around the place until the afternoon. There's stuff to do here, and I really like being at the park. When I was eight, I got my first baseball job, as a bat boy in Little League. And then I became a groundskeeper. When my folks went off on vacations, I'd sleep at the park. So I guess it's natural that I feel so at home here."

A graduate of Weber State University of Utah, he played two years of minor-league baseball before a torn rotor cuff ended his playing career. "After that happened," he remarked, "I went back to school and earned a master's degree in physiology. I figured I'd be involved in sports in some way or other, and I thought that the knowledge would be valuable." Zeke taught school for 28 years in Mesa, Arizona, and was the baseball coach for Mesa Community College for 21 years. "Ten years ago I began to coach for the short-season clubs in the Angels' farm system. It worked out really well; as soon as school and junior college were over, the pro season began. It was over just in time for me to start teaching again. Last fall I retired from teaching and college coaching, and the Angels invited me here to coach at the full-season level."

Zimmerman viewed the advanced Single-A California League as the place where the Angels' best younger prospects really began their development. "In short-season ball, you try to get them to understand the business of being a pro ball player. You want them to develop adult routines because, if they develop consistent daily patterns in their lives, they should be able to bring these habits to the field. Some of them are very young. In the Pioneer League, I've had kids just out of high school in the starting rotation. Those who make it to Cedar Rapids [in the low Single-A Midwest League] learn about the rigors of a full five-month season. Most of the ones who should have been weeded out have been."

The 12 players that made up Zeke's pitching staff were not only just three steps away from the major leagues, but they also had a lot of developing to do. Among them, they had played a total of 30 professional seasons—only three more than the entire major league career of Hall of Fame pitcher Nolan Ryan. Two—Cliff Smith and Dan Jackson—had only one pro season under their belts. The staff averaged 22.7 years of age. The oldest, Mike Brunet, was 25, although he'd only played two seasons since being drafted out of college in 1997. Three—Phil Wilson, Richard Fischer, and Pedro Liriano—were only 21. Only five of them had been chosen during the first 10 rounds of the draft, with Wilson, a third-round choice in 1999, the highest pick. Wilson and Fischer were the only Quakes among the Angels' pitching prospects listed by *Baseball America*, being ranked 16th and 28th respectively. Entering the sixth week of the 2002 season, the Quakes' pitchers were, euphemistically speaking, struggling. Their 5.35 earned run average was ninth in the 10-team league. They had given up 43 home runs (worst in the league), and 137 bases on balls (seventh in the league). Their 293 strikeouts were only seventh-best.

And yet Zimmerman spoke positively about his young charges: "All of my pitchers are upwardly bound. They may not all make the major leagues; but they certainly have at least two more years of development." He sounded like the father and teacher that he is: wanting the best for his students and encouraging them to maximize their potential. He'd been with six of them before, when they were beginning their careers in Butte, Provo, or Boise. "The key," he went on, "is how willing they are to learn or to be taught." All of them could throw excellent pitches—but not on a regular basis. "The role of the teacher," he explained, "is to get them to remember what they did when things went well—for a pitch, an at-bat, an inning, or an entire appearance. 'How did you do that?' I'll ask. And when they can tell me, then they can work at repeating what went right. When they can repeat regularly during the games, you know that their game will start to take off."

While Zeke talked about the game he loved and loved to teach, the players began to arrive in a clubhouse that was much smaller than those many had spent time in as university athletes. One of these rapped on the door, stuck his head in and asked the pitching coach if he knew where the yellow ball was. He was referring to an inflated rubber sphere the size of a volleyball that Zimerman used in teaching pitching mechanics. "I saw it earlier under the bench in the bullpen," the coach answered. "Check there, and I'll be out in a few minutes—we can go over the things we worked on yesterday." And while the young man went searching, Zeke slipped a warmup jersey over his T-shirt, tightened his cleats, and walked through the clubhouse, down the tunnel to the field, and out to the bullpen. A few moments later, he was doing what he most enjoyed—teaching baseball. He had said earlier, "Most coaches are in the minor leagues because they hope a job here could lead to the majors. I'm not—I'm here because I love to teach."

Shortly before the game that evening, a seventy-something-year-old man entered the seasons' ticket and suite holders' entrance of the Epicenter. Dressed in a pair of khaki pants, an open-necked sports shirt, and a slightly rumpled gray windbreaker, all of which looked like they could have been purchased not too recently from the racks of Wal-Mart or, at best, Sears. He greeted the ticket-taker by name and, remarking that it was a bit of a cool night for baseball, entered the elevator. On the third floor, he talked briefly with group sales representative Janice Selasky, one of the veterans of the staff, now in her eighth year with the Quakes, and headed for the suite next to the press box—the owner's suite.

The friendly and unassuming man was Hank Stickney, who, in addition to the Quakes, owned the Las Vegas 51s, Shreveport Swamp Dragons, Dayton Dragons, and South Georgia Waves. Before he purchased his first team, the Ventura County Gulls, in 1987, Stickney had served in the United States Air Force as a second lieutenant and then become founder and president of Western Medical Specialties and Reimbursement Dynamics—health care companies. "I learned the importance there of customer satisfaction," he explained. "I'd ask myself what I'd expect if I were doing business with one of my companies, and then I'd apply it to the way we did business. When I became involved in baseball, I used the same principles."

Stickney and fellow Gulls owners, one of whom was actor Mark Harmon, moved the club to San Bernardino, where the renamed Spirit took up residence in Fiscalini Field, which had primarily served as the site of American Legion contests. "1988 was an interesting year," Stickney recalled. "First we rehabilitated an amateur facility, then we fielded an independent team. We finished 70 and 70, but we drew four times as many people as the Gulls had the year before. It was the first time in the California League that a club had an attendance of over 150,000." When, a few years later, officials of neighboring Rancho Cucamonga talked to him about becoming a tenant in their planned stadium Stickney felt "it was a situation too good to be ignored. I love the challenge of opening up new areas. But," he quickly added, "we helped San Bernardino land another team."

The new park into which Stickney's team moved was not without its problems. "The city hired an architect with no baseball stadium experience," Stickney explained. "The owner's suite is bigger than the press box and the players' clubhouses are very small. The seats were configured in a way that made expanding the stands very difficult." He spent over four million dollars working to rectify those problems that could be rectified.

And he emphasized to his staff the importance of fan involvement at the park. "In the minor leagues, you don't know what kind of a team you'll get from year to year. So you work on entertainment." At that moment, Aftershock, the team's second mascot, entered the suite and received warm embraces from Stickney and his wife, Dee. After the Rallysaurus had left, Stickney related him to the family entertainment element. "Tremor could only work one side of the field at a time. And the people on the other side weren't involved. And so we created another mascot, one who could work the other side, especially on weekends, when we have the most kids."

When Pat Filippone came in to discuss problems he was having with the firm to whom the catering operations had been leased, Stickney offered a couple of suggestions. Pat departed and the owner noted that he left virtually all the day-to-day operations to his general manager. "He's very experienced; when we come to the park, Dee and I can relax and be fans." Then he added, a note of excitement in his voice, "I'm really looking forward to our project in Frisco, Texas." He was referring to the $30 million sports complex that, in 2003, he, along with Texas Rangers owner Tom Hicks, would be opening in a wealthy suburb of Dallas. "I visit every couple of weeks to check on design and construction. The people are really excited—we are way ahead of where we were when we built the stadium in Dayton, Ohio, especially in terms of suite sales and advertising." He alluded to the tremendous success of the Dayton Dragons, who had attracted over one million fans in their first two seasons in the Ohio city. "Right now," he continued, "we're making plans to announce the new Frisco nickname and logo." At this point, Dee, who had been closely following the action on the field, turned to her husband. "Don't tell him what it is," she urged. "It'll spoil the surprise—and that's half the fun"

The game Dee had been watching had been proceeding slowly and, for Zeke Zimmerman's starting pitcher Dan Jackson, badly. At the end of the second inning the Quakes led 3-1, thanks to Mike Campo's two-run homer in the first and an RBI double by Casey Smith in the second. But in the top of the fourth, the Storm sent 10 men to bat and scored six runs. When the inning was over, Jackson's 4.00 earned run average had risen to 5.23. The Quakes came back with two runs each in the bottom of the fourth and fifth to tie the game. They went ahead with two in the seventh, but lost the lead in the top of the eighth, when reliever Alan Wawrzyniak gave up two walks and a home run. The Quakes tied the game at 10 and went on to win in the bottom of the eleventh. As the crowd of 6,312 watched the postgame fireworks, Lake Elsinore radio announcer Sean McCall wrapped up his broadcast with comments about the ugliness of the game, in which the two teams committed nine errors between them. "And so," he concluded, "after three hours and fifty minutes of so-called entertainment, the final score is Rancho Cucamonga 11 and Lake Elsinore 10."

Saturday, May 11

The hallway leading to the breakfast room of the Best Western Heritage Inn is decorated with a mural depicting two of the "heritages" of which Rancho Cucamonga is most proud: the old Route 66 and the new Epicenter. But this Saturday morning very few people passed by the mural. The hotel was relatively empty: the businessmen who stayed during the week had departed, and—although it is the official hotel for visiting California League teams—the Storm had taken the bus home the night before. But the baseball connection remained. An elderly hotel guest approached the room's only other occupant and asked if he had finished with the sports section of the paper he was reading. "My nephew hit a home run last night," he explained. "And I want to see what they wrote about it."

He introduced himself, Dom Jordano, from south Florida. The great uncle of Quakes' left fielder Mike Campo, he'd flown to watch his nephew play ball, something he'd done for many years. "And when I still lived in New Jersey, I'd go to all his Legion and high school games. Then I traveled to watch him in the playoffs when he was at Penn State." Jordano provided details of the young man's accomplishments, which included selection as a second-team college All-American. "And he didn't get a cent for signing a pro contract. Some of those guys get millions, and they can't hit half so well. It's not right." He glanced through the paper, snorted when he found that Campo's home run of the previous night had received only brief mention, and headed down the hallway past the mural depicting his nephew's place of work.

At eleven o'clock, a good hour before most players wake up and eight hours before game time, Jordano's nephew was at work. Along with teammate Johnny Raburn, Mike Campo had reported to the parking lot of Mountain View Tire, where, for the next two hours, the players, along with Tremor, would greet customers who had come to do business with one of the baseball team's important sponsors. "It's something extra we like to throw in for our advertisers," explained Quakes' community relations director Heather Williams. "It gives the club and the sponsor more visibility in the community, and the players seem to have fun." She glanced over her shoulder where the two athletes were performing a high-stepping line-dance with the Shakers, a group of high-school-aged dancers who regularly performed at the Epicenter.

Heather, who had played varsity softball at New Mexico State University and had worked for the legendary minor-league owner and promoter Jim Paul, was responsible for executing the Quakes' new mandate for greater interaction with the community. "It's a 12-month-a-year project," she explained. "One of the biggest activities is the Quakes' Reading Challenge. It involves visiting schools in San Bernardino, Riverside, and Los Angeles Counties. We read the story *A Dream Team for Tremor*, and Tremor interacts with the kids. Then we talk about the reading program: if they read five books, they get two free tickets." She also directs the Rancho Cucamonga Quakes' Community Foundation, which, during the upcoming season, would be sponsoring such fund-raising events as "Hit a Home Run for Education" and "Basebowl," a bowling evening, the proceeds from which would go to various charities.

His line-dancing duties completed, Mike Campo, puffing in a most unathletic manner, sat down in the shade and talked about his life in baseball and the unusual path that had led to Rancho Cucamonga. Going into this evening's game hitting .365, second highest in the California League, Campo had posted .358 and .313 averages in his first two professional seasons. And in his final two years at Pennsylvania State University he'd hit .351 and .425. "I've loved to hit all my life," he remarked. "When we were kids, a group of us would play home run derby for hours—whenever there weren't any games scheduled." He hadn't been drafted out of high school or after his junior year at Penn State. "I was disappointed, but I took my schooling seriously. So I went back another year, played ball, and graduated in business management." His graduation was in early June, a few days before the 2000 draft. He'd had a letter of inquiry from the Anaheim Angels, but on June 6 and 7, the two days of the draft, he received no phone calls notifying him that he'd been picked. "I already had a job offer from a Washington, D. C., firm, working in corporate catering. I kept pushing my start date back, hoping to be drafted. When nothing happened, I asked the company if they could wait a couple of weeks."

They did, and Mike drove to Waterbury, Connecticut, where he'd been offered a tryout with the Spirit of the independent Northern League. "I worked out, they were happy, and they put my name into that night's starting lineup. When the general manager brought me the contract to sign, he said that there was a call from my mother and that I was to contact her right away." Telling him that he'd be right back, Campo phoned home, fearing bad news. But it wasn't: the Angels had called his home with a contract offer. If he accepted, he was to report to Butte of the Pioneer League. Campo thanked the Waterbury Spirits for their interest, changed out of his uniform, and drove home to southern New Jersey. The next night, he stepped off a plane in Montana.

Although his life had changed suddenly, adapting to professional baseball wasn't as difficult as Campo had expected. The pitchers were bigger and faster than he'd been used to in the Big Ten, but they weren't as precise. The Nittany Lions had traveled mainly by bus, including a trip from Pennsylvania to Minneapolis–St. Paul, so he was prepared for all-night rides across the western states. And he'd played in the wooden bat Shenandoah Summer League, so he didn't miss the fact that aluminum bats were outlawed in the professional leagues. Playing in the California League this year was almost a luxury: travel distances were comparatively short, the weather was mild, and the level of play was much higher than in his first two minor-league seasons.

Mike did not share the annoyance felt by his great uncle Dom about the fact that he was an undrafted player surrounded by highly-touted prospects, some of whom had received considerable bonuses for signing. He'd come from a school where baseball was not a major sport, where players were not so highly scrutinized as they were in such places as Louisiana State or Stanford. His baseball had been played in climates where the sport could not be pursued year-round. But he was following his dream; he had progressed steadily in his profession; and he was doing well what he loved doing best—hitting a baseball. Moreover, he got to spend a Saturday morning line-dancing with some very attractive, although quite young women, while most of his teammates had nothing better to do than to sleep late.

At 1:00 P.M., as the line-dancers in the parking lot of Mountain View Tire broke up, another line began to form a quarter of a mile away. A dozen or so people carrying camp chairs strolled up the palm-lined walkway leading to the main gate. Once there, they unfolded their chairs, sat down, and began the five-hour wait for the gates to open. They weren't people with time on their hands and no place to go; they were members of an unusual classification of baseball fan, the bobblehead doll collector, and they wanted to make sure they would be some of the 1,200 people to receive tonight's giveaway, a miniature replica of Mike Piazza, one-time Los Angeles Dodgers catcher. Until the mid 1990s, ballpark fans had received such giveaway items as caps, T-shirts, water bottles, and lunch bags—each stamped with the team's and the sponsor's logo. The Quakes, and most other minor league teams, still distributed these. But a decade ago, when the Beanie Baby collecting craze hit the country, clubs began passing out the dolls dressed in the home team's uniforms. That's when the lineups began. Some fans bought several, even dozens of tickets, so that they could acquire arms-full of dolls which commanded big prices on the collectors' market. When bobbleheads replaced Beanie Babies, the collecting and selling of the prized giveaways continued, so much so that teams started giving out only one doll per customer, no matter how many tickets a person had purchased. It made good business sense: an individual buying a dozen tickets would consume only one person's worth of concessions, and 11 people who didn't get dolls would be extremely unhappy.

Jon Deavers, the first person in line, had begun his quest for a Piazza doll at six in the morning. That's when he'd left his home in Lodi, California, and begun the nearly 400-mile drive south to the Epicenter. He had gathered over 40 of the collectibles in trips that had taken him as far as Camden, New Jersey. When it was possible, Jon liked to acquire three of each figure: "One to keep, one to trade, and one in a safe place in case of an earthquake," he laughed, although he went on to assert that his far-flung travels weren't made just for the dolls: "I really like visiting different parks. I'd never been to the Epicenter and today seemed like a good idea—two things for the price of one."

Although Jon gathered the figures to keep, not all people did. Often they would arrive early, gather the giveaway and leave before the game had even begun. There was enough profit in resale to make the wait worthwhile. Ed Green, the second in line, reported an incident that he'd read about when the San Bernardino Stampede had a Ken Griffey, Jr. bobblehead night: "He was a real favorite when he played there in 1988, although he only stayed for a couple of months before moving up. Even before the gates opened, there was an ad in ebay for one of the dolls. I don't remember what the price was, but it sure wasn't cheap." When the gates opened at 6:15 that evening, the line extended down the promenade and into the parking lot. Within 15 minutes all the dolls had been distributed.

While many of the fortunate 1,200 sat in the stands opening the small cartons, extracting the dolls, and admiring them, the evening's two umpires sat in their small, windowless dressing room also opening cartons and extracting their contents: the five-dozen regulation California League baseballs that they would rub with a special mud to remove the protective gloss. "It's a dirty job," crew chief R. J. Thompson quipped, repeating the tired umpire cliche, "but somebody's got to do it." Not surprisingly, the umpires looked very young, in their mid-twenties, not much older than the players over whose games they presided. "We're like them," he said. "We want to make it to the big leagues." That wasn't surprising either. What was surprising was how he and his partner, Hitoshi Uchikawa, entered the profession.

"When I was in high school," R. J. remembered, "my mother was called by God to be a minister. We were filled with joy; but she had to take a big pay cut, so I needed to get a part-time job. They were paying people $12 to umpire baseball games, and I decided to give it a try. After a while I began to attend umpire clinics in the off-season, and, at one of them, Dale Ford, who was a major-league umpire, was impressed with my work and suggested that I enroll in a professional umpire school. I went to Harry Wendelstedt's school, passed, and was invited to attend the professional

Along with Tremor, two unidentified fans, and Quakes catcher Ryan Budde, umpires R.J. Thompson (center) and Hitoshi Uchikawa (left) stand for the playing of the National Anthem.

umpire evaluation course. I didn't get a pro job the first year, so I saved my money, went back there in February of 2000 and landed a job in the advanced rookie Appalachian League."

Thompson was promoted to the low Single-A South Atlantic League in 2001 and, this year, to the California League. Discussing the differences of the three levels of professional baseball he'd experienced, he remarked: "The game gets cleaner as you advance. It's easier to see the catches and the pitches. And the players are more respectful. They realize that we're all learning and that mistakes are part of the game." One thing that hadn't changed, he recognized in his third professional season, was his enthusiasm for umpiring. "When I started the job, it was strange. I felt a different kind of excitement. I realized that the Lord was showing me what he had in store. And last night, I was behind the plate and near the end of the game, I thought, 'I've been working for nearly four hours and this is great.' The Lord showed me the right calling."

His partner, Hitoshi Uchikawa, a native of Osaka, had played amateur baseball in Japan. When he was a senior in college, he read about umpire schools, something he knew nothing about. He wrote to the United States and, in January 1996, enrolled in the Jim Evans umpiring school. "I couldn't speak English, except to say 'yes' and 'no,' so I smiled a lot. I used to arrive to class with two rule books—a Japanese one in one hand, an English one in the other. I didn't pass the first time, but Jim Evans told me that the big problem was my English. So I went to Sacramento and enrolled in English-as-a-second-language courses." It took two more attempts before he successfully completed the umpire's course, and, that done, he received a job in the Arizona League, an entry-level rookie league. In 2001, he was promoted to the short-season Single-A Northwest League; and, midway through the season, he was moved up to the South Atlantic League. He never considered returning to his homeland to continue his career. "In Japan, there's no respect for umpires," he explained. "And all the jobs go to people who played in the Japanese major leagues. I wasn't one of those, so there was no chance in Japan. I've got a much better opportunity in America. Sometimes," he laughed, "R. J. even lets me rub up all the baseballs by myself." And he scooped up some mud with his fingers and resumed his pregame duties.

Only a few of the people who showed up at the Epicenter left after collecting their Mike Piazza dolls. But when the game ended at nearly 10:30 P.M., well over two-thirds of the announced crowd of 5,464 had departed. During the game, the Quakes players had provided no fireworks and there were none after the game to wait for. Led by Xander Nady, who opened the scoring in the first with a towering two-run homer to left field and later added an RBI double and a single, the Storm scored 10 runs in the first six innings and went on to win 10–2. The Quakes struck out 11 times and managed to get only three runners in scoring position. They committed three errors to bring their series total to seven.

After the game, Nady, another member of the Storm on injury rehabilitation, chatted about the roller-coaster ride that his less-than-two-year-old professional career had been. Even though his three-for-four evening had increased his batting average from .272 to .288, Nady was not completely happy. He expressed his intense desire to leave Lake Elsinore. His frustration was understandable. It wasn't that he was upset with the Padres' organization, his team, or the city of Lake Elsinore; he was annoyed at the slowdown of his career since the fall of 2000. A highly acclaimed college player at the University of California, the Salinas, California, native had been named three times to the All-Pac 10 team, was twice selected an All-American, and had played two seasons with the United States National Team.

However, he was selected lower in the 2000 draft than was expected, partly, according to *Baseball America*, because he'd had a sub-par junior year and because teams expected he'd be difficult to sign.[3] Selected in the second round, 49th overall, he did not agree to contract terms until September 17. Then, two weeks later, he appeared in a game against the Los Angeles Dodgers, singling and later scoring in his only at-bat. His appearance made him only the 19th player since 1965, the first year of the draft, to play his first professional game in the major leagues. "I was very excited and nervous," he recalled. "I still get chills when I watch the tape. The count was two and two, and I hit a fastball right up the middle."

The major-league season over, Nady reported to the Arizona Fall League, where the top Double and Triple-A prospects from each major-league organization spend two months honing their skills. But after one game, he was sidelined, a victim of tendinitis. Physical therapy did not help and, when the 2001 season began, he found himself at Lake Elsinore, playing first base and designated hitter, positions that would not place too much stress on his increasingly tender right arm. He had a banner year, with a .302 average and 26 home runs. Named the Padres' minor-league player of the year and the California League's most valuable player, he'd have been fast-tracked to Triple-A Portland had his arm been healthy. But it wasn't, and during the off-season he underwent Tommy John surgery. According to the 2002 San Diego Padres Media Guide, "Drs. Lewis Yocum and Jan Fronek reconstructed the ulnar collateral ligament in his right elbow with a right plantaris tendon graft."[4]

The surgery went successfully. However, when the 2002 season opened, Nady was judged not sufficiently recovered to play in Triple-A. The team felt he was ready to face Double-A pitching and would have liked to send him to Mobile, their Southern League club. But because, in that league, the designated hitter was not used in games between National League affiliates, of which there were seven, Nady would have been forced to play two-thirds of his games in the field, something his arm could not yet handle. And so, he found himself back in the California League, at a level he'd clearly mastered a year ago. "The people here have been great, but ..." and Nady's voice trailed away. He climbed on the bus to return to Lake Elsinore, no doubt wishing he were boarding a plane heading to Portland.

Sunday, May 12

Batting practice was optional for the Quakes before their Mother's Day afternoon game. But by eleven o'clock, the clubhouse had begun to fill up as several players wandered in and suited up. Most of them were pitchers, and they had come to attend what one of them jokingly referred to as "Zeke's Sunday School." However, even though the session had a silly nickname, the players took it seriously. And, in a few minutes, they were gathered around their coach as he stood in his classroom—the left field bullpen—clipboard in hand and talked briefly with his pupils, all the time

Quakes pitching coach Zeke Zimmerman demonstrates a technique to Dan Jackson.

illustrating his points with arm gestures and body movements. The general lesson over, he assigned the players to different spots in the area, where they began working on elements of their deliveries.

As they went through the motions, all without baseballs, Zimmerman met with each one in turn. His over three decades of experience as a teacher and a baseball coach and player were readily apparent. He spoke enthusiastically to Dan Jackson as the young pitcher worked on the positioning of his feet: "There you go, that's good. The hip had to activate. Do you see how that helped? Keep at it." "Let me ask you this?" he queried Cliff Smith, with whom he'd worked last year in Provo, and, after asking a detailed question, listened intently to the answer. One had the feeling that, like all good teachers, he knew generally what the answer would be but wanted his student to understand that answer and make it his own by articulating it fully. A couple of minutes later, he barked out instructions to Brandon O'Neal, pacing like a drill sergeant as he did so: "I think you can do it. You've got to repeat!" Then he remarked to a bystander, in a slightly annoyed voice that was loud enough for all his pupils to hear: "I told them last night, if they don't have the discipline to learn, I can't teach them. I said, 'At this point you shouldn't need me any more, unless your spirit gets out of whack, unless your spirit doesn't tell your body what to do!'"

One of the spectators of Zeke's Sunday School was Justin Parker, the Quakes' strength and conditioning coach. A graduate of San Diego State University, he, like the pitching coach, held a master's degree in physiotherapy. After graduation, he'd worked for eight months for a professional motocross organization before joining the Anaheim Angels for his first job in professional baseball. "It's been a great learning experience," he remarked, "and Zeke has been a very big part of it. He has a great knowledge of baseball and life and a wonderful approach to the players. I learn every time I talk to him."

While the pitchers worked with their teacher, members of the front-office staff began preparations for the afternoon game. "Mother's Day sucks," muttered one man. He hastily went on to explain that there was nothing wrong with the day, that he loved his mother and wished he could spend the whole day with her. The problem, as he saw it, was that most families didn't spend the occasion at the ballpark. Attendance usually wasn't great, but just as much preparation had to go on. "Somebody said that a lot of mothers send their husbands to the park with the kids so that they can have a quiet afternoon." And he set about unpacking the hundreds of carnations that the players would present to those mothers who did show up at the Epicenter.

In a small change room behind the umpires' locker room, Aaron

Bishop and Shawn Lawrence were going over their Mother's Day plans. They were the people inside the Tremor and Aftershock costumes respectively, and they were working out the details of a brief between-innings skit. Aaron declined to divulge the nature of the short entertainment, but said that he'd been working on it with his wife and Shawn for some time. "I keep a notebook of ideas that come to me and that my partner and my wife bring up. We talk them over a lot and then note how well they seem to go over."

Although the coloring-story book *A Dream Team for Tremor* implied that the Rallysaurus's antics were a spontaneous expression of his fun-loving character, they were, in fact, the result of careful preparation and organization. After the planning was over, Aaron bought any small props that were needed: "I don't get reimbursed, but that's OK. I want the stunts to work. It's important that none of the acts interfere with the game. So I make sure that the umpires and players know about our onfield activities. Sometimes the players even want to join in."

And, when he donned the suit that cost the Quakes $10,000 to create, Bishop had to be physically fit: the Tremor costume was hot and heavy. He maintained a healthy diet, noting that he'd learned the value of fresh fruits and vegetables. And he drank a lot of water—but not during the two hours just before the game. "The suit's too awkward to get into and out of—so I don't need my bladder sending me messages during the game." Nourished and hydrated, he jogged and stretched before suiting up.

And he did the job, seventy games a year, without quitting his day job. By day, from September to June, he was a high school teacher and basketball coach; and in the evenings, a husband and father. And he spent his free time working around the yard of his house. "The fan's can't see this," he remarked, turning around, "but today Tremor's a redneck. I got too much sun this afternoon while I was weeding."

Asked how he became one of the most popular mascots in the minor leagues, Aaron modestly suggested that it was because he had a great deal of fun thinking up new things to do. After five years, he still looked forward to showing up at the Epicenter for each game. Actually, his mascot career began a decade ago while he was a student at the University of California at Santa Barbara and he accepted a friend's dare to try out for the position of the university's mascot, Phantom. He had been the previous Tremor's keeper, following him around the stands protecting him from the bane of all mascots, young teenage boys. Then he began some dancing with the mascot, including playing the role of the dancing umpire.

In 1994, he worked as Pongo the Orangutan, a San Diego Padres' mascot. "I'd drive two hours after teaching school to San Diego, perform, drive back, and then plan my next day's lessons. One day during a Padres game, I realized that the best fun mascots have is in the minor leagues. They're really close to the fans and the game. So, when Lake Elsinore needed a mascot, I applied. It was a lot closer to home. I became Hamlet the Sea Monster. Then the previous Tremor left in 1998, and here I am."

At this moment, umpires R. J. Thompson and Hitochi Uchikawa came into the adjoining dressing room. "Hey Aaron, " R. J. shouted, "have you called your mother to wish her happy Mother's Day?" Receiving an affirmative, he began mock-scolding his partner. "Hitochi hasn't—he doesn't love her." "Of course I do," came the reply. "It's just that we Japanese aren't as demonstrative as you Americans."

In the game that followed, the Quakes looked like they had recovered their winning ways. Starter Rick Fischer retired the first 12 batters he faced, striking out five. The Quakes scored a run each in the third and fourth. At the end of the fourth inning, Tremor performed the Mother's Day skit. Aaron Bishop may have called his mother, but Tremor hadn't called his. As the Rallysaurus pranced happily onto the infield to celebrate the Quakes' lead, a raucous, scolding voice erupted over the public address system and a smaller Rallysaurus burst from the first base dugout. She wore a dress and a wig of blond curls and brandished a bat while she chased her forgetful son toward third base. When he kneeled in a begging posture, she forgave him, planted a kiss on his nose, and, hand in hand, the two walked off the field.

In the top of the fifth inning, back-to-back doubles by Jeremy Owens and Wikki Gonzales reduced the Quakes' lead to one. And in the sixth, a wild pitch on a strikeout, a line drive single, a steal, and a walk gave the visitors a 4–2 lead. Rancho's Sergio Contreras's two-run homer in the seventh tied the game. However, in the top of the eighth, a single, steal, walk, two wild pitches and a sacrifice fly gave the Storm a one-run lead. Lake Elsinore won going away, scoring three times in the ninth. The final score was 8–4. Closer Todd Shiyuk allowed one hit and gave up a walk, but struck out four batters.

Shiyuk, who earned his first save of the year, was appearing in his seventeenth game of the season, the most appearances of any Storm pitcher. While the number was not unusual for this time of year, the fact that the 25-year-old left hander was playing for the Storm at all was. A native of Richmond, British Columbia, a suburb of Vancouver, Todd had never fantasized about following a career in Canada's national sport, hockey. "I never really got into it as a kid," he explained as he waited for the bus to head back to Lake Elsinore. "My grandfather used to play baseball, and he began to play catch with me before I even started school." With its mild weather and early springs, Richmond enjoyed a long baseball season, close to eight months, the longest in Canada, and so Shiyuk had plenty of time to play the game. But if he wanted to become really competitive, he knew that he'd have to move to the United States. "The coach I had when I was 16 and 17 was from Blaine, Washington, and one of his friends was the head coach Middle Georgia Community College. They arranged a scholarship for me."

And so the young Canadian headed 3,000 miles diagonally across the continent to the town of Cochran to further his on- and off-field education. "It was quite a culture shock," he remembered, "the customs, the way people talked, the weather. But I was getting baseball training that I could never have received if I'd stayed at home." Asked how he adapted his pitching to meet the more competitive brand of baseball he was now playing, he quickly explained that he was an infielder. "The only way I was connected with pitching was that John Franco was my favorite player, which was funny, because I always disliked the Mets when I was a kid." He became a pitcher almost by accident. The college held a scout day, when recruiters for four-year colleges, along with scouts from major-league organizations watched members of the team perform a number of drills. "Everyone ran, hit, threw, and pitched. So when my turn came, I got on the bump and did my thing." One of the observers was Bobby Pierce, coach of the University of Alabama at Huntsville, who offered Shiyak a scholarship— as a pitcher for the NCAA Division III school.

The young Canadian infielder who didn't like hockey finished his university playing career on the mound and, along the way, earned a degree in general business. He hadn't been drafted after his junior year and so, after graduation, having no high hopes of being drafted the second time around, he headed to Michigan to play in a semi-pro league. He'd enjoy one last baseball summer before using his university degree to find a job back in Canada. "I got back to our apartment after a game in early June when one of my roommates told me a guy had called but hadn't left a name or number." The "guy" was Mark Wasinger, a San Diego scout, who called again and informed Todd that he'd been chosen in the 10th round. On June 7, 1999, the accidental pitcher signed a contract and soon after joined the Padres' Pioneer League club in Idaho Falls.

Shiyuk performed well during his first season; used in relief, he won five and lost one, while earning four saves. "We all had a wonderful time; to us it was as if we were in the big leagues. The bus travel was kind of rough, but we were so excited to be there that it didn't really matter." He started the 2000 season with Fort Wayne of the Midwest League and in mid-season was promoted to Rancho Cucamonga, which was in its last year of affiliation with San Diego. His career was progressing very well; but all was not right. During spring training, he'd noticed what he'd thought were lumps in his testicles. The Padres medical staff had told him that they were harmless. "I felt weak during the last half of the season, and when I reported to spring training the next year, they told me again not to worry. Later, my roommates said that I'd seemed moody and listless. By mid-season, I'd gotten into 50 games and pitched 72 innings, the most of any season so far, so I thought maybe this was why I felt so rotten."

But with six weeks to go in the 2001 season, doctors gave him another examination. Cancer was discovered, and Shiyuk was operated on the following day. "I could have headed home, but I didn't. Being around the game, being with the guys was a really important part of my rehab. They were really supportive; I tried to come to the clubhouse each day. I feel much better now. A couple of days ago, after I'd finished running with the other pitchers, I thought, 'I don't feel tired at all.' This time last year, I'd have been wiped out after a couple of laps."

Just then two other members of the Storm's rehabilitation corps came up the tunnel leading from the visitor's clubhouse. Wikki Gonzales would be back with the big club in a matter of days, and Xander Nady was scheduled to be promoted to Triple A Portland by the end of May. Shiyuk would most likely spend the remainder of the season in the California League. The Canadian former infielder had suffered the most serious medical problem of the three and would probably need a year to regain his strength fully. "But," he said enthusiastically, "I feel great, and I'm doing what I love to do, throw a baseball."

He followed his teammates to the bus. Just before he stepped aboard, he said a few words to Sean McCall, who was loading his broadcasting equipment into the luggage compartment. He accepted the lollipop the radio guy offered, climbed the steps of the bus, and settled down for the 45-minute commute home from work.

Postseason Postscript

The Quakes did not make the playoffs, finishing with a 54 wins 86 losses record, poorest in the league. However, they did capture their 10th-straight California League attendance crown, drawing 292,150 fans to the Epicenter, just over a thousand more than in 2001. Mike Campo finished the year with a .313 batting average, third-highest in the league and was named to the All-Star team as a designated hitter. Lake Elsinore went all the way to the league finals before losing to Stockton. Nady, Wikki Gonzales, and Todd Shiyuk all left the Storm for higher leagues. Nady moved to Portland where he hit .283, with 10 homers against Triple-A pitching. Gonzales's rehab stint lasted longer than expected. He spent 19 games with Lake Elsinore before returning to San Diego. After 45 games, in which he posted a 3.31 earned run average, Shiyuk received a promotion to Double-A Mobile of the Southern League, where he appeared in 10 games. Nady returned to the Arizona Fall League, hitting .323 there before being sidelined with an injury.

4—Cincinnati's Kids Come to Billings: The Mustangs of the Pioneer League

June is the month when a great many young baseball players make their first steps toward fulfilling their life-long dreams of becoming major leaguers: they are selected in the major leagues' annual draft, sign their first contracts, and play their first professional games. Young men who, a few weeks earlier, were competing on high school and college diamonds now discover themselves playing for money with one of 181 minor-league teams in the United States and Canada. Some become instant millionaires, receiving signing bonuses that in a couple of cases have exceeded $5 million. Others, happy to be in professional baseball, work for less than minimum wage and daily meal money that can easily be exhausted with two super-sized orders at a fast-food restaurant.

A few players are fast-tracked, beginning their professional careers at the high Single-A level, joining teams that begin their seasons just over two months before the draft takes place. A larger number of college players, as well as high school players selected early in the draft, usually begin their seasons with one of the short-season Single-A teams; lower college draft choices and most high schoolers, in the advanced rookie leagues; while the rest report to the rookie league teams that operate out of major-league training complexes in Florida and Arizona.

In 2002, 157 newly-drafted athletes would begin their careers in the Pioneer League, an eight-team advanced rookie circuit that extends from Medicine Hat, Canada, to Provo, Utah. The numbers represented just over 10 percent of all players selected and nearly two-thirds of each team. The remainder of each club in the league would be made up of players promoted from the lower rookie levels or others returning to their teams for a second year of seasoning.

Chris Gruler, Cincinnati's top pick in the 2002 draft, exercises along the sidelines just before the Mustangs' first game, which was played in Medicine Hat, Canada.

The Pioneer League has been in considerable flux since 1994, with five clubs moving to new cities and seven clubs becoming affiliated with different major-league teams. The Billings Mustangs are the third-oldest club in the league, having been continuous members since 1969, and hold the longest affiliation with a major-league team, having been with the Cincinnati Reds since 1974. Their record both on and off the field has been very strong: their nine pennants are tops in the Pioneer League. In 2001, the community-owned club, one of few in the minor leagues, enjoyed its most successful season, drawing a record 104,000 fans, and winning the league championship. It has been suggested that the continued success on the field results from the fact that, because the Reds do not have a short-season Single-A affiliate, Cincinnati sends most of its top draft choices to the Mustangs.

Monday, June 17

Before they arrived in Billings during the second week of June, probably none of the new members of the Mustangs had heard of the small city of Medicine Hat. But at 1:30 P.M., Sunday, June 16, they boarded the Trailways bus parked in front of Billings' Cobb Field to make the 373-mile trip to the Canadian city where, the next night, two of them would make their professional baseball debuts. Twenty-six hours later, they again gathered beside the bus, this time dressed in their warm-up uniforms and carrying their game shirts and other baseball gear in their new bright red Cincinnati Reds equipment bags. They would be on the bus for only ten minutes as they traveled one mile to Athletic Park, a baseball stadium whose visiting clubhouse was so small and cramped that visiting teams changed and showered at their hotel.

The 29 athletes were tall, physically fit, young, and inexperienced. Only five were listed at under six feet; at six-seven, Joe Curran was the tallest and, at five-nine, Domonique Lewis, the shortest. Although today marked the opening of the Pioneer League season, all were in good physical condition and had been playing from four to six months already this year: in Caribbean winter leagues; in high school, junior college, and university leagues; and at the Cincinnati Reds' spring and extended training camps in Sarasota Florida. Tanned and trim, they were athletes about to enter their prime playing years. But they were young: over two-thirds were under 22. Chris Gruler, the kid on the team, wouldn't turn 19 until September 11. At 23, Jeremy Ison was the veteran. Twelve members of the club had only recently signed professional contracts. Gruler, the most heralded of these, was a right-handed pitcher who had played for Liberty High School of Brentwood California, and on June 4 became Cincinnati's

first-round draft pick, and third overall, agreeing to a $2.5 million sign-
ing bonus. By contrast, Troy Cairns, a second baseman for the University
of New Mexico Lobos, was a 46th round pick and probably received a
bonus worth at least $2.4 million less than that of his new teammate.

After driving past the police station, the curling rink where many of
Canada's best-known "men with brooms" have trained; the hockey rink,
where this year's projected number one National Hockey League draft
pick, Jay Bouwmeester, played for the local Tigers, the bus pulled in front
of Athletic Park. As they filed out, a couple of the players looked at the
signs around the outside of the park which bore the names of former
Medicine Hat Blue Jays who had made it to the majors: David Wells, Jimmy
Keys, Pat Borders, and others. It was a reminder that the long and winding four-to-six-year road to the big leagues began in small rookie league
stadiums like this one.

Built in 1977, Athletic Park was situated between a neighborhood of
small, older, frame houses, and the South Saskatchewan River. Beyond the
outfield wall rose a levee along which joggers trotted during games, occasionally glancing at the diamond to their south. The levee was built in the
late 1990s after a heavy spring runoff resulted in the river's overflowing its
banks and flooding the park—fortunately before the opening of the
Pioneer League season. Capacity of the park is generously listed at 3,000;
although that must include the grass berm along the right field line. The
stands themselves, which extended from third to first and are backless aluminum benches, could probably hold 2,000, if fans were snugly seated.
Even that number of seats was more than enough to handle last year's
nightly "crowds" of just over 700, the worst per-game average in the
Pioneer League.

While the home team Blue Jays, an even-younger squad than the
Mustangs, with 10 players under 20 years old, took batting practice, the
Billings players stretched, jogged and played catch under the watchful eyes
of strength and conditioning coach Matt Sanders. As the Blue Jays headed
to their clubhouse—only slightly larger than the visitors'—the Mustangs
gathered around the batting cage. They were relatively quiet as they awaited
their chance to work on their swings against the tosses of coach Jay Sorg.
Their shyness was understandable. Many felt pre-opening-game jitters.
More important, they had been together as a group for only a week and
hadn't had a chance to form the buddy-groups or, at worst, cliques that
characterize sports teams. Only the Latin players, drawn together through
language and culture bonds, seemed to cluster together.

Today, Walter Olmstead, who had played college ball at Texas Christian
University, would make the first steps in the actualization of a dream he'd

had since he was a little boy. After the TCU season had ended, he'd been invited to Cincinnati for a brief, pre-draft workout and then returned home to San Antonio, where, on June 4, he and his family gathered around the computer to listen to the draft. The big first baseman—he's 6-5, 230 pounds—didn't have too long to wait. By two o'clock central time, he was selected by the Reds as their eighth-round pick. "Things moved pretty quickly after that," he remarked, waiting his turn in the batting cage. "I cleared out my apartment back in Dallas and by Sunday I was in Billings." Ninety minutes before his first pro game, he admitted he was excited, nervous, and anxious to get going. "At times I can't believe it. I've imagined this day since I was little, cheering for Oakland, especially the Bash Brothers [Jose Canseco and Mark McGwire]."

Troy Cairns, the next in line for batting practice, had to wait until the second day of the draft before he'd been chosen. Relatively small for a baseball player—he weighs only 160 pounds and was listed on the roster at six feet, somewhat of a stretch—he played at the University of New Mexico, a good but not dominating club in the Big Sky Conference. Late the second day of the draft, in the 46th round, the then-second baseman heard his name announced; he had been picked by the Reds as a shortstop. "I really wanted to be drafted," he admitted, enthusiasm in his voice. He didn't feel disappointed at being chosen so late. "I got a chance, and I'm taking it." He arrived in Billings and began working at his new position.

The opening game was, if not ugly, certainly not pretty. Both teams seemed to have first-game jitters. Cairns and Olmstead were the only two Billings rookies to play. Medicine Hat started three—Carlo Cota, Zeph Zinsman, and David Smith—and later brought in Jose Salas and relief pitcher Jordon DeJong. Lead-off Mustang Domonique Lewis, who played for Billings last year, blasted a 2–1 pitch into right field where, aided by a brisk wind, it cleared the fence. In the second and fourth innings, lead-off Mustang batters Jason Vavao and Onix Mercado also homered. However, the Blue Jays countered with blasts by Smith and Zinsman, and the score after four was 4–3 for the visitors. The clubs traded runs in the fifth, but Billings added eight more before the game ended. It was a night of long balls—six home runs, four doubles, and a triple—and of errors—only one by the Mustangs, but six by the Jays.

The rookies excelled at the plate, collecting nine hits. Troy Cairns doubled to left in the second and to right in the eighth, and singled in the ninth to lead the Billings attack. Olmstead struck out in two of his first three trips to the plate, fanning on sinking fastballs. He then singled, was hit by a pitch, and drilled a home run to right that would have gone out even if it hadn't been hit in Medicine Hat's bandbox of a park.

The weather for the game was mild, in the high 60s. However, the Opening Day crowd was a disappointing 712. A large number of these were in their 50s and 60s, and there were few young adults and fewer families. Although schools were still in session, most students had completed exams and more families might have been expected. By the end of seven and a half-innings, with the Blue Jays trailing by eight runs, fans seemed to be lingering in the seats only to hear the lucky numbers for the 50/50 draw. When these were announced in the bottom of the eighth, most began heading for the exits.

Both the attendance figures and the game result marked a disappointing start to the Blue Jays' 25th anniversary celebration. "Keeping the Dream Alive" read the slogan on the cover of the program. However, since 1999, when local owner Bill Yuill sold the club to American David Elmore, Jr., fewer and fewer southern Albertans had been showing up to watch the beginnings of baseball dreams. In three years, an average of 26,000, down nearly 15,000 from the preceding three seasons, had attended. Rumors circulated that the club was contemplating relocation to Calgary (after its Pacific Coast League team had moved to Albuquerque) or to northern Colorado.

After the game, the managers of both teams expressed fairly cliched thoughts. Rolando Pino explained that the Jays were just over-anxious, that everyone was bound to be nervous on Opening Day. Billings' Rick Burleson, while admitting that it was nice to get the first win, cautioned that "things can fall apart in a hurry in this league. Last year, Missoula started 0 and 6; but came back to win 13 in a row. We barely beat them for the first-half championship." Walter Olmstead remarked that he'd been a bit tight during his first two at bats, but felt in the groove when he sent a fastball out of the park. Troy Cairns discovered to his surprise that he felt more comfortable during the game than he'd expected. Making a good play early in the game on a ground ball to his left helped him to relax.

Tuesday, June 18

By 9:00 A.M., a threatening low-pressure area had moved into Medicine Hat from the west. The ensuing rain, which would have been welcomed a year ago, brought unhappy looks to the faces of townspeople and area farmers. In late May, a two-year drought which had reminded old-timers of the "dirty thirties" dust-bowl era had ended. Torrential downpours had caused rivers to flood and fields to turn into quagmires. Although rivers were slowly dropping back to normal levels, further rains could spell trouble.

At 9:30, Billings' manager Rick Burleson stood at the entrance of the Medicine Hat Inn, looking skyward. "What is this?" he questioned in mock anger and then, more seriously, asked: "Does anyone know if its going to keep raining later today?" A rainout on the season's second game would be, to say the least, inconvenient. Not only would it necessitate a double-header the next night—something enjoyed only by the most fanatical of die-hard fans—it would disrupt the daily rhythms of training and playing that were so important to establish early in the season. Pitching rotations would be scrambled and position players would be hindered from getting in the groove. As Burleson waited in vain for an answer, the players, who were gathering around in shorts and sweats, put towels over their heads, clutched their Walkmans, and sprinted to the bus. They were pitchers bounded for a special workout at the YMCA adjacent to the ball park.

While Matt Sanders led them through their paces, the weather question was being raised two hundred yards to the east in the double-garage-sized yellow brick building that served as the Jays administrative office. General Manager Paul Fetz contemplated the possibility of only the third rainout in the over three seasons he'd been with the club. "We don't have a big tarpaulin; we've never needed one." That explained why a rainout would be so devastating to the club. The Blue Jays, he explained, had a fairly low attendance, but, because they had a low overhead, they generated a small profit each year. "Our staff is mainly interns who work for low wages in order to gain experience in sport-related businesses. We've worked to increase advertising revenues for our yearbook, which is now twice the size of what it was when we took over in 1999." An important part of revenue generation was sponsored group nights, and three of these had been scheduled for the first home stand. Tonight was designated "Youth Safety Patrol Night" and "Prairie Rose School Division Night." A good crowd would spend money at the concessions and souvenir stand. Rain would not only keep these young spenders away, but walk-up customers as well. "A day of rain" was one of the factors in the Boston Braves' winning the 1948 National League Pennant. But to small minor-league operations like Medicine Hat, a day of rain could cause considerable financial hardship.

Over lunch back at the Medicine Hat Inn's Back Lane Cafe, Troy Cairns, who had started at shortstop for the Mustangs the night before, freely admitted that 13 days ago he hadn't heard of Medicine Hat, or even Billings. "I never dreamed of being here because I didn't know it existed. This is my first time out of the United States." He'd hung around his family's home in suburban Kansas city most of Tuesday and Wednesday, June 4 and 5, but not with high hopes. "I'd talked to a couple of scouts in the spring, but nobody had promised anything. On Wednesday morning, it was nerve-racking; the phone hadn't rung." And so he took some friends back to their houses and said good-bye as he was getting ready to head to Maine to play in a summer college league. "When I got home, my family told me I'd been selected. I thought they were kidding. Then a Reds scout called. It was one of the best days of my life."

The next few days were a blur for Troy. He hung out with buddies for a few days and then flew directly to Billings, where he signed a professional contract and joined his new teammates. Through one of his uncle's connections, he located lodgings in a basement suite, which he shared with fellow draftees Jared Humphries and Walter Olmstead. "We pay a bit of rent; but they're really good to us," he enthused. "They feed us and chauffeur us around."

Adjustment to his new surroundings, both on and off the field hadn't been as great as he'd expected. "I think that having had three years of university has helped me. There are things a junior at college has experienced that a senior in high school hasn't." With so many of the new players coming from universities, homesickness and meeting new people hadn't been that much of a problem. He liked using wooden bats, as opposed to the aluminum ones of college, feeling that they were more traditional—"the way baseball's supposed to be"—and he had played shortstop in high school.

Troy expressed pleasure at his successful first game, but emphasized that it was only one game, that baseball was in many ways a game of failure, and that learning to deal with that was a crucial part of developing as a professional. He had his first chance in the field in the bottom of the first when he took a low and away throw from catcher Onix Mercado to kill lead off Jay batter Juan Peralta's attempted steal of second. And in the sixth he made a fine play to his left to turn a ground ball into the hole into an out. "I was glad it was to my left, because with those ones, if you don't reach them, it's OK." His first hit, a double came in the top of the second. "On a one and two count, I hit a fast ball on the outside of the plate. I was anxious and nervous when I came up for my first at-bat, but after I swung and missed on a pitch, I told myself, 'It's like any other game.'"

As a 46th-round draft pick and a relatively small middle-infielder, Cairns faced challenges that higher draft choices did not. With little money invested in him by the Reds and a player in what is increasingly becoming a big man's game, he would have to make himself noticed or risk being considered a roster-filler, a body necessary to complete a requisite quota of players. "It's really important that I gain weight," Troy admitted. "I'll have to pay attention to diet and weight training." As for his work at the plate, he believed it was important to know his role, to "set the table" so

Mustangs pitcher Jose Gomez sits in the lobby of the Medicine Hat Inn, talking to his girlfriend in Chihuahua, Mexico.

that the heavier hitters could drive him in. "And I do want to learn to be more patient at the plate. I don't take a lot of pitches; when I see one I like, I just want to swing at it. I might not see it again." Did having been taken very late in the draft bother him? "One thing is," he laughed, "I won't have to worry about how to spend all that money." He noted that a key element of his contract was having the Reds pay for him to finish university. "Whether I'm drafted in the first or fiftieth round isn't the important thing. The big thing is that I got drafted. Now its up to me how far I can take my dream. I can't understand how some guys turn down $four million and sit out a year. How much money can you use? And you don't get to play ball!"

In the early afternoon, Jose Gomez sat in the hotel lobby talking quietly on his cell phone to his girl friend in Chihuahua, Mexico. A couple of players waved to him as they headed out the door to look in nearby stores for souvenirs of their first trip to Canada. Trainer Steve Baumann spoke to the desk clerk, checking his list of players' room numbers against that of the hotel. "I've got to call everyone to let them know that batting practice has been canceled. The bus won't be leaving to the park until just before five. After I've done this, I've got to call our travel agent. The Reds want Chris Gruler to fly to Cincinnati after he pitches on Friday. They want to do an MRI on his shoulder and hold a press conference for the southern Ohio media."

Perhaps the busiest member of the Billings Mustangs, Baumann not only performed the athletic therapy duties for which he'd trained at the

Mustangs trainer Steve Baumann hangs up one of the special patriotic uniform tops worn by Billings for the home opener. The tops would be worn again on July 4.

University of Cincinnati, but also acted as a traveling secretary, a clubhouse attendant on the road, and, at 24 years old, a big brother confidant to the young players. His many duties for this trip had began Sunday morning as he packed his trainer's bags and oversaw the collection of other equipment the team would need on the road. Just before the team bus reached Wild Horse, a tiny border-crossing station on the Montana-Alberta line, he collected birth certificates, passports, and immigration certificates from coaches and players. "I'm the team spokesman at the border, and I try to have everything organized so that we can get through as quickly as possible." After Monday night's game was over and the team had gone back to the hotel, he'd collected the players' soiled warm-up and game jerseys, which he would wash at the hotel laundry. On Thursday, he'd make sure the players left nothing behind at the hotel and, the game over, have food ready for them to eat when they boarded the bus. Then, before they settled down to an awkward, fitful eight-hour sleep, he'd again collect their documents to present at the border.

As Baumann talked about his relationship with the Cincinnati Reds, his listener got the impression that if Tommy Lasorda bled Dodger Blue, Baumann bled Cincinnati Red. Steve grew up watching the great Reds' teams of the 1980s. "I saw Johnny Bench's last game and Pete Rose's 3,000th hit. I had a TV fan's loyalty; now its a professional loyalty. I'm a fan of the front office and all the players in a very different way. I look forward to helping the Mustang players realize their dreams of playing in the major leagues. And I'd certainly like to be there with them some day. But I enjoy what I do now. I'm young, and it doesn't bother me to live out of a suitcase."

Fans attending the games seldom saw Baumann. He might run onto the field to check a player who'd been hit by a pitched ball or shaken up sliding into second trying to break up a double play. His most important work, however, went on behind the scenes, and not all of it took place in the training room. "I can be an intermediary between the players and the coaching staff. Because I'm not that much older, I understand where they're coming from, things like their music. They can talk to me in a way they couldn't to Rick, Jay, Ed, or Matt. But I also know the staff side, what Rick Burleson wants." He didn't consider himself a psychologist, but Steve recounted how more than once he'd had players lying on the training table talking for more than an hour about the pressures of adjusting to their new lives as professional athletes: being a long way from home for the first time, missing mother and girlfriend, no longer being the only superstar on the team.

"They have to learn to make the adjustment," Steve explained. "I can't force them. But I do try to help them to get out of the college or high school mind-set, to understand that now they are all professional athletes, an equal among many. I try to help everyone to be on the same page. Sometimes it can be a little thing, like calling the manager "Rick" or "Skipper," not "coach" like they did in high school and college. Other times, it's big things. Sometimes players from major college programs can be a little cocky and take the attitude, 'It worked well for me before; why should I change for you?' Some players can't make the adjustments, mental and physical, and are soon out of the game."

Last night's game was a win in more ways than on the scoreboard, Steve noted. "It was a blow-out, but a huge confidence-builder. I saw 30 guys cheering each other on." However, the postponement of batting practice today could be counter-productive to the momentum created by Monday night's victory. "The guys want to play, not go to a movie or sit in a hotel room watching a video. We're trying to help them develop the day-to-day rhythms that are so different from their previous playing experiences. This year it will be every day for twelve weeks, and next year it will be for five months. Missing batting practice will break the pattern just as we're starting to establish it."

When the team arrived at the park, the members of the three-man grounds crew, who were also the assistant general manager, marketing assistant, and media relations director, moved around the infield working on the many puddles and wet spots. Their one wheelbarrow was loaded with bags of drying clay, much of which had been generously spread around the home plate area which had been left uncovered, the only tarp, a small one, having been spread over the mound. A small pump beside the visitors' dugout putted, sending a garden-hose-sized jet of water onto the grassy area in foul territory. One of the grounds crew used a large rake squeegee to push a big puddle of water off the warning track onto the grass. As they did their work, dark, threatening clouds advanced from the west. Just after six, fans trickled into the park. Many were armed with umbrellas, most had donned late-winter jackets brought out of back closets, a few clutched sleeping bags.

For the game that followed, the anticipated crowd of schoolchildren failed to show up. Paid attendance was generously announced at 249. Also failing to show up was the Billings' hitting power; their bats produced only five hits as opposed to 16 on opening night. Five home runs sailed out of the park; three hit by the Jays. Two were hit by the Mustangs: one by Mike Bassett, appearing in his first pro game, the other by Walter Olmstead, his second, a moon shot that would have cleared any Pioneer League fence. Trailing by a run coming into the ninth, the Mustangs tied it at five. But with two out in the bottom of the ninth, Michael Galloway singled and took second on a wild pitch and third on a passed ball before Morrin Davis's infield single to deep short sent him across the plate. There were few people left in the stands to cheer the home team's victory. The winning 50/50 number had been announced in the seventh inning, and, with the temperature in the mid 40s, most of the fans departed. By 10:30, the bus was back the hotel, Baumann had collected the laundry, and the players had headed to their rooms to contemplate what was, for most, their first professional defeat.

Wednesday, June 19, and Thursday, June 20

After Tuesday night's game, Matt Sanders announced that the next morning's conditioning workout had been canceled. The rain continued during the night and through the morning. By noon, the diamond at Athletic Park, barely playable on Tuesday night, was declared unplayable. Both batting practice and the game were canceled and a double-header scheduled Thursday, the last date in the season's opening series. Having virtually exhausted the shopping possibilities of downtown Medicine Hat, the players lounged about listlessly waiting for seven o'clock, the time their game should have started. Now it marked the time that the multiplex cinema across the street would begin the evening's showings. *The Bourne Identity* was the movie of choice for the unwillingly off-duty Mustangs.

Rick Burleson and his two coaches remained busy in the early afternoon discussing the team's performance to date. The manager then retreated to his room to call Tim Naehring, the Reds' director of player development. The call over, he then relaxed in the hotel's coffee shop and discussed his playing and managerial career and his goals for this year's Mustangs. During the 1970s and 1980s, Burleson played with the Boston Red Sox, California Angels, and Baltimore Orioles. A member of the Red Sox' 1975 American League championship team, he participated in the famous sixth game of that year's World Series, the one in which Carlton Fisk's dramatic twelfth-inning home run enabled Boston to tie the series against Cincinnati. "It was fun; but I was young, and I thought I'd soon get another chance to play in the Series. That didn't happen, and I learned that you have to appreciate things while you can."

Burleson's coaching and managing career began because, like many retired players, he found he missed the game and wanted to find a way to stay involved. He began as a minor-league roving instructor, then a scout, and a major-league coach. "At one point," Burleson remembered, "I found myself coaching at third base and really liking it. I was much more a part of the game on the field and felt I could have a bit of an influence on the outcome. One time, Don Zimmer explained that he wanted all of his major-league coaches to have had minor-league managing experience. When I heard that, I realized I'd have to become a manager if I wanted to stay in the game."

In 2000, after managing successfully at high Single-A Lancaster and San Bernardino and Double-A San Antonio, he found himself at a crossroads. When the Dodgers transferred their Double-A affiliate to Jacksonville, Florida, he could either move with them or move out of the game. Because he didn't want to live a continent away from his wife and family in Ontario, California, he chose the latter option. "I'd started working with a landscaping business, when Cincinnati phoned to ask if I'd be interested in coming to Billings." Not only was the job considered one of the best in the lower minors, it would allow him to spend more time with his family. "My wife was getting tired of baseball after living with me for 37 years. Billings was the best of both worlds." The last two years, he'd attended spring training in March, spent most of April and May at home, and managed with Billings in the summer. "I've actually had a chance to see my son pitch at junior college."

Working with players younger and far less experienced than those he'd managed in the California and Texas Leagues was, he said, a rewarding challenge. He tried to teach them the everyday work ethic that was needed to succeed in the professional ranks. "In college and high schools," Burleston explained, "there are only two or three games a week. Here, we only have four days off in eighty-one and two of those are spent on the bus." By successfully dealing with the physical and mental stresses of the short-season rookie league, players would be better prepared for the five-month, 140-game marathon of the full-season leagues. "They have to learn to concentrate, to stay focused for nine innings day-after-day," he noted. The overall goal was to make each individual better as a member of a team. "We explain to them the Cincinnati philosophy: the team name on the front of the jersey is more significant than the individual's on the back. When I talk to a specific player about something, I emphasize the word 'we,' not 'you'. By learning to contribute to team wins, each player is showing real development." Of course, he was pleased with the success of each person and would be pleased and satisfied in two or three years when the first of his Mustangs played in a Cincinnati Reds uniform. "I'll be proud to have been the manager they got their start with."

By 9:30 Thursday morning, the rain had stopped and the clouds had broken up. Several players boarded the bus and headed to a conditioning session at the YMCA. At three the entire club entered the bus, suitcases in one hand, equipment bags in the other, pillows under one arm, and Walkman earbuds firmly attached. At six, they began the first game of the double-header, this time before a much larger crowd, 1,005, which raised the Blue Jays' attendance average to 655, barely the subsistence level. The Mustangs managed only three hits, one of them a home run by Elvin Beltre-Andujar, a fourth-year pro, and lost 3–2. They took the second 9–7, and again found their bats, with Junior Ruiz, Walter Olmstead, and Ryan Peters each belting home runs. Shortly after midnight, they again climbed onto bus, this time heading back to their new summer home— Billings.

An unidentified Billings player emerges sleepily from the bus after an all-night trip from Medicine Hat to Billings.

Friday, June 21

By 9:30 A.M. on the first day of summer and the longest day of the year, Cobb Field buzzed with activity. The outfield signs were being firmly attached on top of those of the stadium's co-tenants the American Legion teams of Billings. Near one of the entrances to the stands, a carpenter put the finishing touches to a small ramp leading to the newly installed handicapped elevator. In the Mustangs' office, sales director Adam Bryant, who had played for the team in 1994 and 1995, began printing tonight's general admission tickets, grumbling as the finicky printer slowly spat them into his waiting hand. A customer came in to purchase four of them, no doubt spurred on by a headline in the morning *Billings Gazette* that announced "Fans Encouraged to Arrive Early" because of an anticipated sellout of 4,600. At another desk, assistant general manager Gary Roller talked earnestly on the telephone about problems with the team's Web site, referring to "a really bad guy" and to someone "wearing the black hat." His biggest concern was that fans unable to attend, especially those beyond the limited evening range of KBUL's signal, would not hear the Internet broadcast. And rural Montana listeners represented potential weekend customers.

While he was conversing, a stadium worker stuck his head in the door and called out, "They're here!" The Mustangs had just completed what what one sleepy player muttered was the "trip from hell." Rubbing their eyes, the young professionals stumbled from the bus and rummaged through a pile of equipment bags looking for their own. Many also reached for their cell phones to call host families to come to the stadium to pick them up. The return from Billings had begun later than originally planned. Because of the double-header it was after midnight instead of eleven before they left Medicine Hat. Rimrock Stages' driver Ira Presinger explained other difficulties. "We had to take a roundabout route to the border because the immigrations and customs offices on the direct route closed at midnight. I called another driver to get the quickest way—but it turned out to be 60 miles of dirt and gravel. Then, when we showed up at the border, two of the Dominican players had forgotten to bring the papers they needed to get back into the States. That ate up another half an hour."

This was the kind of endurance training that Burleson had talked about. Not only had the young Mustangs played close to five hours of baseball the night before, followed by eight hours of at best fitful sleep on the bus, but also, they would be playing ball again in less than ten hours and would be back at the park in less than six. The journey to Canada five days earlier had been easy in comparison to the one just finished. Then they had made the trip in eight hours and had a night and day in Medicine Hat to prepare for the game. Later this season they would travel overnight from Casper, Wyoming, to Great Falls, Montana, and another time from Medicine Hat to Missoula and two days later to Great Falls. This season's travel itinerary would certainly be a baptism by "tires."

In addition to its story about the anticipated large crowd, the *Gazette* carried two other related Opening Day pieces. A front page article bearing the headline "Ailing, aged Cobb Field Plays Hurt," reported that a park to replace the present one, which was built in 1948, was at least four seasons away—that is, if a proposed bond issue passed. This year, the city would be spending $100,000 repairing water-damaged decking and renting a new wheelchair elevator. Although Billings attracted close to 100,000 fans a year, making it one of the best-drawing Pioneer League clubs, the park was outmoded and deteriorating. Without a new park, the city could lose the club to another area or, at least, lose its thirty-year affiliation with the Cincinnati Reds, who might become reluctant to let their young prospects perform in a substandard facility.

The third story, by baseball beat writer Mike Scherting, profiled Chris

Built in 1948, Cobb Field has been the home of the Billings Mustangs for the 50 years the team has been a member of the Pioneer League. Before the 2002 home opener, fans arrived early so that they could select the best general admission seats.

Gruler, perhaps the hottest attraction to play at Cobb Field since Austin Kearns, now with the Reds, in 1998. His presence as the game's starting pitcher was one of the factors that caused the rush for tickets. In addition to Kearns, Billings fans have seen a great number of Cincinnati players open or continue their professional careers at Cobb Field. Adam Dunn, who'd been picked in the second round of 1998, also debuted as a Mustang. In all eight members of the Reds' current active roster had started their climb to the majors in Billings. The Mustang Hall of Fame wall beside the front office included photos of such other major league stars as Paul O'Neill, from 1981, and Dick "Dr. Strange Glove" Stuart, from 1952 and 1955, George Brett, from 1971, and Larry Shepard, from 1949 to 1951.

Also pictured on the display was Bob Wilson, a Mustangs' shareholder since 1971, two years after they rejoined the Pioneer League, and, since 1985, their president and general manager. In the early years, Bob Cobb, the Hollywood restaurateur had, with such friends as Bing Crosby and Cecil B. De Mille, held the largest portion of the original stock. "Cobb," Wilson laughed, "is the only person to have had both a salad and a park named after him."

This stock had gradually been acquired by local people, none of whom expected any money on their investment. In fact, the 2001 Mustangs posted a net profit of only $12,324, down over $4,000 from the previous year. Travel expenses rose $18,000 over the same period, and dues to the National Association doubled. Sources of revenue were limited. Season tickets were much less expensive than other Pioneer League cities. The 550 box seats, all of which had been sold, cost $114 for a 38-game season; general admission, $95. In Casper, such seats were $231 and $119, a difference which perhaps explains why, this evening the Mustangs would draw around 4,600 fans, while Casper, for the opening game in its new park, would attract under 2,000.

Until two seasons ago, the Mustangs' other major source of revenue— outfield fence advertising—had not existed. All the signage and its revenue belonged to the American Legion clubs. Now, when the Mustangs were on the road, their 26 signs, which sold for $2,000 a season, were flipped over the outfield wall uncovering the Legion signs. When the team returned, the signs were refastened. Without this new source of income, the small profit might turn into a larger loss.

Cincinnati Reds player development director Tim Naehring is seldom far from his cell phone. Here he talks with the Reds' home office as he watches the Mustangs take batting practice.

Over the past decade, the Mustangs had been the most consistently successful club in the Pioneer League, averaging 97,000 fans a season. Only the former Salt Lake City Trappers, who, in 1992, attracted 217,000 people in a market 10 times larger than the Mustangs', and Ogden, who, playing in a new park has exceeded the Billings' totals by an average of 5,000 four times, have done better. When asked why the team has been so successful, Wilson admitted that the low prices were a draw, but emphasized that in a traditional baseball town the Mustangs offered good baseball. "We're the summer place to be. We sell baseball, not carnival acts. We've never had a mascot, and we won't as long as I'm here. A mascot trivializes a team. And we don't have dizzy bat races or onfield contests. I don't want people to say I watched a mascot and some funny races and incidentally saw a game."

And the baseball had been good. The Mustangs had been in the playoffs in seven of the past ten years, winning pennants in 1992, 1993, 1994, 1997, and 2001. Much of the success was due to the quality of players sent by the parent Cincinnati Reds. At a time when affiliations change as often as some Hollywood stars change spouses, Billings has had a working agreement that has lasted since 1974, one of the longest of the current affiliations between the 30 major-league clubs and their farm teams. It began because the then Cincinnati farm director Chief Bender had liked Billings since the time that both he and the Montana city had been affiliated with the St. Louis Cardinals. When he joined the Reds, he encouraged them to link up with Billings. "I think that it has worked," Wilson explained, "because of what we do for them. Our fan club is very active in providing homes for the players; we provide a car for the manager and other things that aren't in our contract with them. They, in turn, have signed variances which overlook several aspects of Cobb Field that don't meet minor-league standards."

By five o'clock, an hour before the gates opened, over 100 fans lined up on the plaza in front of the main entrance to Cobb Field. There were no giveaways—unless the magnetic schedules that clubs generally give out on Opening Day count. The early arrivals had heeded the *Gazette's* warning about a capacity crowd and wanted to stake their claims to the best of the 4,200 general admission seats.

Inside, Tim Naehring leaned against the batting cage. He'd taken the early Delta flight out of Cincinnati, transferred in Salt Lake City, and, on arrival in Billings, had headed to the ball park to watch his newest players, most of whom he hadn't seen since the draft. He shook hands with them as they stepped out of the cage and then walked over the dugout to talk with Rick Burleson about the club's first four games.

Domonique Lewis, returning to Billings for a second season, signs autographs for young Mustangs fans.

The gates opened a few minutes before six and several people proceeded directly to specific parts of the park, put down their cushions and blankets to mark their spots and then headed to the Cobb Grill for a dinner of ballpark food. Along the first base line, five school-aged boys leaned over the railings extending programs, a glove, and a bat to Domonique Lewis, the club's leading hitter with a .385 average after three games and one of six returning Mustangs. Their treasures autographed, the kids ran to find their parents. Lewis headed to the left field bullpen area for pregame stretching.

The exercises were led by Matt Sanders, a 30-year-old former university and junior college coach, working his first season for Cincinnati. After three years of part-time scouting for the Reds, he had eagerly accepted the role of strength and conditioning coach, a relatively new position in professional baseball. "It all began in the early 1990s, when Louisiana State was winning so many College World Series," he explained. "They were developing baseball-specific conditioning programs, and, after their success, others began to imitate. It's a lot different from football conditioning, where muscle development has been stressed. Flexibility is really important in baseball." A rookie pro, Matt admitted that this year had been a learning process: "In college, the coaching decisions are made by two or three people. Here you're working with a large organization that has an overall philosophy of player development. I'm learning a whole new pattern of people skills."

At 6:30 P.M., Chris Gruler, the person many of the fans had come specifically to see, headed to the right field bullpen where, after a brief conversation with pitching coach Ed Hodge, he began his warmup tosses. A small group of people gathered at the end of the first base stands watching the starting pitcher's tosses. "I don't collect autographs," remarked a father standing with his young son. "But this is one I'd like to get for my boy."

Before the home opener, Manuel Paula (left) and manager Rick Burleson (43) display the Pioneer League pennant the Mustangs won in 2001.

The infield dirt watered down and the lines freshly painted, Gary Roller walked to the grass in front of the mound with the returning players. Together they held the Pioneer League pennant that the Mustangs had won last year. Soon it would fly on the center field just below the American flag. Then the teams were announced. "Your 2002 Mustangs" lined up along the first base line wearing special uniforms: navy blue with red and white trim, the shoulders and arms were decorated in an American flag motif. They would be used only twice: tonight, in memory of the victims of September 11 and on the Fourth of July. After that they would be auctioned off.

As seven o'clock neared, the public address announcer asked fans to sit closer together: "We've got a lot of people outside who want to get in. Please help us." As the general admission fans shifted along the bench seats, Tim Naehring; Manny Guerra and Carl Cassell, scouts for St. Louis and Texas respectively, and reserve players from both teams, armed with radar guns and clutching pitching charts, settled into the box seats right behind the plate. The audience rose for the singing of *God Bless America* and *The Star Spangled Banner*, umpire Brian Frisch called "Play Ball," and Chris Gruler leaned forward for the sign from catcher Steve Booth. The right-hander's career began with a high and outside fastball clocked at 93 miles an hour. The three individuals involved in the pitch were all rookies: Gruler's delivery was caught by Booth, a twenty-two-year-old and a ninth-round draft pick from the University of San Francisco. Frisch, who called the pitch a ball, was a recent graduate of umpire school.

In the top of the first, Gruler seemed a little uncertain, throwing 18 pitches, 11 for balls. He retired leadoff batter Brandon Simon, another rookie, on a comebacker to the mound, but gave up a bloop single and a walk. He retired the side in order in the second with the help of a fine running catch by center fielder Alan Moye, and threw nine pitches in the third, when he faced three batters. The fourth opened with shortstop Troy Cairns making a fine backhand play in the hole for the first out. Gruler gave up a walk and a single and threw 13 pitches. He left the game after the fourth. Although not spectacular, he showed good control. His 12 to 6 dropping curve ball was particularly effective, and he used it to ring up two of his three strikeouts. The game over, he returned to the home of his host family to pack. Having just returned from an 800-mile road trip, he would be catching the early Saturday Delta commuter to Salt Lake City. From there he would fly to Cincinnati for his scheduled MRI and press conference.

After the game, pitching coach Ed Hodge, another rookie who joined the pro ranks this year after several seasons of college coaching, talked about his star performer: "He was really excited. It reminded me of a race horse at the starting gate. He wanted all the pregame ceremonies to be over so he could get to it. He wasn't right on at first, but he got stronger as the innings progressed. His curve ball worked really well." Tim Naehring was extremely pleased with the performance of his top draft pick. "He has great talent," the Reds' director of player development commented. "He's very mature, the kind of kid you root for." He explained that for Gruler and the other '02 draft picks, the Cincinnati organization's job now was to develop a plan and establish a routine that would enable them to develop both mentally and physically. He had drafted players who not only were within his organization's budget, but also had the talent and passion to succeed. "We explain to them that the really big dollars are at the other end of the rainbow, not this one." The Reds had gone into the draft looking for starting pitchers, and Gruler's performance tonight had confirmed what Tim and his scouts had noticed in the many months they'd been watching him: he had the potential to win in the majors.

When Gruler left the game, the Mustangs held a 3–0 lead. However, the Missoula Osprey picked away at this with a run in the fifth and two in the eighth. In the top of the ninth they scored three unanswered runs to win their first game of the young season, 6–3. The Mustangs' record dropped to 2 and 3.

Very few of the capacity crowd of 4,731 left the game until the final out. True to Bob Wilson's word, there were no carnival acts. The spectators spent most of their time watching, cheering, and commenting knowledgeably on the plays they witnessed. They enjoyed standing, singing, and dancing to *YMCA*, *Cotton-eyed Joe*, and *Take Me Out to the Ball Game*. But that seemed to be all the non-baseball entertainment they required. The game over, several of the fans stopped to talk to Wilson, who greeted each by name. One of these, Aaron Hoffenbocker, had made a 223-mile drive from Butte, as he had done for all weekend Mustang home games for the last two years—since his town had lost its team to Provo, Utah. Wilson remarked to one fan, a pleased grin on his face: "Who could ask for anything better? A great game, and," he added, to no one in particular, "not a single person asked for a mascot!"

Saturday, June 22

Saturday, the first full day of summer, began more quietly than Friday had begun. The players, after their all-night road trip, followed by the excitement of the home opener, were presumably at their "foster homes" sleeping in. The clubhouse was locked—not even that 24-hour-man Steve Baumann was around. In fact it would be close to two o'clock before he'd show up and the players would begin to straggle in. In the front office, Bob Watson and Gary Roller finished up the paperwork from last night's game. The Website had been returned to working order; the ticket printer was functioning smoothly; and—because a smaller crowd was expected this evening—less preparation was necessary. In the stands, cleaning crews gathered paper cups and wrappers, swept peanut shells into the main aisles, and then began power-washing the grandstand. "There was an awful lot of beer and pop spilled last night," explained one of the workers.

His paperwork completed, Roller surveyed the freshly cleaned grandstand, sat down on a shaded bench, and talked about the kind of work that was essential to keep the Pioneer League's most continuously successful franchise successful and the real challenges it would face over the next half-decade. The 39-year-old Billings native had earned a master's degree in sports management at Idaho State University and, realizing he wanted to follow a career in baseball, talked with Bob Wilson. In 1993, he began to work for the Mustangs as a part-time intern and, within a few years, had become assistant general manager, gradually assuming more and more duties.

"Last night was great," he remarked and then cautioned, "but it's the biggest crowd we'll have this season." When asked for reasons for both statements, he explained in detail. He began by noting that the Mustangs have been supported exceptionally well in the community. "People were anxious to see the team again, especially since we won the pennant last year." They really liked Rick Burleson's no-nonsense approach to managing, so they were glad to see him back. And they looked forward to welcoming back last year's "Most Favorite Player," Onix Mercado. He admitted the fact that Chris Gruler's presence might have sold some tickets, but went on to say that, although fans followed the game on the field very intently, not that many kept up with background information such as the draft.

As good as the average attendance was, it would need to grow, Roller continued. "We'll need more revenue to keep up with rising costs. People weren't happy when we increased ticket sales last winter—fifty cents a game and $20 for a season ticket—and that just went toward maintenance of the park. We don't want to alienate the fans we have, so we'll have to find other sources of money." Because they had become so firmly established in the community, the Mustangs hadn't had to market their product aggressively; people knew what to expect, and they'd been getting it. But that would have to change, especially in the two or three years before the opening of the new stadium, which, if approved, was expected to be completed by 2006. The change included marketing in communities as far away as Sheridan, Wyoming, 120 miles to the south, and aggressively booking group outings from the area's businesses, clubs, and churches. "As well, we'll have to encourage the casual family fan," Roller continued. "And that means more non-baseball related promotions and contests. But we'll still make sure that our main focus is always the game itself. As long as I'm involved, there will be no circus—ever!"

At 2:30 P.M., most of the Mustang players who had arrived at the park were clustered around the clubhouse's 19-inch television set, sitting on ice chests, an exercise bike, a couple of rickety folding chairs, and the edges of locker stalls. They were watching the final game of the College World Series between the Texas Longhorns and South Carolina Gamecocks. Most of the viewers had played college ball, and some knew the players they were watching. But, interestingly, much of the conversation was about the uniforms and uniforms in general. The comments, about various likes and dislikes, may have been prompted because of the patriotic uniforms that the team had worn last night. The Mustangs' attitudes were perhaps best expressed by one player, who muttered, "I'm all for patriotism. But the best I can say about the tops we wore last night is that they were," and he paused as he considered the best adjective, "they were—uh—interesting."

Most of the players not watching were jogging back and forth on the outfield track or taking extra batting practice in the cage in left field foul territory. The majority of these were Latin players who had no links to or much interest in the college game. Like most clubs at the lower levels of the minor leagues, the Mustangs had a large contingent of Spanish-speaking players—nine, nearly a third of the roster. Their opponents this week, Medicine Hat and Missoula, had six and eleven respectively. The majority of these Caribbean players, five on the Billings' squad, were from the Dominican Republic. On the Mustangs, there was also one each from Puerto Rico, Venezuela, Mexico, and Brazil. On average, Billings' Hispanic players were both younger and more experienced than their American counterparts. That is because, being exempt from the free agent draft, they could be, and often were, signed after they had turned sixteen. Only Chris Gruler was younger than the youngest Latin player, Jason Matooka. However, three of the Latin players had at least three seasons of professional baseball experience. Victor Jumelles, Elvin Beltre-Andujar, and Manuel Paula each began his career with the Reds' club in the Dominican Summer League—a 31-team circuit designed to filter out the best players in this baseball hotbed and refine their skills before they were sent to the American rookie leagues.

Much has been written about the challenges faced by Latin players, particularly Dominicans, who come to America to play professional baseball.

While a few high-profile players, like the San Francisco Giants' Hall-of-Fame pitcher Juan Marichal and Chicago Cubs' home-run hitter Sammy Sosa, had achieved great success and tremendous wealth, many others failed, slipped into obscurity and returned to their homelands. Baseball, it has been said, is a young man's only ticket off the island. By signing pro contracts, young men carried on their shoulders the enormous expectations of families and friends. On arrival in the United States, they found themselves in a land whose culture was totally alien—language, food, and customs. All their games were, to use the title of a book by Marcos Breton and Jose Luis Villegas, *Away Games*.[1] In that book, the authors followed the career of Oakland Athletics' shortstop Miguel Tejada and delineated the loneliness, prejudice, and misunderstanding surrounding the lives of his less successful countrymen.

Although the Mustangs had coalesced as a team amazingly well in the less than two weeks they'd been together, a gulf nonetheless existed between the English and non–English speaking players. Jose Gomez sat alone in the lobby of the Medicine Hat Inn, talking on his cell phone to his girl friend in Mexico. Victor Jumelles from the Dominican Republic and Luis Valera from Venezuela sat by themselves in the hotel's bar in Medicine Hat, ordering a Labatt Blue because it was the only brand name of beer they knew. Along the sidelines of Cobb Field, Carlos Rincon stood silently and awkwardly beside coach Ed Hodge, awaiting the arrival of Onix Mercado, the only really bilingual member of the team, who would then translate the coach's instructions to the pitcher. And more than one American player had privately admitted that he wished he'd paid more attention during high school Spanish classes.

Unlike many rookie-level teams, the Cincinnati's Pioneer League club did not employ a Hispanic coach who could both offer playing advice and serve as a translator. That duty on the Mustangs fell to Mercado. When he was a little boy in Isabela, Puerto Rico, his mother had given him a plastic baseball bat as a birthday present. "I just grew up playing baseball. I didn't get a chance to develop any heroes, because my mother and my sisters were always watching soap operas and sit-coms on TV." At age 11, he spent a year in Miami living with his father and picked up English so easily that he was soon called on by other Spanish-speaking children to translate for them. A year playing junior college ball in Iowa increased his language skills. He left college after one year and, in the winter of 1999, signed with the Reds as a free agent.

Although he posted fairly low numbers in two seasons—a .247 average and one home run in 74 games with the Gulf Coast League Reds and then the Mustangs—he was both popular with fans and respected by his teammates and coaches. Extremely valuable as a battery mate for the Hispanic players, he also helped them adapt to life in a foreign country. "It feels good to help take care of them, to get them used to the Reds' way of doing things," he said. Because Steve Booth, a ninth-round draft pick this year was most likely to be the Mustangs' first catcher, Onix's chances of moving quickly up the Cincinnati ladder were limited. But, with his strong work ethic, cheerful disposition, and helpful nature, he represented the kind of team player that Tim Naehring said he hoped all of the young Reds' players would become. And, if he had a limited future on the playing field, his demonstrated people skills suggested that he could certainly be an important part of the Reds' organization.

One of the Hispanic players Mercado was helping was Victor Jumelles, at 22, the oldest, along with Beltre-Andujar, of the Caribbean players on the team. Signed by the Pittsburgh Pirates in 1998, he spent two seasons with their Dominican Summer League team and another with the Chicago White Sox in the same league. He was released by Chicago in January of 2001. In three seasons, he'd won seven, lost 12 and posted a 4.45 earned run average over 111 innings. Used primarily in middle relief, when he was picked up by Cincinnati in July of 2001 and sent to their fall instructional league in Sarasota, he represented a useful athlete for the Reds, who could use him to take over when their youthful starters had reached their pitch counts. If, in its affluence, the Florida resort town represented a far cry from conditions in his barrio in Santiago Rodrequez, how much more different must Billings have been, where his first road trip took him across a distance greater than the length of his home country, but with a population ten times smaller than his present home of Santo Domingo?

Through his interpreter Onix Mercado, he spoke about the changes in his life in the last 10 months. His shyness and short answers were a contrast to the gregariousness of his translator and may have reflected a sense of culture shock and uncertainty in his new surroundings. He'd begun to play ball at the relatively late age of 15, when he'd acquiesced to the urging of friends to join their team. Two years later, he noticed scouts attending his games. The Dominican League had been a learning experience as he'd had to develop different kinds of pitches to be successful. Coming to the States was difficult because he didn't speak English, and he'd had to adjust to a different kind of food. He missed his family very much, but enjoyed traveling to new places. And then, though the words came in Spanish, he proved that he was developing an understanding of the clichés that can be served to sports writers: "The Cincinnati Reds have given me a chance. Now I've got to go out, work hard, and make the most of it."

This had been a week of professional debuts—not only for the recently drafted players, Billing' coaches Ed Hodge and Matt Sanders, and Missoula manager Jack Howell, but also for the umpires for this series: Jayson Milsap and Brian Frisch. "They don't look any older than the players," a fan had exclaimed on Friday night as she watched the pair standing at home plate discussing ground rules with the managers. This wasn't exactly correct, but very close. Milsap, a management and marketing major from Texas A and M, and Frisch, who had studied environmental biology at the University of Kansas, had enrolled in umpiring school a few months after their graduations from university and, after that, had been assigned their first jobs in the minor leagues—in the Pioneer League.

As they sat in the umpire's dressing room—a cubicle with three folding chairs, three coat hooks, a shelf for towels, a shower and toilet—before Saturday's game, the two discussed the roads that led them to Billings and where they hoped the roads after that would lead. Both began umpiring when they were in high school. Later Jayson worked the regional Junior College finals, while Brian umpired in the newly formed independent Northeast League.

Why, they were asked, would they want to go through the boot-camp-like rigors of professional umpire school and then travel thousands of miles in three months to work games for low pay, putting up with the abuse of fans and confrontations with disgruntled players and managers? "I guess I'm like the players," Jayson explained. "I want to make it to the major leagues. I'm not making much money this year, but it's the best job in the world. I get paid to watch baseball three hours a night and I travel to places I'd probably never see otherwise." Brian agreed and added, "It's the American game, and I love being a part of it."

Both admitted that umpiring school was stressful. Jayson attended the Harry Wendelstadt school, which emphasized field work, and Brian, the Jim Evans school, where the initial focus was on knowledge and interpretation of rules. However, each school, the rookie umps emphasized, taught that it was how you applied the rules you knew that would determine how successful you were on the field. "It was a mental strain at the school," Jayson remembered. "In the afternoon, games were being played on three diamonds, and you never knew when the evaluation team might be at your field. Then at night, you'd spend hours studying your rule book." For the 50 successful candidates—25 from each school—the next stage in their education, 10 days at the Professional Umpire Corporation camp, was more stressful. "There were 50 of us trying for 35 jobs," Brian commented. "I'd not made the group of 50 when I first attended umps school; but I made it this year. And now we had to go through another evaluation process. On the final day, they lined us up in alphabetical order and began calling us forward one by one."

"It's what I figure going in front of a parole board would be like. I stood in front of the seven bosses and they asked you what you felt about how you'd done," Jayson added. "Then they told you if you'd earned a job." He had to wait five months before reporting to Missoula to umpire his first professional game. "They brought us onto the field in a limo. Then a Fed Ex truck delivered the mascot, and they introduced all the players and coaches of both teams. I'd been waiting for months and I was anxious and nervous. I was working the infield. The first guy hit a ground ball and when he reached first, he slid into the bag. He must have been more nervous than I was. After that first play I felt OK."

Brian admitted that he, too, was nervous, more than he realized. "I don't know if I should tell this, but," he went on, "I was behind the plate and in the second inning I called the bat boy to bring some new balls. He put them in my mask and I began to transfer them into the pouches on my belt. I thought I'd emptied the mask, but when I put it on, there was one left and I bashed it on my nose." That was not so painful as what had happened in last night's game, when a foul tip ricocheted off his mask: "I felt like I'd been hit by a freight train. But, hey, it made the paper," he laughed, referring to a photograph of the incident in this morning's *Gazette*.

Both emphasized that, although they'd passed their basic training, their education was continuing each day. Every game presented new situations that required accurate and quick interpretations of basic rules. And they were working with young players who were still learning both the physical and mental aspects of their games. "I learned," Jayson remarked, "that I couldn't assume that they'd make the correct play and throw the ball where you'd expect. Not only could they bobble the ball or throw it wildly, they could make mental errors. I had to let the ball take me to where the play would occur."

In the game that followed, few of the erratic plays that Milsap had talked about occurred, although each team committed four errors. In addition, there were five hit batters, two wild pitches, and a passed ball. Unfortunately for the nearly 2,900 Billings fans who showed up at Cobb Field, the home team lost 3–2. The Mustangs managed only six hits and struck out 12 times. Five runners were stranded in scoring position. After six games, the Mustangs' record had slipped to 2 and 4.

After the game, a dozen or so fans hung around the exits from the stadium, chatting with each other about the evening and glancing toward the closed doors of the Mustang club house. Except for the fact that most were in their mid-fifties to mid-sixties and it was Saturday, they could have been parents waiting to take their children home from a Friday night high school athletic contest. They were, as one joked, "recovering empty-nesters," and they had offered spare bedrooms and finished basements to the Mustang players, most of whom were younger than their departed children. "In a way you feel like a parent," commented Bob Hofmann, who was housing Onix Mercado for the second year and Junior Ruiz for the first. "You just keep the lid on and offer fatherly advice. Last year, when Onix wasn't playing much, I lent a sympathetic ear and cautioned patience. He's a super person. He's very trustworthy and a real team leader. I was happy to have him stay with us again this year."

Bob was standing with Dean Fuller who was, as it were, the "Dean" of the host family program. A member of the fan club for ten years and active on its board for most of them, Dean and his wife Jen had been sharing their home with young ball players for eight summers. He had become involved to help out Gary Roller, or more precisely, to free the assistant general manager from the time-consuming and sometimes stressful business of matching players and families in a way that didn't bruise egos of prospective hosts. The players were charged a nominal fee by the families. "I didn't think it was good for them to get everything given to them. My players each pay $150 a month. That includes food, use of a TV, the computer, phone, and washer and dryer." Rules were minimal—no overnight female visitors, respect for the furniture, staying off the phone after 10 o'clock, and keeping rooms clean. The benefits far outweighed the rules—boating excursions on nearby lakes, barbecues and picnics. And the players' parents were often guests when they visited Billings. "Last year, I think we had more parents and family members than players," Dean commented. "There has been an occasional problem with players; they're kids, after all, and a few get carried away. But it's a rewarding experience. We still hear from some of them several times during the season, long after they've left Billings. They've become extended family."

At this point, the newest member of Dean's family came from the clubhouse and climbed into the car, the last in the parking lot. It drove away and a quiet descended. Aging Cobb Field began its night's rest.

Postseason Postscript

Although Billings finished the first half of the Pioneer League's split-season in third place in the four-team North Division, they won the second half to earn a playoff berth. They were defeated in two straight games by Great Falls in the semi-finals. Eleven Mustangs were promoted to low Single-A

Dayton during the season, including Onix Mercado, Domonique Lewis, and Chris Gruler. Troy Cairns, who saw action in just over half of the Mustangs' 76 games, hit .324. Walter Olmstead, bothered by eye problems much of the season, hit a disappointing .189. Rick Burleson was named the league's Manager of the Year. Billings again finished second to Ogden in the attendance standings, with over 98,000 people coming to Cobb Field. Back in Canada, Medicine Hat attracted 26,000 fans, and, shortly after the season ended, the club announced that it would be relocating to Helena, Montana, which had lost its previous Pioneer League team two years earlier.

5—Down in a West Texas Town: The El Paso Diablos of the Texas League

"Where Future Stars Shine." This marketing slogan used in the mid–1990s by the Knoxville Smokies could easily have been applied to all of the teams in the three Double-A Leagues: the Southern League, the Texas League, and the Eastern League. From El Paso, in western Texas, to Portland, Maine, on the northern Atlantic Coast, Double-A stadiums have been, to paraphrase a Connie Francis song, "Where the Prospects Are." Usually under 25 years old, they have moved quickly through the various classifications, often bypassing one and not infrequently two or three of the five lower levels. Many players on each Double-A team have legitimate shots at becoming major leaguers. Five of the starting 1998 position players of the New Britain Rock Cats moved to the Minnesota Twins within two years. In 2002, 138 of the top 300 prospects chosen by Baseball America, *10 for each major-league organization, would play all or part of their seasons with Double-A clubs.*

The Texas League is the oldest of the Double-A leagues. Formed in 1888, it has been in continuous operation since 1902, except for a three-year period during World War II, when two-thirds of all minor leagues suspended their seasons. It is also the second-oldest of all minor leagues still in existence; the International League began play in 1884. In its long history, the Texas League has fielded teams in 39 cities located in seven states. During the 1960s, it, like most minor leagues fell on hard times, with membership falling to six clubs and frequent franchise shifts occurring. However, between 1987, when Wichita joined the league, and 2000, when the Jackson, Mississippi, Generals became the Round Rock, Texas, Express, membership in the eight-team league remained constant. El Paso has been a member of the Texas League since 1962, with a one-year absence in 1971. From 1975 to 1983, the club led the league in attendance.

Dudley Field, former home of the Diablos, is now used for poorly attended minor-league soccer games. During the 1970s and 1980s, capacity crowds came to the park as much for the zany between-innings contests and activities as for the baseball games.

During the first half of the 1990s, it was in the top three; however, figures have declined in five of the past seven years.

Saturday, July 6

Dudley Field, bordered on one side by the barrio and on the other by the main highway leading to Juarez, Mexico, is old. Three of the large blue and white aluminum sheets walling the back of the main grandstand are missing. The girders supporting the roof are rusted. The grandstand's bench seats have been removed, leaving only large concrete strips. The washrooms are dimly lit and, while clean, have the musty smell of old basements. Behind the third base bleachers stand two Porta-Potties. The park looks like what it is, an aging baseball stadium, a decaying relic from the middle of the 20th century. Something important is missing: no red dirt area marks out the infield base paths, creating a contrast to the green grass. That is because baseball is no longer played here. Dudley Field is now the home of the El Paso Patriots, a minor-league soccer team.

Until 1990, the diamond was the essential feature of Dudley Field, the focus of attention to the 3,000 or more fans who came out 70 nights each spring and summer to cheer the El Paso Diablos. But by the late 1980s, the park's age was readily apparent, and the club relocated to Cohen Stadium, a $6 million state-of-the-art facility, 10 miles north on U.S. 54. In fact, its age was already showing in 1973 when Jim Paul and three friends purchased the financially struggling Sun Kings. That purchase and the activities in the stands and on the sidelines that Paul began to orchestrate the next season signaled what many people consider the first step in the creation of the "new" minors.

In his air-conditioned office in a new commercial building on El Paso's west side, Jim Paul, who sold the team in 1996, making a $5 million profit on a $1,200 investment, talked about the years at Dudley Field and the current state of baseball.

He opened the conversation by discussing an incident that had occurred two days earlier, on July 4. "I was riding my exercise bike and watching *Good Morning America* when they did a feature on 10 great patriotic photographs. And one of them was from our then-new ballpark on the 4th of July." He reached over to a shelf that contained, among other things, a picture of his shaking hands with former president Ronald Reagan and a plaque from *Baseball America* proclaiming him the top minor-league executive of the past 20 years. From the shelf, he picked up a framed picture,

Former Diablos owner Jim Paul proudly displays a picture of an El Paso player used on the cover of *National Geographic*.

the cover of the April 1991 *National Geographic*. In the foreground, a player wearing uniform number one, looked out to the center field scoreboard on which was displayed an electronic image of a waving Stars and Stripes and the words to the national anthem. "I'm really proud of that picture—not just the fact that it was on the cover of *National Geographic* or that it was featured on network TV. It's what baseball is all about—the great American game." An image of the new park, published just as the minor leagues were beginning their most prosperous decade since the 10 years following World War II, the picture seemed to say: "Look! Minor-league baseball, the great American game, is not just alive, it's thriving, and El Paso is a big part of that!"

It wasn't so at the close of the 1973 season. The minor leagues were struggling to stay alive and, indeed, were mainly being kept alive by the major leagues as places in which to develop talent. The Sun Kings were sharing in the malaise and, in 1973, drew only 63,081 fans, the second-poorest attendance total in the Texas League. Not surprisingly, the club was for sale for assumption of debts and a few thousand dollars in cash. "I inherited the job of general manager of the team," Jim Paul remembered, "because I used the position as a bluff to get the athletic director's job at the University of Southwest Louisiana State." His friends were part of a group buying the woebegone Sun Kings and wanted him both to be part of the ownership group and to run the organization. His bluff called by the university, which did not offer him a position, he returned to his home-town and began his new job. Paul turned the franchise around quickly. In 1974, attendance rose to 112,470, second-best in the league, and increased for each of the five following years. In 1982, a record 282,272 fans jammed Dudley Field, the best in the Texas League since Fort Worth attracted over 354,000 in 1948.

How did Paul do this at a time when fans around the country were not coming to ballparks in record numbers? "I think," he explained, "that my greatest asset was that I didn't know anything about baseball. When I lived here before, I used to take my little brother to the park a couple of times a year. And, in 1973, when I asked myself how, as a teenager, I chose the games we attended, I remembered that it wasn't for the games them-selves, but for the promotions. That was the fun part." In those days, pro-motions were few and far between: country days, which featured egg tosses, greased pig races, and milking contests; pony giveaway day; and the appearance of Max Patkin, the clown prince of baseball who would later enjoy a supporting role in *Bull Durham*. These few promotions resulted in the best attendance days of a team's entire season.

Shortly after assuming his position, Paul attended the annual winter meetings in Houston and was disappointed to discover that everyone was talking baseball, but that no one was dealing with declining attendance and the challenge of how to get people back into the parks. "When you went into the lobby," he remembered, "there was a lot of cigar smoke and not a lot else. Then on the final day, I attended a seminar given by Fred Whitaker, who said, 'If you want people to show up, you've got to make it fun; you've got to get them involved.' That's just what I wanted to hear, and, after his talk, I followed him around asking all sorts of questions."

When he had taken over the team offices in El Paso, Paul had noticed a large chalkboard nailed to the wall. A grid had been traced on it with columns indicating the date, opponent, time, promotion, score, and attendance for each game. In the past, most of the promotion spaces had been usually vacant and the corresponding attendance slots filled with low figures. "I realized that if you marketed well, a good promotion would bring people in. Once you got them there and impressed them with the activities—once you made it fun—there was a very good chance they'd come back on their own." And so Paul began to fill the chalkboard on the wall with off-the-wall promotions.

But the first thing he did was to change the team's nickname—from Sun Kings or Sun Dodgers, as they were called when the club was a Los Angeles affiliate, to Diablos. "I remembered that when I was a kid, mothers would call their children 'Poco Diablito,' little devil, when they'd been exasperating and mischievous. And that's what we had in mind—not something darkly satanic, but something sly, mischievous, something fun. And we wanted something Hispanic, because Hispanics were the largest part of our market." It would be another 15 years before other minor-league teams would follow suit, dropping the names of their parent clubs for catchy monikers like "Alley Cats," Crawdads," "Warthogs," and "Sand Gnats." To go along with the new nickname, the club created a logo that emphasized the fun. A horned black devil wearing a cape pranced or tiptoed non-threateningly forward, its eyes radiating mischief.

Paul also turned misfortune into advantage—a point he frequently stressed in talks he later began giving around the country. "Shortly after we took over, our organ was repossessed. So I went to Radio Shack, bought a cheap cassette tape recorder and a packet of tapes, went home and taped a bunch of my 1950s and 1960s 45s. That night, when I went to the park, I gave them to our PA man. Between innings, he'd turn the thing on and put the mike near the speakers. The crowd really liked the lively music. I always thought organs were for funerals, and I didn't need that if I wanted more people to show up."

Paul Strelzin, the PA announcer to whom Paul handed the cassette recorder, has since become legendary in minor-league circles. A high school principal from New York, he pushed the off-the-wall principle to the limit, often calling out greetings to individuals walking along the concourse and leading almost ritualistic chants in the late innings. "Do you believe?" he'd cry out. On receiving a response, he would intone in a more heightened evangelistic manner, "No! Do you *really* believe?" and receive a chorus of much louder shrieks of faith. He would also introduce each Diablo with a nickname that he and Paul had concocted: "The Enforcer," "Doctor of Batology," or "Teen Angel." "It was," Jim Paul recalled, "part carney act, part camp revival meeting. It really upset the purists. But Texas League president Bobby Bragan supported me. When he got complaints, he'd tell people: "He's filling his park. Are you filling yours?"

Unlike contemporary practices, where expensive bobblehead dolls and back-to-school backpacks are common giveaways, Paul's were frequently very inexpensive and were designed more to enhance the interactive fun of the fans at the game than to bring more people into already packed Dudley Field. "One time, I discovered a close-out sales of cartons of kazoos. They weren't more than 20 cents each. Paul Strelzin led the crowd in playing *Three Blind Mice* when the umpires came on the field (umpires had a better sense of fun in those days), and *Take Me Out to the Ball Game*. We didn't have a sophisticated sound system, so he'd blow his kazoo into the mike with the "charge" bugle call and the crowd would join in." Another time Paul picked up caseloads of bubble-blowing kits at a price of 10 cents a kit and had his PA announcer coordinate a between-innings bubble-fest. "There were thousands of bubbles floating in the air—everyone was laughing and having a great time."

The fun could not continue forever at the old park. Security had always been a problem. Some of the young residents of the nearby barrio considered the hubcaps of parked cars fair game. And, with the bridge to Juarez only two minutes away, car thieves found the parking lots very inviting. Even Paul returned to the parking lot after one game to find his car gone. "Nonetheless," he emphasized, "we had pretty good relationships with the neighborhood. We hired a bunch of local kids to work with the cops to supervise the parking lots. And we worked out a deal with McDonald's to give away coupons for families to get into the park free on Mondays and Tuesdays. It worked well for all of us." McDonald's got customers, families got to be together at ballgames, they bought concessions, and the event generated good will for the Diablos.

These security problems, along with the condition of the park and the rising costs of operating in the minor leagues, meant that the Diablos would need to have a new park or move to a new city. "We lost money in all but three years at Dudley," Paul explained. "Something had to be done." A bond issue was scheduled, and Paul enlisted the help of baseball friends Sparky Anderson, Tommy Lasorda, and Fernando Valenzuela to film a series of commercials about the need for a new stadium. "The same night that an *El Paso Times'* poll predicted that the bond issue to fund $6 million for a new park would fail 3–1, we began to run the commercials. The vote passed by half a percent."

The new park, named after a local sports editor who'd advocated its construction, was situated 10 miles north of the old park. The area was chosen because, in good traffic conditions, it would be less than 20-minutes' drive from anywhere in the Diablos' target area. Out of the cramped park which was difficult to get to, the Diablos had moved into one closer to the rapidly expanding suburbs—a park with 20 revenue-producing luxury boxes, which rented for $12,000 a season, a lounge for private catered parties, and 400 box seats. Attendance jumped, reaching all-time highs in 1994 and 1995, the years of and following the major-league strike and cancellation of the World Series. Three hundred twenty-seven thousand and 329,000 showed up in successive seasons. "We had to work a lot harder than we did before, and we became a year-round activity. We had the luxury boxes and a lot more box seats to sell and we had to provide a product that would keep people returning year after year."

Located in the northern suburbs of El Paso, Cohen Stadium was the first of the new generation of Texas League parks. Unfortunately, only the outfielders have a view of the Franklin Mountains rising behind the stands.

In 1996, Paul sold the Diablos. "After 24 years, I felt burned out. The challenge to keep fresh, to do something new every year so that people would come back, was getting much harder. It got so it wasn't fun getting up each morning to go to the park." Since then, he'd served as the athletic director of New Mexico State University in nearby Las Cruces; run the operation of the Buzzards, the town's minor-league hockey team; entered the appliance business; and raised racehorses. Yet he remained proud of his years as one of minor-league baseball's most revitalizing and successful entrepreneurs and happily listed the promotions and activities that the Diablos inaugurated and that have since been picked up across the minor and major leagues. "I think the way to be number one is to make your fan number one. If you're loyal to the fans, they will be loyal to you. I think major-league owners and players forget this far too often."

And, he noted, it was important that players and owners at both the major- and minor-league levels respected the game of baseball. More than once in his conversation, he applied the term "sacred American game" to the sport. "It has survived so much," he noted, "wars and depressions. If I were the commissioner, I'd make every professional player watch the full nine hours of Ken Burns' documentary on baseball. If they know the history, they'll respect the game." And Jim Paul looked over to the framed *National Geographic* cover. With the number one on the back of player Greg Edge's uniform and his reverential posture as he looks across the grass of the recently completed Cohen Stadium toward the American flag on the scoreboard, the photo symbolized the meaning to Paul of the game he had done so much for because of his great love and respect for it.

By two o'clock that afternoon, activity at Cohen Stadium had begun to pick up. Although the team had been on the road for four days, the park had been the site of a Fourth of July concert and fireworks display on Thursday. The post-celebration cleanup had been completed Friday morning, and the team would not be taking batting practice this afternoon. Thus the grounds crew had a little time to work on the dry and bald patches on the infield grass. These had developed because fungus and grubs, which had increased greatly in number because of the mild winter, had eaten away at large areas of the turf.

The morning *El Paso Times* had referred to the upcoming eight home games as the Diablos' "marquee homestand." Beat reporter Bill Knight wrote: "All stars seem to be in alignment for a special El Paso Diablos' homestand. The Diablos might just be playing their best baseball of the season. The club has some of its best promotions lined up over the next eight games. And the weather is … well, it is summer and warm and beckoning for baseball."[1] The Diablos were, indeed, playing their best baseball—

not just of the season—but in recent years. Now in the third year of an affiliation with the world champion Arizona Diamondbacks, the club was stocked with Arizona's best minor-league players. Nine of the Diamondbacks' top 30 prospects, as evaluated by *Baseball America*, were on the Diablos' roster. These included top prospect Luis Terrero, an outfielder, and second-round pick Mike Gosling, a left-handed pitcher. Although Terrero was hitting only .282, Gosling owned a 9 and 3 record, second-best in the league. The best season was being enjoyed by Chad Tracy. The 17th prospect, who led the league with a .368 batting average, had been above .400 for the first two and a half months of the season. Moreover, all but two members of the 23-man roster had spent their professional careers in the Diamondbacks' organization. This year's Diablos thus represented Arizona's first home-grown minor-league affiliate. The club had been in the race for the Western Division's first-half championship until the second-to-last day of the season. They had started the second half on a tear, coming home with a 12–4 record, which put them three games in front of second-place Midland.

The lineup of promotions and giveaways, as important to many of the patrons as the game itself, was equal to that of the baseball team. Tonight would be the final of three bobblehead doll giveaways. After receiving replicas of Diamondback stars Luis Gonzalez and Curt Schilling, fans could now own one of Randy Johnson. Sunday would feature the antics of "Krazy Karacters," a group of costumed mascots. Baseball card and backpack giveaways, 50-cent tamale and 25-cent hot-dog nights, and the season's second appearance of the Famous Chicken and the third of five fireworks displays would be featured later in the homestand. Anyone who didn't care about the Diablos could eat cheaply, watch non-athletic events, and take a freebie home for the price of a $5 general admission ticket to Cohen Stadium.

And the weather would be great. El Paso had escaped the rains and floods that had devastated central and west-central Texas. And the 100 degree plus temperatures that had baked the area for the past week were gone. Game temperatures would be in the mid–80s and only occasional gusty winds and very scattered thundershowers were forecast.

The Diablos' organization needed this marquee homestand to be successful. In 45 home dates, they were averaging 3,243 fans a game, over 6,000 less a game than Round Rock and fifth-best in the eight-team Texas League. Only five of the 21 Friday, Saturday, Sunday, and holiday home dates—generally the best-drawing game nights—had attracted over 5,000 fans. The largest crowd—8,026—had arrived for a school-day matinee in which tickets had been distributed at a deeply discounted rate. If average attendance levels did not increase, the Diablos would finish the season with a total paid attendance of 225,000, the third-straight year in which attendance had declined and the lowest figure in 12 years. At a time when revenues were flat and operating costs were increasing, such a total would be a cause for alarm.

At five o'clock, half an hour before the gates opened, no more than 50 people were lined up at the park's main entrance, a far cry from the thousand who had started arriving at Rancho Cucamonga's Epicenter hours before the California club had begun handing out its bobbleheads. "Some people may have been discouraged by the weather reports," operations manager Jimmy Hicks suggested, referring to the possibility of thundershowers.

In the press box, general manager Andrew Wheeler suddenly found himself saddled with a new duty. Because of family matters, Bernie Olivas, the regular scorekeeper could not make it to the game. One of Wheeler's first baseball jobs had been keeping score for the Boise Hawks of the Northwest League. "But that was all manual. I've used this computerized program a few times—but it will be interesting," he remarked as he reached down the counter for the program's thick spiraled instructional manual. Over the next 2 hours and 45 minutes, as he entered plays into the computer and on the paper score sheet beside it, he used the telephone, a cell phone, his walkie-talkie, and his raised voice to communicate with reporters, game-day workers, press-box visitors, and his father.

"Andrew," came a distressed voice over the walkie-talkie, "there's a guy who came in from Arizona. He's really mad because they told him at the ticket window that there were lots of bobbleheads left; but when he got to the gate, they were all gone. He's furious—what do you think we should do?" Later, his dad called his cell phone to ask about good places to eat in Las Vegas, and the dutiful son dispensed culinary advice about locations and the special items at various restaurants. On a more serious note, he advised staff on the procedures they should follow when a fan, who may have had more beer than necessary, had slipped on the steps and been taken to a hospital. He called out his decisions on various scoring plays for the information of radio broadcasters, writers, and scoreboard operators. And interspersed with all these communications was a running conversation about various trips to the golf course, an evaluation of today's trade between the Arizona Diamondbacks and the Pittsburgh Pirates, one which involved former Diablo Duaner Sanchez; and his trip on Tuesday to the Double-A All-Star game in Norwich, Connecticut.

When the night's attendance, 5,153 was announced, Wheeler seemed to be disappointed, but said nothing. He did, however, express disappointment at the Diablos' performance on the field. "Before the game, you could feel an excitement in the stands; the fans really wanted to cheer, to get into the game. But the team isn't giving them anything to cheer about." The Diablos started Oscar Vallerreal, another top prospect. But the visiting Round Rock Express got to him quickly. Although he struck out the side in the first inning, he also gave up two runs on three hits and a wild pitch. The Diablos came back with a run in the bottom of the first, but four Express runs in the top of the third put the game out of reach. By game's end, the Express had nine runs on 15 hits, to El Paso's two runs on seven hits. Round Rock starter Nick Roberts pitched his first complete game of the season. It was his third victory against the Diablos this year. By the time the game was over, a large percentage of the fans and their bobblehead dolls had gone home.

After the game, Wheeler placed the defeat in perspective. The Diablos had played a 15-inning game on Thursday, two seven-inning games on Friday, and their plane had arrived from San Antonio at 3:30 Saturday morning. "They're bound to be tired. The Express flew in from Austin early this afternoon, so they had a good rest at home. And they only played nine innings last night. Moreover," he continued, "we didn't have our manager or best hitter." He was referring to the fact that early in the morning, manager Chip Hale, along with Chad Tracy, had flown to Milwaukee, where on Sunday, the former would coach and the latter play in the Future's Game. This contest, a part of the major-league All-Star festivities, would feature the top prospects from the minor leagues. Hale and Tracy would return to El Paso in time for Monday's contest with Round Rock.

Sunday, July 7

When it opened in 1990, Cohen Stadium was the first of the new-style parks in the Texas League. But, in 2003, when the Shreveport Swamp Dragons would move to a multi-million dollar complex in Frisco, a very wealthy suburb of Dallas, it would become the third-oldest. Nevertheless, the Diablos' home maintained a fresh and new appearance. Located next to the Patriot Freeway, 10 miles north of downtown El Paso, it stood between the new suburbs of the foothills to the west and the relatively undeveloped plains to the east. A movie complex was to the north, a campus of El Paso Community College to the south. Unlike many more recently created downtown parks, which had been constructed as part of inner-city rejuvenation plans, Cohen Stadium was conceived as a destination point, a place to which people drove with the sole purpose of

attending a ballgame. Although it was situated in an area which civic officials expected would become an integral part of the city's northern expansion, it was located near the Diana Drive off-ramp mainly because it could be reached by car in 20-minutes' driving from anywhere in the Diablos' target audience area. It was not surprising, therefore, that the stadium was surrounded by acres of parking lots, enough to handle easily all the vehicles on the occasional nights when there were capacity crowds of over 8,000 people.

Although the park was visible from the freeway—the light standards could be spotted a mile away during the day and much further at night—it was not an imposing structure. The outside walls were faced with rough pale lavender bricks that harmonized with the nearby college buildings. Only after entering the main gates did a visitor get a sense of the park's size. The playing field was recessed, so that the first image was of the entire park. A wide concourse ran from the left to right field foul poles behind the stands, providing fans with easy access to the gift shop, the numerous concession stands, and the arcade game center that bordered it. In front of the concourse, rows of aluminum benches fanned out to the foul poles; below them, red box seats, and then the brown dirt of the warning track and the green of the infield grass. At the far edge of the outfield warning

(*Above and facing page*) A painting in the luxury suite area depicts the canopies that were to be an integral part of Cohen Stadium. By the 2002 season, they had yet to be installed.

track rose a twenty-foot-high fence adorned with 69 eight feet by 16 feet signs, each of which sold for $4,500 a season. These fees, along with the $8,000 each for the signs on the giant right field scoreboard, accounted for a significant amount of the Diablos' revenue.

A person walking along the warning path under the double row of signs quickly realized that the left and center fielders had the finest view in the house. If their attention ever wandered and they decided to look above the sky boxes, they'd see the Franklin Mountains. Looking over the third base stands, they'd see an interesting and if, they paused to consider it, curious sight: five white poles looking like the masts of a flotilla of tall ships inexplicably dry-docked at the edge of a baseball stadium located in the southwest desert.

A paragraph in the promotional kit that was sent during the winter to prospective advertisers explained what the poles were. "The single largest change [in the ball park this year] will be conspicuously evident on Opening Day. A canopy of massive white translucent fabric that will provide shade and protection from inclement weather to most of the third base concourse area will cover a large portion of Cohen Stadium. Once erected, the canopy will give Cohen Stadium the look that was originally intended by its designers when the structure was built in 1990. It will make Cohen Stadium strikingly visible among the growing surroundings of Northeast El Paso." However, three months after Opening Day, the white masts stood bare and the white translucent coverings remained in their packing, each one of them strapped to a mast's spar.

On Sunday, in his second-floor office, Andrew Wheeler explained the history of the canopy, along with his own personal history in minor-league administration and the challenges his staff faced running this Double-A franchise. "When the city was building the park, the costs were more than they'd anticipated. So they dropped the plans for the canopy to save $300,000," he explained. "It was to be the design signature for the ball park, something that set it apart from other parks, and it would provide shade for our customers. The city has finally secured the funds as part of a larger bond issue. Now it will cost $2 million." He expected the canopy to be up by the end of July, in time for the club's last dozen home games. Wheeler also noted that, with the canopy in place, the Diablos could rent the concourse for such outdoor events as car shows, craft displays, and even weddings.

Wheeler's spacious second-story office reflected the two greatest loves of his life: baseball and golf. The TV in the cabinet facing his desk was set on ESPN, which was playing highlights from the day's major-league games. On the wall, two large framed prints depicted famous landscapes from the

Pebble Beach and Augusta National golf courses. Wheeler talked about his college baseball career at UCLA and an off-season invitation from a family friend, Bill Pereira, to spend a summer in Boise working for his newly acquired Northwest League team, the Hawks. "I cleaned up trash and did the scorekeeping, both on a volunteer basis. But I got really valuable experience; I saw great young ballplayers; and, as often as I could, I fished and golfed." After graduation, he worked on a full-time, paid basis with Pereira's Sioux City Explorers of the independent Northern League. "After Bill acquired the Diablos from Jim Paul, I came down here to be assistant general manager. A bit later, I took over the general manager's role."

Assuming the leadership of a baseball franchise that had been run by a well-known, respected, and very popular local businessman was no easy task. Wheeler explained the challenge that the present management team faced. "The previous owner didn't have a large financial investment in the team and he was able to pay himself a salary as president and general manager," he began, referring to Paul. "He was able to give out a lot of free tickets without any financial strain on the operation." By contrast, the Pereira group that took over the Diablos spent $6 million just to purchase the team. At the same time, the Professional Baseball Agreement, along with Texas League dues, took away a larger portion of the gross revenues than before, and operating expenses, most noticeably team travel, increased drastically.

"Our revenues are flat, our expenses are increasing," Wheeler continued. "And we live in one of the poorest cities in the minors. Our ticket prices have risen only $1.50 in 13 years. Our challenge now is how to keep our general admission at $5 while meeting increased expenses. We've been working hard at selling corporate sponsorships and that's helped. But we've also had to raise our concession prices; some people have complained, but they have to realize that that's the price they'll have pay if they want to keep the $5 general admission."

Wheeler discussed the problem faced by most operators of full-season minor league teams: the length of the season, 140 games over five months. "April is really difficult everywhere, not just up north where the weather can be brutal. Kids are in school and sports fans are watching basketball and hockey playoffs. And by mid–August, football is starting up, and the kids are going back to school. It's really hard to sell single-game tickets at the beginning and end of the season. "Moreover," he continued, "having 70 home dates makes selling individual season tickets difficult. Probably only a dozen or so people would attend all home games or even 90 percent of them. So it makes no sense for people to invest $300 for a season ticket."

Wheeler also believed that the long season was unnecessary for the ballplayers, explaining that most of them played in the fall or winter months and followed rigorous training programs all year. "In the old days, a lot of players didn't stay fit in the off-season, and they didn't usually play any baseball then, so the major leagues needed their minor leaguers to play for five months." He also noted that the April weather in half the country was brutal on the players and that over the five months they would benefit from more off-days during the season. "They only get 15 off-days and nearly half of these involve travel."

He was pleased with the Diablos' new affiliation with the Diamondbacks. "Most of our fans don't follow the minor-league teams and the progress of prospects, but for those who do, having the world champions as our parent club is interesting. When our players move up to Triple-A, some people will travel to Tucson to watch them, and, after that, when they make the majors, to Phoenix. And we may see Arizona sending some of their big leaguers here to rehab."

For the rest of the fans, what the Diablos focused on was providing affordable, safe family fun in a clean, secure environment. "But that's hard to advertise," Wheeler went on. "What we need to do is get families here for the first time and provide an evening's entertainment that will make them want to come back. The stadium experience is our best advertisement. That's why we work very hard on customer service." At that point in the conversation, the phone rang. It was a customer, and Wheeler listened for a minute before offering a solution to the problem. The solution accepted, the general manager hung up the phone, flicked the TV to a station showing golf, and, after studying the leader board, turned the set off and headed to the diamond where the Diablos were about to begin their stretching exercises.

In left field, strength and conditioning coach Sean Renninger stood in the center of a circle of pitchers, leading them through their paces. One of them, Mike Gosling, was facing the rigors of a 140-game schedule for the first time. Like Chad Tracy, who at this moment was no doubt suiting up for the Futures Game at Milwaukee's Miller Park, Gosling had been fast-tracked by the Diamondbacks. However, there was a significant difference between the hard-hitting third baseman and the hard-throwing left-handed pitcher. While both were playing their first season in Double-A ball, 2002 was Tracy's second professional season; it was Gosling's first. He had bypassed the bottom four levels of Arizona's farm system.

As he relaxed in the clubhouse after the workout, Gosling spoke about his baseball life to date. Born in Madison, Wisconsin, the 21-year-old had grown up in Salt Lake City. He'd always wanted to be a pitcher, "ever since

Mike Gosling, highly ranked Arizona Diamondbacks pitching prospect, relaxes during afternoon stretching exercises. In 2002, his first professional season, Gosling won 14 and lost 5, earning a spot on the Texas League All-Star team.

I began to play catch in the back yard with my dad. And since I was left-handed, everyone encouraged me." Like all kids, he indulged in fantasies about World Series heroics. But whereas others smashed dramatic home runs, he dreamed of shutting down the opposition's most dangerous slugger and then being mobbed by his teammates as he strode triumphantly off the mound.

He'd excelled on the mound with Salt Lake City High School and, not surprisingly, was drafted—in the 14th round. "I was flattered," he remembered, "but I'd signed a letter of intent with Stanford. I really wanted to go to college, and Stanford had a great academic reputation. Their baseball team, the Cardinals, had a history of producing good pitchers. I don't think I could have gone anywhere else and received such a quality education—athletically and academically." He began his college baseball career as a reliever, but was switched to a starting role at the beginning of his junior season. It was a learning experience, he said: "I had to develop a different mind-set. I had to prepare myself for a pace that would get me as deep into the game as possible; before I'd just gone into the game and given it all I had for a few batters. And, as a starter, I had to work on three or four pitches that I could throw for strikes. But I was happy to make the shift. I'd always felt I was best suited to be a starter."

After the college seasons, Gosling went to summer school—baseball style. Between high school and college he'd pitched for the Anchorage Glacier Pilots of the Alaska Summer League. The next year, it was off to the east coast to play with the Orleans Cardinals of the Cape Cod Summer League, generally accepted as the best of all college summer circuits. And just before his junior year, he summered with Team USA His summer education would prove invaluable when he turned professional; he would bring to the minor leagues a great deal of experience pitching against batters who used wooden bats, not the aluminum ones of high school and college. This would be one less adjustment he'd have to make as a pro. "The summer leagues," he went on, "had more of a pro ball feel. You were more on your own than in college, and you had to adjust to a new group of guys. The competition was great."

Like most college players, Gosling was drafted after his junior year. But unlike most of them, he finished his season pitching in the ultimate college game—the final of the College World Series in Omaha's Rosenblatt Stadium. The converted reliever was charged with his team's 12–1 loss to Louisiana State, having given up seven earned runs in four innings. However, he had performed well during the season, winning seven and losing three, with an excellent 77 strikeouts to 28 walks ratio.

Two weeks before the big game, he'd been drafted in the second round—67th overall—by the Diamondbacks. Even though Gosling knew that he'd probably be chosen in the early rounds, he admitted to being nervous and anxious. "I was at the university, and my girlfriend and I were listening on the Internet. We kept hearing names called out, but not mine. Then I heard that the Diamondbacks had picked me. I was very happy; my advisor had said they really wanted me." The Diamondbacks wanted him so much that they signed Mike for $2 million, one of the highest amounts ever offered a person taken in the second round, and sent him to the Arizona Fall League where he played with and against the top prospects in baseball, athletes with Double- and Triple-A and even major-league experience. "Going to the Arizona League," he remembered, "I wasn't quite sure what to expect. I looked at it as a learning experience—even if I got knocked around. I might be able to prove myself, or at least get a taste of what top-notch minor-league hitting was like. It was a win-win situation."

The Arizona Fall League learning experience over in mid–November, Gosling embarked on two more learning experiences before reporting to the Diamondbacks' minor-league camp in mid–March. "The guys in the fall league told me that fatigue was a real problem over 140 games and that you had to prepare yourself over the winter. When you realize that baseball will be your full-time profession and you have three or four months when you're not playing, you need to work out. I spent two or three hours in the gym each day doing cardiovascular and strengthening exercises." The rest of the time was spent at Stanford, completing his bachelor's degree in medical biology. "I'd made a commitment to my education, and I'd taken extra courses along the way. I only had a quarter and a couple of hours to go, so I completed my requirements during the winter quarter. It was over just before spring training. During the [Texas League] All-Star break I went back to my graduation at Stanford," he said, a note of quiet pride in his voice.

When Gosling reported to the Diamondbacks' minor league camp in Tucson, he found himself assigned to the Double-A clubhouse. "My goal was to try to be on the Double-A roster when camp broke. I was pleasantly surprised. I thought I could compete at this level, and now I had a chance." Just halfway through the season, Mike had made the most of this chance. He'd won his first four games, one of which was a complete game, lost the next two, and then won five of his next six, the last a 3–1 victory on July 5 against San Antonio.

Not scheduled to pitch for another four days, Gosling changed out of his sweaty T-shirt and joined three teammates at a game of cards. One of the aces of the Diablos' mound staff, he now looked for success with the aces he'd just been dealt.

As Gosling settled into his card game, his pitching coach, Mark Davis, leaned against the batting cage watching the visiting Round Rock Express players take their practice swings. The winner of the 1989 Cy Young Award as the National League's top pitcher when he earned 44 saves for the San Diego Padres, M. D., as the players called him, was in his fourth year coaching in the Diamondbacks' organization. He had first worked with Gosling last October in the Arizona Fall League and offered his explanation for the young pitcher's excellent professional start. "Stanford has one of the top college baseball programs in the country and has a very high percentage of their games against top-ranked opponents. The level of ability of the players Mike faced day in and day out was higher than most college pitchers would encounter."

Davis had been impressed with Gosling's work in the Arizona Fall League, remarking, "He was different from the average college guy. He didn't have the metal bat phobia so many have; he wasn't afraid to work both sides of the plate. I think now that he's doing the job like a guy who has two years of pro ball behind him." Moreover, the pitching coach believed that Gosling's obvious intelligence helped him. "When you give him advice, he wants to know why you're making the suggestion. Then he'll try what you've suggested and come back after and say, 'I see what you mean.'" Asked if there were any dangers in fast-tracking young players, as the Diamondbacks were doing with Gosling, Davis said no. "Fast-tracking is only for the guys who can handle it. You always make sure players start their careers at the levels that are best for them. Mike started at Double-A because that's where he was ready to begin his development as a pro."

Sunday night's special attraction was an appearance by the "Krazy Karacters," a traveling group of performing mascots who danced on dugout roofs, mingled with fans, and performed a series of short, between-inning skits. In one of the funniest of these, a character who looked a little Grover from *Sesame Street* chased Oscar Villarreal, last night's starting Diablo pitcher, from the left field bullpen, behind the plate, and toward right field. As he did so, the blue chaser tossed water balloons at Villarreal in several failed attempts to douse him. But as pursuer and pursued passed the visitors' dugout, the tables turned. Several members of the Express, each with water balloons in both hands, surged onto the field, successfully rescued Villarreal, and dampened both the spirits and the costume of the "Krazy Karacter."

In addition to the entertainment provided by the visiting mascots, the fans also enjoyed good baseball provided by the hometown nine. The night marked the first start by El Paso pitcher Blake Mayo since August 31, 2000. A rising star in Arizona's minor-league system, Mayo had undergone Tommy John arm surgery in the spring of 2000 and had missed all of last season. He'd returned just a week ago and had allowed one earned run in two brief appearances. In this, his first start, he threw 82 pitches over five innings and limited Round Rock to one earned run. He struck out six, while walking one. A bobble by Jack Santora to open the top of the third and then three hits gave Round Rock a 3–1 lead, and so Mayo did not earn the win. That went to Jay Bellflower who succeeded him. During Jay's stint on the mound, the Diablos scored six runs to go ahead. When El Paso closer Jesus Silva earned the save in spite of allowing two runs in the top of the ninth, one press box wag asked writer Bill Knight if he was going to lead off his story with the phrase "Jesus Saves." The final score was a not-completely satisfying 7–6 for El Paso. The announced attendance of 2,970 was less satisfying to Andrew Wheeler, who earlier had been very upset when he received a report from Milwaukee that Chad Tracy had only entered the Futures Game in the sixth inning and then only as a defensive replacement. "Unbelievable!" he exclaimed more than once. "The best hitter in the minors, and he doesn't even get an at-bat."

Marcy Hammock, Jodie Cervantes, and Louise Edgeworth were, perhaps, happier with the evening's results than were the rest of the fans. The first two were the wives of Robby Hammock, Diablo catcher, and Chris Cervantes, Diablo pitcher. The third was the girlfriend of P. J. Bevis, another pitcher. Louise had just arrived in El Paso a week earlier from Brisbane, Australia, where she'd just completed her degree in biology. Marcy and Jodie had been Cohen Stadium regulars since 2000, when their husbands had been promoted from the Diamondbacks' low Single-A affiliate in South Bend, Indiana. Accompanying them were their small children, ages seven months to three years. As the women watched the game, they chatted with each other as though they were neighbors enjoying morning coffee in their back yards, called encouragement to Diablo batters, changed diapers, and occasionally left their seats to retrieve Gentry Hammock, a two-year-old, who was a great favorite with the regulars sitting nearby. They talked about themselves and their baseball-playing husbands as if all were part of an extended family. When the Diablos' third-baseman broke the plate glass window of a luxury suite with a foul ball, the women shook their fingers at him in mock-admonition and one remarked: "That's Jack Santora; he's always stirring things up."

When Marcy met Robby while he was a student at the University of Georgia, she knew he was interested in baseball. "But," she noted, "I had no idea that it would lead to a professional career." That career began at eight in the evening of June 3, 1998, when the Arizona Diamondbacks called to tell Robby he'd been selected in the 23rd round of the draft and that he was to report to the Lethbridge (Alberta) Black Diamonds of the Pioneer League. "He was so excited that we went over to the university baseball stadium to play catch for half an hour. After he'd had his little fix, we came home, and he started to get ready to head out." Marcy didn't accompany him to western Canada, but in less than a month, he called her to say that he wanted her to be a part of this. In the winter of 1999, the two were married, and Marcy began the life of a baseball wife.

"Some people think that I've put my own life on hold," she remarked. "But I don't think I've given up a lot. I think that my role is to support him—that's my career. With me here, the season is easier for him. I try to encourage him to talk to me about the game; when he does, he feels better." It certainly hadn't been the glamorous life that many people unfamiliar with minor-league athletics frequently think it is. "It's a financial strain, living on one income. Minor-league players don't make a lot of money," Marcy continued. "And moving to a new city every year or two can be tough. You have to get to know new people. And you're always thinking, 'If he gets called up to the next level, that's great. But I sure hate the thought of packing up and moving all over again.'"

Jodie Cervantes met her husband in December 1999 at an American Home Furnishings Store where the two worked in their hometown of Tucson. He was working there after his second professional season, and the two were married a year later. When Chris returned to South Bend for his fourth pro season, she moved with him. However, before he even got into a game, the Diamondbacks promoted him to El Paso, and she followed. With two small children and a husband who was home only in the mornings, and then only when the team was in El Paso, she found life a little hectic. "Sometimes when the team is on the road, I head back to Tucson to visit my family for a few days."

Although, like Robby Hammond, Chris Cervantes didn't generally bring the game home with him, things had been a little more difficult this year, Jody noted. "He's had a lot of days between appearances this season," she explained, alluding to the fact that during the first three months of the season her husband had pitched only 54 innings. "He used to be a starter until last year. After three or four days of inactivity, he starts to get antsy around home. Once he didn't pitch for nine days." Like Marcy, she emphasized that minor-league life was not at all glamorous. "But it's worth it all to see him when he comes home happy from the game he loves. Chris and baseball go hand in hand."

Twenty minutes after the game, the stadium was nearly empty. With the help of Louise Edgeworth, Marcy and Jodie packed baby bags, gathered children and placed them in strollers, and headed along the concourse toward left field. There they stood quietly, awaiting the appearance of Robby and Chris—baseball wives picking up their husbands after a hard night at work.

Monday, July 8

The morning edition of the *El Paso Times* predicted that the heavy rains that had flooded west Texas over the weekend would arrive in town late in the afternoon. While this was relatively welcome news for area firefighters, it was not for the front-office staff of the Diablos. Shortly after two in the afternoon, operations manager Jimmy Hicks called the weather service and learned that the advancing rain clouds were only half an hour away. He informed the front-office staff to be on stand by for tarp duty and headed to the field to examine the large, rolled-up protective covering, something that saw very little use in El Paso's arid climate. Gusty winds soon announced the arrival of the front, and people appeared from all portions of the park, hurried down the steps leading to the first base area, lined themselves up in front of the big roll, grabbed two handfuls of the waterproof covering, and, on command, began to pull. As they did so, the raindrops began, and, when they increased, those Diablos who had been running laps along the outfield warning track headed for the protection of the clubhouse.

Moments later, a couple of them returned with folding chairs to the small covered porch of the clubhouse. They unfolded these and sat down to survey the rain which, by now, had become a steady, but not heavy drizzle. One of the watchers was Jack Santora, a 25-year-old third baseman from Monterey, California, who was listed in the Arizona Diamondbacks' media guide as 5 feet 9 inches tall, on the game day roster as 5-8, and in *Baseball America's 2002 Almanac* as 5-7. "Actually," he confessed, "I'm only 5-6." In a game where anything under six feet is considered short, Santora was one of the shortest players in the minor leagues, and, at 160 pounds, one of the lightest. He made up for lack of size and weight with an aggressive, feisty style of play.

Jack had never really considered becoming a professional player and didn't play American Legion or college ball with the sense of mission that characterizes so many future professional players. "The idea just gradually developed when I was at UCLA. I spent a summer in the Cape Cod League, and I really liked the wooden bats. They took us all to Fenway Park one day, and I got to meet Nomar Garciaparra. I think that summer was when I realized that pro ball was for me." When draft day rolled around in 1999, Santora and many of his fellow Bruins gathered together. It was a time of pranks and good spirits. In the early rounds several of the players received phone calls, Santora included: "I was really surprised. I had no idea that I would go so quickly; the scouts who'd talked to me left the impression that I'd probably have to wait until the second day. Well," Jack paused and then laughed at the memory, "the caller said he was from the Dodgers. It turned out to be the friend of a friend who knew that I was a Giants' fan, that I really hated the Dodgers. He used to razz me all the time about going to university in Los Angeles."

Then, an hour or so later, he received a second call, this one for real. It was Hal Kurtzman, the Diamondbacks' central California scout informing him that he'd been selected in the nineteenth round. "And even that was a surprise." It didn't take Jack long to sign. In fact, a day later he affixed his name to an Arizona contract and got ready to join Arizona's rookie team, the Missoula Osprey.

At first, life in the small Montana city as a member of a new club was a bit of a shock. "For the first time in three years, I had to become a member of a new team—we all did. And it was a much different kind of mixture than I was used to: about a third were college guys, a third were just out of high school, and a third were Latin players who only spoke a few words of English. In the beginning, it seemed sort of cutthroat," Santora remembered. "I thought, we're not here to win, like we were in college. But as soon as I realized that it was really the same game, and I started having fun. I started to see the team as a family. In fact, over the years some of them have become closer than my own family. I'm with them every day for six months, and we share a lot of confidences. It's much different from college, where you also had your life in class and a social life away from the team." Two other members of the 1999 Osprey team, P. J. Bevis and Kevan Burns, were still teammates.

When Santora moved to South Bend in 2000, he acquired four more members of his new extended family: Chris Cervantes, Billy Martin, Tim Olson, and Oscar Villarreal. He also acquired a valuable baseball lesson: a 140-game season was a long grind. "About June I felt tired and weak, and I got into a slump. We didn't have a strength coach then, but I realized that I'd have to spend more time in the gym to maintain my stamina for the entire season. That year, I got the best advice I've ever had in baseball: 'Come to the park ready to play every day.' I live by that rule."

Santora began the 2001 season in El Paso, having skipped advanced Single-A. Asked what difference he perceived between Double-A and low Single-A ball, he noted: "The game is much faster; everyone is fast here. The pitchers are all really good. You can't rely on luck; you have to work at the plate. You have to be thinking all the time, to be able to make adjustments from at-bat to at-bat. We see the teams here much more often than we did in the Midwest League, so it's a challenge to adapt each time you meet them." Last year, Jack added more family members: Brad Cresse, Jamie Gann, Mike Gray, Robby Hammock, Matt Kata, and Javier Lopez. Over a three-year period, individuals were coalescing into a team, the first team in the Diamondbacks' history to have been formed nearly completely from their own draft choices.

During his first three years as a professional ballplayer, Santora did not put up big numbers; his average hovered around .250, and he hit only two home runs. But he played aggressive baseball, working for the team. In 2000, he was third among all minor leaguers with 18 sacrifices. He had been patient at the plate, striking out on average only once every two games. And once on base, he was a good runner, successful in 60 out of 85 stolen base attempts. His fielding had improved since his first season, when he committed 20 errors in 51 games. He strove to be there when his extended family needed him.

Unlike many players drafted while they were still in college, Santora completed his degree quickly. When his baseball career is over, he might consider teaching and coaching. "But it's hard to play this game when your mind is in some other time and place. Life is short and baseball life is even shorter. So I try to stay focused, to take advantage of it now." And the immediate now involved taking batting practice. The threatening clouds having passed away, the staff had removed the tarp, spilling what little moisture had collected onto the outfield grass. A tractor pulled the batting cage into position, and Jack folded up his chair, put it back in the clubhouse, and trotted to the cage.

Midway through batting practice, Chad Tracy and manager Chip Hale, recently arrived from the airport, emerged from the clubhouse and came to the batting cage. Tracy took his swings and returned to the clubhouse, while Chip picked up a bat and began hitting ground balls to the infield. Later, he talked about the whirlwind trip he was in the middle of. He was asked why he and Tracy had come from Milwaukee when they would have to leave for Connecticut after only 14 hours in El Paso. Wouldn't it have been easier and more restful to have proceeded directly to the Double-A All-Star game from the Futures Game? He remarked that both of them had a job to do here tonight and went on to explain that the grueling travel schedule had been part of Tracy's education as a professional ballplayer and future major leaguer. "I wanted Chad to learn about the long early morning flights he'll be making when he's in Triple-A. And there'll be a time soon when he'll be called on to make a very quick flight to join the big-league team. Then in a couple of days, he'll be with them on a long road trip or, perhaps, getting on a plane to head back to his minor-league team. After this week, that kind of travel won't come as quite so much of a shock."

The Diablos' manager went on to talk about the fast-tracking of two of his young stars: Gosling and Tracy, who had had only 64 professional games—half a season—under their belts before this year. "I think fast-tracking is partly a matter of opportunity. Some organizations don't have the openings at this level. I think that if a player is ready to move up quickly, he'll really learn from it." Of Tracy's hitting, he noted that the 22-year-old had been a hitter since he was a Little Leaguer. "He has a good quick bat, and he makes good contact with pitches anywhere in the zone. He doesn't hit a lot of home runs, but he doesn't strike out a lot. With two strikes on him, he's able to put the ball in play. He's done well so far; now we'll see how high he'll go. Next year he should be in Triple-A."

Hale himself had been fast-tracked as well, moving from managing rookie ball to Double—in only his third year as a manager. Like many former players, he'd begun managing because he'd missed the game he loved and wanted to stay involved. In his first year in Missoula, he led the Osprey to second-place finishes in both halves of the split season; the next year, the club lost the North Division title to the eventual league champion Billings Mustangs. The two seasons were learning experiences for both himself and his young players. "I think the biggest thing I learned was to be patient, to remember when I was their age. I had to let them make mistakes and learn from them. The most important thing I could impart to them was to respect the game both on and off the field. That respect has been lost by too many major leaguers, and I didn't want my players to imitate some of those guys."

He admitted that jumping four levels from rookie to Double-A ball had required adjustments on his part. "I haven't led players through each of the steps or observed those stages of development. I quickly discovered that I didn't need to work on fundamentals that much; by now those should be almost second nature. I find we spend more time on strategy—the players at this level are smart and quick. A lot of them could compete at a major-league level. All they need is consistency and fine-tuning. That's my job here, to help them do things well—all the time!" And then he returned to the clubhouse to talk over strategy with coaches Scott Coolbaugh and Mark Davis.

Three scouts, Gregg Miller (white shirt) of the Minnesota Twins, Joe Sparks (black shirt) of the St. Louis Cardinals, and Dale Sutherland (glasses) of the Anaheim Angels, watch intently as the Diablos play the Round Rock Express. Scouting in the minor leagues is a major activity for all big-league organizations, who use the information scouts gather to access younger players available in trades and as part of a data bank on players who may some day be major-league opponents.

An hour before game time, four middle-aged men sat talking in the press box. Their conversations ranged from comments on the just-completed batting practice, to rumored major-league trades, to the recent death of Ted Willaims. They had an easy, yet slightly guarded camaraderie, as though they were employees from different and competing companies who'd accidentally found themselves standing in the same concession lines at a movie or ballgame. In a sense they were. The four were professional scouts for major league teams, and they were in El Paso to observe and evaluate the talent on the Diablos and Express. They were in some ways, a fraternity, a group of men sharing a common lifestyle—the lonely, seemingly never-ending road life of the scout—and they enjoyed sharing time with people who understood the joys and stresses of the job. Joe Sparks worked for the St. Louis Cardinals, Gregg Miller for the Minnesota Twins, Dennis Cardoza for the Florida Marlins, and Dale Sutherland for the Anaheim Angels. As game-time drew closer, three of them closed their briefcases and headed to the concession stands for their typical evening meal for nearly two-thirds of the year: soda and a hamburger or hot dog.

Dale Sutherland remained behind for a few minutes arranging his files and talking about the life of a scout. He was nearing the end of a 27-day road trip, which, when over, would have involved watching as many games in Orlando, Houston, Arlington, Tulsa, El Paso, Tacoma, and Portland. A brother of former major leaguers Gary and Darrell, Dale had not played pro ball, but had begun part-time scouting while he was coaching in youth leagues. Over the years, he'd worked for the Expos, Indians, and Padres and, since 1991, for the Angels. He explained that scouting wasn't restricted to the amateur leagues, that after players had been drafted, it was important to keep track of their progress and development. Each major-league club had an enormous data bank covering every player in the minor leagues. "It's important to know their strengths and weaknesses so that when one of them reaches the major leagues, you'll know how to play against him when he faces your club." In addition, minor leaguers constantly become available for trade or sale to other organizations. "Only when you have this information do you know when a player is worth picking up."

And so, every year, beginning in spring training and through to the end of the major league season, Dale watched the Double-A, Triple-A, and big-league clubs of six major-league organizations. "I see each club for five or six games early in the season and then again later," he explained. Armed with a radar gun, stopwatch, and charts, he recorded every player's at-bat, noting what pitches the batter swung at—type, speed and location—and the result of the swing. Before the second visit to each club, he carefully studied the charts. "That way, I have a good idea about which players I want to concentrate on." He kept parallel charts on the pitchers.

Unlike some major-league organizations, which assigned scouts to specific geographical areas, the Anaheim Angels assigned theirs to organizations. "When you spend a lot of time studying an organization, you really get to know it, where it's strong and where and when they might have someone available," Dale explained. "I have to know the six organizations as well as they do themselves. I'm almost a shadow 'farm director' for each organization." In his office at home in La Crescenta, California, Sutherland had a wall chart for each of his six organizations, listing what he considered their prospects. "And these lists," he remarked with a smile, "are often quite different from the ones that *Baseball America* puts out each spring."

With his focus on individual players, Dale didn't have much time to watch the games themselves. "Sometimes after I've seen all the players I've come out to watch, I'll leave in the seventh or eighth inning, and when people ask me what the score is, I have to say that I don't know. But I love coming to the park," he went on. "Sometimes when I'm sitting there behind home plate, I hear the fans talking about the players making evaluations. And I think, 'That's what I'm doing, too. But they had to pay to watch the players, and I'm getting paid to do the same thing.'"

Shortly after Dale Sutherland had departed from the press box, picked up his baseball supper, and taken his place on "Scouts' Row"—a group of box seats behind home plate—Bill Knight, baseball writer for the *El Paso Times* arrived. Now in his 24th year of covering the Diablos, he talked about the hundreds of games he covered at old Dudley Field. "I used to show up early," he said, "and jog and take grounders with the team. Then I'd shower and get ready to cover the game." Dudley Field, he recalled, was cozy for both fans and players. "It was a real hitters' park. One game we beat Beaumont 35–21 and the next day they won 20–13. And the stands were not big; that made it fun for everyone. PA Announcer Paul Strelzin would get the crowd really up. He even got tossed out by the umpires for something he said. You miss that cozy feeling at Cohen Stadium; there's more room here for everyone, and so it's not as intimate."

As his comments during previous games had indicated, Knight still found it fun to come out to watch the Diablos 65 to 70 times a year: "Each year the players are new and different; but they all have a high level of skill and they all have the same hopes and dreams. It's wonderful to see that." Did writing about a game every night ever become routine or even a chore? "Not really," he said and went on to explain. "I've only got 10 to 12 column inches to fill each night. So I keep the play-by-play details to a minimum.

I try to make each story a little feature essay, to give an overall sense of the game and to focus on one or two main aspects."

In his story for the next day's *Times*, Bill didn't have to wait long for his angle. "The tone was set with the first two batters of the game," he wrote later that evening, "quicker than you could play the national anthem, just a handful of pitches into this Texas League Western Division duel. After leadoff batter Eric Bruntlett singled, Henri Stanley sent a towering fly ball over the right field wall. The first home run of the series, it gave the Round Rock Express a 2–0 lead and they never looked back. Although El Paso pulled to within one run with a three-run fourth inning, Round Rock triumphed 8–5, their 11th win against El Paso against 10 losses, and their 10th victory in the last 14 games against the Diablos."[2] While Knight worked on his story, Hale and Tracy packed their gear for tomorrow's early morning departure for Connecticut, and the crowd—announced as 1,950—filed to the exits.

Postseason Postscript

The Diablos, who had just missed first place in the first-half of the season, fared worse in the second half: they finished third in the Western Division, missing the playoffs. As the Diablos slumped, so too did attendance. The final total was 234,971. The figure marked the third year attendance had declined and the lowest total in a dozen years. Individual Diablo players did, however, have good years. Chad Tracy, whose .344 average was 22 points ahead of the second-place finisher, was named Texas League Player of the Year. He, Matt Kata, Andrew Good, and Mike Gosling, who won 14 while losing only five were, were named to the league's All-Star team. Later in the season, Brad Cresse, Mike Gray, and Oscar Villarreal were promoted to the Triple-A Tucson Toros. The canopies were erected as promised while the Diablos were out of town in late July. But before the club had returned to Cohen Stadium, a severe wind storm tore them down. Officials promised that they would be in place before the start of the 2003 season.

6—Turning Diamonds into Lugnuts: Lansing of the Midwest League

The lower Single-A Midwest League, which expanded by two teams in 1988 to its present size of 14 clubs, has, perhaps, been most influenced by the changes taking place in the minor leagues since 1990. Beginning in 1991, there have been eight franchise moves, including two each from Springfield, Illinois, and Madison, Wisconsin. The first move, from Wausau, Wisconsin to Kane County, a western Chicago suburb, included two essential characteristics of the majority of the relocations. Clubs went from smaller cities and older parks to larger population centers with new stadiums. Wausau had a population of just over 37,000; Kane County, of close to 320,000. Wausau's Athletic Park, which was over 30 years old, seated 2,500 fans. Like the stands, the field was also small: 318 feet and 316 feet to the left and right field foul poles respectively and a mere 365 feet to dead center. In 1975, the year the city joined the Midwest League, 63,000 fans attended games; after that the figures steadily diminished. By contrast, the Cougars, in their first year in brand-new Elfstrom Stadium—which included luxury suites and a walk-in gift shop—drew 240,000 and then posted attendance increases in eight of the next 10 years, reaching a high of 523,000 in 2001.

Fort Wayne, West Michigan (Grand Rapids), Lansing, and Dayton, that had also relocated to bigger cities and new and bigger parks, also posted significant attendance increases. Only the Michigan Battle Cats, who played in an older park in the relatively small city of Battle Creek, did not experience the incredible success of the other shifted franchises. Three of the eight clubs that did not move—Appleton, Peoria, and Cedar Rapids—enjoyed significant increases in attendance when they moved into new parks in their host cities.

Along the way, most of the old clubs acquired new nicknames. The South Bend White Sox became the Silver Hawks; the Beloit Brewers, the Snappers;

the Appleton Foxes, the Wisconsin Timber Rattlers, and so on. The new teams adopted fierce or catchy monikers: Cougars, Battle Cats, Lugnuts, Whitecaps, and Wizards. The new nicknames for both old and new clubs proved to be excellent marketing devices and spurred merchandise sales.

But a transfer of city, change of nickname, or move to a newer park were not, in themselves, guarantees of continuing success. South Bend had enjoyed its best year at the gate in 1994; Appleton in 1996, the second year in their new park; Fort Wayne, in 1993, the franchise's first year in a new city and park. After drawing 171,000 fans in the first year in Battle Creek, the Battle Cats' attendance dropped drastically. West Michigan, still one of the most successful franchises in the minor leagues, reached a high of 536,000 in 1997 and has declined each year since.

The owners and operators of the Lansing Lugnuts, which drew an average of over half a million fans in their first three seasons and have dropped each year since, have learned what all franchises moving to a new city and/or new stadium have had to learn: after the novelty and euphoria of the first few seasons have worn off, the hard work and creativity that had been as important as the novelty for the early successful seasons must be expanded and intensified if the club was to maintain its place as a major player in its city's summer entertainment scene.

Located in downtown Lansing, Oldsmobile Park was designed to blend in with, not dominate, the rest of the area.

Sunday, August 4

"Ten years ago, this spot was the center of sin city and skid row," said Greg Rauch, general manger of the Lansing Lugnuts, as he sat in the grandstand of Lansing's Oldsmobile Park, taking a breather in the late Sunday morning sunshine. "And look at it now," he continued, gesturing around him. "I think this is the best park in all of Single-A baseball." Behind him, maintenance crews completed tidying up the stands, bagging the soda cups and popcorn boxes, and sweeping away the peanut shells and popcorn husks left by Saturday night's sellout crowd of 11,503, which had come to cheer the Lugnuts to an 8 to 3 victory over the visiting Burlington Bees, to view the year's 14th fireworks display, and to spend close to $80,000 on concessions and souvenirs. On the field, the Lugnuts, a farm team of the Chicago Cubs, took batting practice, sharpening their skills to contribute to another win, which would enable the team to retain part of a three way first-place tie with the Michigan Battle Cats and Dayton Dragons in the Midwest League's East Division.

Now in their seventh season, the Lugnuts had been born in March 1994, two years before they played their first game in Michigan's capital city. Less than a month before the start of the 1994 season, the struggling Waterloo (Iowa) Diamonds were sold to Take Me Out to the Ball Game, a group headed by Chicago advertising executive Tom Dickson, and moved to Springfield's Lanphier Park, an aging structure built in 1925. The club struggled in the Illinois capital for two years before moving to Lansing. In his book *Waterloo Diamonds*, author Richard Panek, who had originally set out to write about the minor-league renaissance of the 1990s, chronicled in detail the death of professional baseball in the Iowa city. He focused on 1992, the club's penultimate season. The Diamonds' season opener was ominous. Four hours before the game, the staff searched frantically for misplaced bases; when the game began, only 728 fans were in the seats; later that night, it was discovered that the programs with the winning stamps for prizes hadn't been put on sale.

The city of Waterloo had been hit by economic depression and unemployment. Memorial Stadium, located in an older part of town, "with a railroad track on one side and a cemetery on the other,"[1] had been built in 1946 and, Panek notes, "belonged squarely to a mid-century style of ballpark architecture, all steel girders and poured concrete that was as blunt and functional as the city itself."[2] However, by 1992, the ballpark had not only aged, it was in such disrepair that it failed to meet virtually all the facility standards established by the Professional Baseball Agreement of 1991. Without a new park or, at least, extensive and expensive renovation to the existing facility, the city of Waterloo would be in danger of losing its professional ball club and, with it, an important component of its "quality of life." The necessary funding was not available and the club became available to interested buyers. Dickson's group purchased the Diamonds for $1.3 million.

Although the success of the Lansing Lugnuts occurred after the publication of *Waterloo Diamonds*, Panek discussed the impact of new parks on other communities in the Midwest League. South Bend's Stanley Coveleski Stadium was his prime example. "For four days," he began, " [the Diamonds] had been playing in the purgatory of Kenosha, a lame-duck franchise in a seventy-one-year-old facility. In South Bend, however, waited the promised land." The players were overwhelmed by the facilities, described as "wonders." Panek's example of South Bend's park suggests an almost religious awe: "the green was manicured so that concentric circles of mowing grace radiated from the pitcher's mound."[3]

Coveleski Stadium had been built specifically to attract a minor-league team. "The mayor at that time envisioned the stadium as an anchor in the redevelopment of a downtown that had been devastated over the two previous decades by the losses of such industrial stalwarts as Studebaker, Singer Sewing Machine, and John Deere."[4] In the year that only 48,000 fans visited Waterloo's aging downtown park, the South Bend White Sox played before more than 200,000 people. Whereas one new ballpark helped to revive an inner city, an old one 300 miles to the west was dying along with the urban core near which it stood.

It seems clear that Dickson's Take Me Out to the Ballgame group had intended Springfield's Lanphier Park to be only a temporary home. The previous tenants, the Cardinals, had drawn only 110,000 before moving briefly to Madison, Wisconsin, and the city did not seem interested in building a new park. Panek reported that the group had wished to relocate in the Chicago suburbs, hoping to duplicate the success of the Kane County Cougars. When these explorations failed to bear fruit, it turned its attention eastward. The Sultans of Springfield drew only 54,000 in 1994, less than half the total of their predecessors, the Cardinals. A lame-duck franchise in 1995, they attracted 39,000.

Michigan had been without minor-league baseball since 1951, when the Central League—which included teams in Flint, Grand Rapids, Muskegon, and Saginaw—folded. But the success of the West Michigan Whitecaps, which attracted close to half a million fans in 1994—its first season—had indicated that baseball could be very successful in Michigan. Lansing, with an area population of close to half a million, was searching for ways to revitalize its downtown area in order to draw people from the suburbs on weekends and to keep the thousands of state government workers after 5 o'clock on weeknights. One of the possibilities was a minor-league team. Take Me Out to the Ballgame and Lansing civic officials struck an agreement and work began on a new downtown park.

The choice of a downtown site followed a pattern that had begun in 1989, with the construction of Buffalo's Pilot Field. Built originally in the hopes of attracting an expansion major-league franchise, it has been credited with playing an important role in the revitalization of that city's urban core. Other similar developments included Trenton, New Jersey's Mercer County Park and Portland, Maine's Hadlock Field. In his study of a number of these downtown parks, Frank Jossi noted "the ball fields use neotraditional architectural design at sites where civic leaders expect a new attraction to spawn new restaurants and businesses."[5] Such parks used "fallow acres in a marginal part of downtown,"[6] blended in with existing architecture, and took advantage of parking lots that were relatively empty after normal business hours and on weekends. Such stadiums became green oases in what had been urban deserts.

The City of Lansing hired the architectural firm of HNTB to design the facility that would be built on a narrow strip of land located between the major north-south arterial roots of Cedar and Larch Streets. It had

The playing field of Oldsmobile Park is in a bowl below street level. Pedestrians walking by can view the diamond through the chain link fences beyond the left and right field areas.

limited space within which to work. The firm created a recessed park so that the steel roof and exposed steel structure would blend in with, rather than overshadow the low brick buildings nearby. Fences near the city sidewalks in the left and right field corners of the playing field were made of chain link so that pedestrians passing by could glance in at the action. The area in front of the main entrances was made into a brick and grass plaza with park benches and bronze statues of baseball players. So well did the completed product harmonize with its urban environment that only the signage and the park's light towers indicated that the building was a baseball stadium. HNTB had since developed downtown parks in Louisville, Kentucky and Toledo and Dayton, Ohio.

As the construction crews spent 60,000 worker-hours creating the stadium from 400 tons of steel and 6,500 cubic yards of concrete, facing the structure with 70,000 bricks and covering part of it with 2,700 gallons of paint, the front-office staff laid the groundwork for fashioning the team's identity.[7] First, they announced that the Oldsmobile Company had purchased naming rights to the stadium for $1.2 million. While the athletes were still playing as the Sultans of Springfield, the team nickname and logo were introduced at a large downtown rally. The Lugnuts and the cartoon-like bolt forming the logo tied in with the automobile theme initiated with the naming of the park. The club opened a downtown retail outlet to sell hats, T-shirts, and other souvenirs, all of which became such hot sellers that, before there had even been a game played at the new park, Lansing Lugnuts' merchandise became one of the top sellers in all the minor leagues. A second outlet in a suburban mall opened just before Christmas 1995. The Lugnuts also introduced their mascot well before the season began. The Big Lug, a purple, baseball-uniform-attired dinosaur with huge lugnuts for nostrils, appeared at a conference held to announce the opening of season ticket sales. As Opening Day approached, the Lugnuts' name and image was thoroughly planted in the minds, not just of central Michigan sports fans, but of young families planning summer evening and weekend outings.

By March 1996, the stadium had been nearly completed. Inside workers affixed signs to concession stands, continuing the automotive theme. The Chome Plated Grill, Dashboard Diner, Hubcap Cafe and Filling Station would offer the standard ballpark fare. Nuts and Bolts, the souvenir store, stocked up on caps, T-shirts, coffee mugs and pennants, many of the items bearing a stylized picture of Oldsmobile Park and the words "Inaugural Season, 1996."

On April 5, 1996, the hometown team played and lost its first game— 9 to 5 against Rockford. The temperature at game time was 35 degrees, which may explain why the crowd of just under 10,000 is not among the 20 biggest crowds to attend Oldsmobile Park in its first six years of operation. The Lugnuts' on-field performance was, at best, adequate during the 1996 season. They finished in fifth and last place in the East Division in the first half of the season and first in the second half. But they lost two games to one to cross-state rival West Michigan in the first round of the playoffs. They also lost the attendance race to West Michigan. In mid–August, the Lugnuts became the first Midwest League club to draw over 500,000 fans in a single season, and, after their final league game of August 28, posted attendance figures of 538,326, an average of 7,802 a game for 66 home dates. But the West Michigan Whitecaps still had three home games remaining and drew capacity crowds for two of these to push their final total to 547,401.

Greg Rauch remembered the inaugural season, remembered losing to West Michigan that first year, both on and off the field. "Sure, we'd have liked to have won the pennant and the attendance crown," he remarked. "But West Michigan at that time was affiliated with Oakland and they were loaded with young prospects. And they had a market twice the size of ours to sell tickets to—but they only drew 10,000 more than we did." At that time, Rauch was the box office manager and, in spite of his pride in what the staff did in getting people into the park, he realized that in the first year, "we oversold the market. We had the best per-capita attendance in the league—everything about the year was big. We knew things couldn't keep on that way." They didn't. Attendance dropped by 15,000 in 1997 and by 38,000 the next year. In 2001 it had dipped to 404,490 and, based on current 2002 figures, it could end up below 400,000.

Although Rauch admitted he'd like to see attendance go up, he was realistic. Given the size of the market, 400,000 to 425,000 a year attendance was to be expected. But now that the novelty of having professional baseball in town has worn off, the always-hardworking staff would not only have to work harder, but would have to develop a careful marketing strategy. "We have to recognize that group sales are our main source of business. And so we focus on that during the off-season. We target 25 dates a year that we'd like to have sellouts, with crowds of over 10,000 a game and work to sell those dates to groups. Then, by late March or early April, we know which games will be sellouts and we select other ones to offer to companies, churches, schools, and the like. We've also sold season tickets to companies and mini-packs to individuals. Our walk-up game-day sales are the least significant aspect of our ticket revenue."

But in addition to getting people into Oldsmobile Park, the Lansing Lugnuts had to provide their patrons with a good time at prices that were reasonable for them and cost-efficient for the club. "We've learned how to run our food, ticket, and stadium operations very efficiently," he explained. "And we've also learned how to listen very carefully to our patrons. We're not just selling tickets to a baseball game—although that's important. We can't market the on-field product because we have no control over that. But the fact that we're a Chicago Cubs farm team is important. People have been watching the Cubs on WGN for decades; in fact, they're almost as popular as the Detroit Tigers in this part of the state. So people have a link with them. And Wrigley Field isn't that far from Lansing—a four-and-a-half-hour drive. Our fans can go there to see players who may have been Lugnuts three or four years ago."

Rauch explained that in providing the off-field product, they worked at keeping Oldsmobile Park looking fresh and new, renovating and repairing the park in the off-season and at polling the fans to discern aspects of the ballpark experience that had or hadn't worked, and making sure that the atmosphere remained neighborly. "In a way," he explained, "we're like an old-time village square. Winter is over and people are coming out of hibernation. They want to see each other and have an enjoyable two or three hours' entertainment. We provide a nice place—friendly surroundings—at a reasonable price and a fun atmosphere. And if the Lugnuts win that's even better. If the people enjoy their time here, with family or friends or as members of a bigger group, they'll probably come back. That's what we're working for."

His few minutes of relaxation in the sun over, the Lugnuts' general manager stood up, stretched, and then looked toward the outfield where a couple of players ran along the warning track. "You know," he said, a little wistfully, "I used to play ball at college, and I decided to get into the minor-league baseball business because I loved the game. But now I'm so busy with what happens off the field that the only time I see players in uniform is when I take a break, like just now." But with gametime approaching and a good family crowd expected, Rauch turned his back on the field and headed to the concourse running behind the grandstand seats to talk with his lieutenants about preparations for today's Family Day crowd.

When the gates opened at 12:30 P.M., Ratchet stood outside the main entrance to Oldsmobile Park in front of a sign that read "Have a Blast." She clutched the strings of a bundle of balloons that she gave out to arriving young patrons. The Lugnuts made an even-greater effort than usual on Sundays to cater to children, hoping thereby to attract larger numbers of families on a day when many parents might decide to take their offspring to nearby lakes or other recreation sites. In addition to Ratchet's welcome, the club had installed a face-painting booth on the main concourse and

Ratchet, one of Lansing's two mascots, poses in front of the stadium. In an hour, "she" will be welcoming children and handing out balloons.

a kiosk at which youngsters could have personalized, plasticized cards made from photos they'd brought with them. The Chrome Plated Grill and the other food outlets were well stocked with kid favorites: pizza, ice cream, and soft drinks.

Ratchet, a smaller version of the Big Lug, was an important element in the team's marketing. During the winter of 1997, the Lugnut staff decided that the main mascot needed a friend, not just to stave off loneliness, but also to provide a new entertainment feature for the families coming to the park. "If we like to make the park seem as fresh as it was on our first Opening Day," then-general manager Tom Gluck explained, "we also want to add fresh experiences each year." Like Aftershock, the second mascot of the Rancho Cucamonga Quakes, Ratchet's smaller size would make her more appealing, less threatening for smaller children. Having two mascots work the stands on days when large crowds were expected increased the amount of off-field entertainment available. The new mascot was not just a smaller version of the Big Lug. Whereas he was a well-intentioned but often bumbling character, she was developed to be more youthful and sprightly.

After having received balloons from Ratchet, having had their faces painted, and having loaded up at the concession stands, many of the kids headed to the low railing in the right field corner, the designated autograph area of Oldsmobile Park. Here, they waved hats, cards, and autograph books at the young men who would be Cubs. "Who did you get?" one youngster asked another as the two headed back toward their seats. On hearing the name, he replied, "I don't know who he is? Do you?" The reply was negative. Their reaction was typical of most young fans, for whom collecting autographs of unknown players was part of the ballpark experience—no more important than racing up and down the stairs and consuming more food than was needed. Many of the autographs, hastily shoved in pockets, would disappear in the next wash. Only a few entrepreneurial children, aware that in a few years an autographed minor-league card of a major-league star could command big money, usually saved the signatures.

Even if the young autograph seeker had been a more informed Lugnuts fan, it was quite possible that he still wouldn't have known who the owner of his newly acquired signature was. The Lansing Lugnuts' roster had been in a state of flux since Opening Day. Only seven members of the initial roster had been on last year's squad. One of last year's team had made it to Double-A ball and 18 were with high Single-A Daytona. Fifteen of the 2002 opening day Lugnut roster had played last year with Boise of the short-season Single-A Northwest League; three, with the Cubs' rookie league club in Mesa, Arizona. By August 4, 12 of April's Lugnuts had departed, most promoted to Daytona and one to Double-A West Tenn. Two had been demoted to Boise. They had been replaced by four selections from the 2002 draft, along with promising members of the Boise and Mesa teams. The two most recent roster additions had arrived at Oldsmobile Park just before last night's game. Aron Weston, who had just been acquired by the Chicago Cubs in a trade with the Pittsburgh Pirates, had come in from Hickory, North Carolina—but his baggage hadn't. Nonetheless he had gone 3 for 5 with three runs batted in. Joey Monahan, the Cubs' seventh-round draft choice this year, had played for the Boise Hawks on Friday night and taken two flights to make it to Lansing. He was 2 for 4 with one RBI.

Monahan went hitless during Sunday's game, but Weston contributed a two-run single and a double in the Lugnuts' 9–2 thumping of the

Burlington Bees. The home team scored its winning runs in the first inning. The announced crowd of 5,120 departed happy. The win put the Lugnuts within one win of last year's total, when they had finished both halves of the season well out of their division pennant races. More important, because the Clinton LumberKings were edged 5–4 by the Michigan Battle Cats, and Dayton had lost, the Lugnuts enjoyed sole possession of first place, one game ahead of the Battle Cats.

Monday, August 5

Next to the manager, the coaches, and the trainer, the person who sees the most of the players on a minor-league team is the bus driver. For 70 games a year, he is their chauffeur, taking them on hour-and-a-half commutes to nearby towns and eight-to-ten-hour rides to cities often two or three states away. If he likes the game, is enough years older than they are, and has the right temperament, he becomes more than their driver— he is a father figure, a person unconnected officially to the team who can lend a sympathetic ear. Phil Johnston, since 1976 the driver for the Reading Phillies of the Eastern League performed the dual role so well that, in 2000, he was elected to the Reading Phillies Hall of Fame. Dean Day, for the last seven years the driver for the Burlington Bees, hadn't had the same honor conferred, but he felt very close to the young ballplayers who rode his bus.

"I've always loved baseball, and I follow it closely," he remarked in the early afternoon as he checked on his bus in the parking lot of the Holiday Inn. "I really enjoy watching young players develop and seeing them move up the ladder. Of course, sometimes they can be annoying, like any kids. This morning I cleaned up seven garbage bags of junk from our trip in on Saturday. Yesterday we were all too tired to do anything but go to the park and get the game in." Saturday, the bus had pulled away from Burlington, Iowa's Community Field with what everyone thought was plenty of time to make the 450-mile trip to Lansing—the club's longest road trip. But no one had taken into account the midsummer Saturday afternoon traffic around Chicago. "Just before we hit the slowdown," Dean recounted, "one of the players put a movie on. It was *Payback,* and by the time it was over, we'd only traveled six miles. The players got impatient and kept yelling at me to change lanes. But that wouldn't have done any good. It was four lanes, bumper to bumper, not even creeping along most of the time."

So far this season, the Burlington Bees, a farm club of the Kansas City Royals, had traveled 7,250 miles on Dean's bus, over 160 hours, or the equivalent of the time it takes to play 58 ballgames, nearly 40 percent of the Bees' 140-game schedule. "The commutes to places like Quad City [80 miles away] are simple. The bus leaves around 2 o'clock from Burlington and returns home pretty quickly after the game," Dean remarked. "On longer trips, the players watch movies, play cards, play games on their laptops or Game Boys. They also spend a lot of time sleeping, or at least trying to. That's particularly the case now. But at the beginning, they were excited to be making trips to see parks that were new to them. Burlington's park is pretty old and the crowds are really small. They'd heard rumors about how great these other places were and how many people came to the games."

Dean had also introduced many of the players to winter. Eight members of this season's Bees were from the southern states, eight from the Caribbean, one from Hawaii, and one from South Africa. Fourteen members of the team had played last year in short-season or warm-weather leagues. This April, the Bees had traveled north to Appleton, Wisconsin for their first road series. Sleet, snow, and cold weather had caused the cancellation of the first two games. Later in the month, Bees games in Burlington, Beloit, and Quad City had been postponed. "I remember once in Beloit," Dean recalled, "it was a beautiful sunny afternoon with temperatures in the upper 60s. But, by the end of the game that night, it had dropped to 34 with a 30-mile wind. It was hard on everyone—and the Latin players couldn't believe it."

Dean noted that not all bus companies and certainly few drivers wanted to be involved with professional and college athletic teams. "But I enjoy it, and it's a good account for the company—around $35,000 a year. Most of the time the kids are pretty good. They know that this year could be their last chance, and they want to make the most of it. It's their sabbatical from the real world, and they want it to last as long as possible. And they learn from the examples set by the manager, coaches, and trainer. The players do what's expected of them—if management runs a tight ship, they'll follow the lead.

"The trainer's very important; he's the link between players and manager. A good trainer really helps the players and the manager create the right atmosphere. However," Day went on to say, "a bad organization can have the reverse effect. Shortly after I began driving the Bees, we were with an organization that didn't care about how foul-mouthed and messy its minor-league teams were. It seemed that everyone—players and coaches and manager—couldn't wait to get the games over so that they could start drinking beer. I remember after a trip back home—and it was only three or four hours—I collected 178 beer cans. And a few of the players didn't drink. I think the attitude began with the owner of the big-league club and filtered down from there."

Day sat in the dugout during most games and stood behind the batting cage during practice, often sharing brief wisecracks and jokes with the players and coaches who came up to chat with him. "Today," he said, "one of the players has a great practical joke. I took him to Wal-Mart where he bought a cheap and very short woman's dress. There's a guy in the bullpen who's been getting out of line, so, during the game, someone's going to sneak into the clubhouse, hide his street clothes and just leave the dress. He'll have to wear it on the bus and I'm going to park in front of the hotel so he'll have to walk through the lobby in the outfit."

Not only did he help the players execute their practical jokes, he also initiated some of his own. "I remember last year," he chuckled, "we were in Fort Wayne and Jason Fingers—he's Rollie's son—had bought a bunch of fireworks. He was letting off a lot of real bombs in the parking lot before the bus left. I went over and told him that he'd better be careful, the cops were pretty strict in Indiana. We got on the bus, and I drove three or four blocks and then pulled over and got off. I came back in and announced that the cops wanted to talk to the guy who'd let off the fireworks. They wouldn't let us go to the park otherwise. Jason was in the back, and he looked pretty shaken as he came down the aisle. I went out with him to the back of the bus—there were no cops. I'd just made it up. But he was pretty scared for a bit!"

Dean Day laughed as he finished telling the story and then stepped back on the bus. "I'd better give it another once-over before the troops arrive. They may mess it up, but if it's clean when they first get on board, they might eventually get the idea!"

While Day readied his bus for the 20-minute trip to the stadium, two members of the Lugnuts' permanent staff took a short break in their offices at Oldsmobile Park. It was midway through their day. "It's funny," said concessions manager Dave Parker, "we're only open for business two-and-a-half to three hours a night and only when the Lugnuts are at home. But Jason and I usually put in 15 hours a day when there's a game." The Jason he referred to was Jason Wilson, director of food services, and, between them, they were responsible for what to many fans was as important as the game and what to the Lugnuts' organization was almost as big a revenue producer as ticket sales. "We estimate," Jason explained, "that the per-person average spending is $8 a game." He went on to note that the average included the more expensive menu items ordered by suite holders, especially food plates that ranged from potato skins at $29 a plate, to shrimp platters at $125, and steak or salmon lunches and dinners served

"Eatertainment" is an important element of the minor-league ballpark experience, whether it be downing the old staple—a hot dog—in the stands or nibbling from a fruit tray in the luxury suites.

along the third base line at the Bullpen Cafe. Given last season's attendance of just over 400,000 fans ate and drank over $3 million worth of food and beverage.

Because "eatertainment," as it has been called by some members of the sports business, was such an important revenue producer, it wasn't surprising that the Lugnuts' two top people in that department spent 15-hour days during homestands. In addition to quantity of time, the two also engaged in detailed, quality planning. "We work at scheduling for two weeks ahead," Parker explained, "particularly for delivery of product. We have to make sure that we always have at least four games worth of product on hand." That includes over 10,000 hot dogs in the main freezer. They also kept an eye on the long-range weather forecasts as they ordered. Cold weather meant that many gallons of coffee would be consumed; ice cream sandwiches were favorites on warm afternoons, particularly Sundays when there were lots of family groups.

Scheduling for a specific home date usually began four or five days ahead. "When we look at how many advance tickets have been sold for a date and look at the weather forecast, we can make a pretty accurate prediction of the attendance," Jason Wilson said. "Then we can decide how much of what to prepare, how many game-day workers to call in, and how many of our concession stands to open." Because the four main concession stands offered roughly the same fare, on nights when a small crowd was expected, Jason and Dave might decide to open only the Filling Station on the third base line and the Chrome Plated Grill along the first. On a big night, such as a Saturday fireworks extravaganza, all four would be opened, along with the small microbrewery kiosk and Winston the Barbecue King's Grill. That night 40 concessions workers would staff the food outlets, while members of volunteer groups would patrol the stands, offering ice cream sandwiches, pop, and beer. "They keep a part of the proceeds," Wilson remarked and went on to explain that only those products that were easy to handle were sold in the seating area—and that didn't include hot dogs. "You don't realize how much work it takes to get mustard on a hot dog," he laughed.

In addition to the fans in the seats and the suites, there were hundreds, on some dates, often over a thousand hungry people in the Tailgate Terrace, Gasoline Alley, and Bullpen Cafe. Here groups of 20 or more enjoyed pregame game meals that cost $9 or more a person and included chicken, hot dogs, hamburgers, bratwurst, salads, desserts, and non-alcoholic beverages. In the Lugnuts' front office, four people worked exclusively in group sales, contacting church groups, civic organizations, and businesses. Much of their work took place during the off-season. The snow might be on the ground, but the Lugnuts reminded people that spring was just around the corner. Such advance group sales provided revenue that helped the club through the sometimes lean and often cold days of April. On event day, Jason Wilson's staff prepared and served the food to the gathered hungry hordes. "Last Saturday night, 60 people worked the picnic areas and the suites," he noted.

Like all members of the front-office staff, Jason and Dave worked year-round. The fall and winter months might not have 15-hour days, but they were busy. "As soon as the season is over," Jason explained, "we clean the food preparation areas thoroughly, review the year—what went well and where we can improve—and start planning our budget for the next year. We consider applications from private vendors, line up food suppliers, and, in late winter, begin hiring game-day staff. A few weeks before Opening Day, we check the equipment carefully to make sure everything is in good working order. Then we get ready for those 15-hour days."

Those 15-hour days were partly a result of the fact that, since 2001, the Lugnuts had run their own concessions. "Before that," Jason explained, "an outside firm who handles the food services at a number of minor- and major-league sports stadiums did ours." But the Lugnuts felt that if they took over, they'd have greater control over both product and service. "We really do work harder to please our customers; it's more time and energy, but based on the feedback from people who come to the park, it's been worth it."

Dave and Jason headed to the large food-preparation room behind the third base Chrome Plated Grill to check on the work being done for parties to be held that evening in three of the 24 luxury suites that overlooked the playing field. On the field, the Lugnuts had completed batting practice and the Bees were beginning theirs. In the outfield, small groups of Burlington players stood together, occasionally breaking their conversations to drift in a desultory way under a fly ball or to stop the progress of a grounder headed to the warning track. Among the group were three or four pitchers who weren't scheduled to see action tonight. They had completed their stretching exercises and wind sprints and were there mainly to throw balls back toward the infield and to fill in time before the game began.

One of the Bees' pitchers held an unusual place in professional baseball. Of the several thousand non–Americans in the minor leagues, Barry Armitage was one of only two from South Africa. Early in 2000, the 23-year-old right hander was working in a sporting goods store in his hometown of Durban. "I never knew what I wanted to do with my life," he said as he sat on a bench along the third base line, resting from his duties in

At 23 years old, South African native Barry Armitage finds himself following an
unlikely and undreamed of career as a pitcher for the Burlington Bees, a farm team
of the Kansas City Royals.

the outfield. "I didn't go to college, but I loved sports. I always felt comfortable on a playing field, especially a baseball field."

In a land where cricket and rugby are the major sports, Armitage had
an unusual background: his father played baseball and his stepfather, fast-
pitch softball. He watched them both and, when he was five, received his
first baseball glove, a hand-me-down from his brother. "I began to play
quite a bit after that, but it wasn't until I was 10 that I began to pitch, and
I was in high school when I got into organized baseball leagues. It was all
softball before that." Playing conditions were, to say the least, basic. School
and club teams used soccer fields in the off-season; there were no cut-out
infields or mounds. "In fact, I didn't throw off a mound until I was 16. But
I'd always had a good arm. I was sort of a natural; I threw hard enough
to get guys out."

Needless to say, Armitage didn't have any major-league heroes as he was growing up. It was only in the last few years that he was able to watch games on ESPN. "Even now, when guys are talking baseball around the clubhouse, I sometimes don't know who they're talking about." He did have a small baseball card collection when he was growing up, but, most of the time, baseball talk was limited to conversations with his friend and coach. "He knew a lot about the game and he always encouraged me. But I'd always hoped that I'd be able to come to the United States to watch some baseball games. I never even fantasized about coming to play here."

That all changed in April 2000. Allard Baird, the general manager of the Kansas City Royals and his chief Caribbean scout, Luis Silverio, had made a quick trip to South Africa to see if there was enough talent to establish some kind of scouting system. By the time they'd arrived in Durban, they'd become totally frustrated and were preparing to return the next day to Kansas City, writing the mission off as a failure. However, they'd talked with Barry's friend, the coach, who made a quick call to the sporting goods store to tell the young pitcher to come out for a tryout. "The day before, I'd had a really good game, with 24 strikeouts in nine innings," Armitage remembered. "It's a pity they couldn't have been in town then, because when they were going to have the tryouts I couldn't get away from work. Finally my boss gave me a half-hour off. I rushed over to the field and told them I could only throw for five minutes before I had to get back to work."

Baird and Silverio liked what they saw and invited Armitage to visit them after work. They explained the organization to him and offered him a contract which they hoped he'd sign before they departed the next day. "There was no bonus; in fact, I didn't even know bonuses existed. The next night, our club had baseball practice, and I had to tell the fellows that I wouldn't be there. I was getting ready to go to America." On April 18, Barry became a member of the Kansas City Royals' organization. "I hadn't even turned 21—it was a remarkable day."

Armitage's coming to America was briefly postponed. "A week after the day I'd signed, I learned that I had a bone fracture. Kansas City wanted me at their Florida camp right away. But after I had an MRI and it was sent to the Royals, they decided I should rehab for three months." He arrived in Florida at the beginning of summer but didn't get into any games with the Gulf Coast League rookie squad until near the end of the season, pitching only 10 innings in five games. Nonetheless, the Royals were still very interested in him and encouraged his interest in playing winter baseball in Australia. In 48 innings there, he posted an earned run average of 3.02, ninth-best in the league.

In 2002, he was promoted to the Spokane Indians of the short-season Single-A Northwest League. "I drove all the way to Spokane from extended spring training in Florida. Beside the road on one of the mountain passes, there was still some snow. I got out and made a snowball—it was the first time I'd ever touched snow, let alone pitched with a snowball." Playing with the Spokane Indians marked two more firsts for Armitage: he played for the first time in front of big crowds and he made long road trips. "At first, I was nervous about the crowds, but I soon found that I loved it. The first time I pitched, there must have been 6,000 at the park. The road trips? Well, they were good practice for this year in the Midwest League."

Armitage played well in the Northwest League. Although his record was 1 and 7, he struck out 70 batters in 72 innings while walking only 26. He developed new pitches and discovered he wasn't cut out to be a starter. "They taught me how to use the slider and began working with me on a change-up. I think I'm really beginning to be comfortable with it. I learned that location was as important as speed for a fastball, and I realized I worked better in relief. As a starter, I'd go five innings pretty well and then the sixth-inning jinx would hit." This year, he'd been used only three times as a starter. His 29 appearances led the club, as did his seven saves, and he'd maintained his strikeout-per-inning average. His won-loss record was 5 and 2. Overall, his performance earned him a berth on the West Division team for the Midwest League's All-Star Game.

"If I were an American, people would say I was living my childhood dream," Armitage remarked happily. "But it never was a childhood dream. But now I have this dream of doing as well as I can, of going as far as I can in professional baseball. All these things are remarkable."

Armitage did not pitch in the evening game. Burlington starter Brian Bass and reliever Brian Melnyk proved ineffective against the Lugnuts, who pounded out six singles, a double and a home run on the way to a 5–2 victory. The Bees did make it interesting in the top of the ninth as a leadoff single followed by two walks loaded the bases. Closer Steve Ellis came in, allowed a run on a sacrifice fly, and then induced two groundouts to end the contest. A crowd of 3,956, quite respectable for the slowest day of the week, left happy. This win equaled last year's season total and the Lugnuts maintained their one-game lead in the East Division. The players left the park almost as quickly as the fans. Tomorrow's game against Burlington would start at noon—there wasn't going to be much time for post-game recreation and then rest.

Tuesday, August 6

The Lugnuts' promotional schedule advertised August 6th as "Summer Fun Day." However, a couple of game-day employees only half-jokingly referred to it as "Wreck the Park Day." The game would begin at 12:05 P.M. so that thousands of children from nearby camps and local parks could enjoy a field trip to Oldsmobile Park. The young fans might not wreck the park, but they would spend a lot of time racing up and down the grandstand steps, lining up at concession stands, and missing the refuse containers with their pitches of crumpled hot dog and candy wrappers and squashed drink cups. Summer Fun Day meant that by the time kids began filing through the gates at 11 A.M., front-office and game-day personnel would have had to combine finishing up cleanup from last night's game and preparation for this one in under three hours, less than half the usual amount of time.

For the members of the Lugnuts and Bees, the noon start would mean that they would be taking the field at a time when most of them would normally have just begun to wake up. The night before, Lugnuts' manager Julio Garcia had announced that the usual activities that comprised the standard four hours before game-time would be optional. Players could elect whether or not to take batting and infield practice, which would be abbreviated. Accordingly most of the athletes, several of them somewhat bleary-eyed, began to wander into the team's clubhouse only around 10 o'clock. As they changed, they chatted quietly with each other, watched Sports Central on ESPN, and scanned the local sports pages for reports of last night's game.

Joey Monahan, the new kid on the block, was one of the earlier arrivals. "I'm still not sure of the drill around here," he remarked. "And, as a newcomer, I figured it was better to be a bit early instead of a bit late." He wouldn't admit to being sleepy, reporting for work so soon after a night game, but he did admit that the last few days had been a little wearing. He explained that his recent call-up from Boise had been somewhat of a surprise. "I'd been struggling a bit there, both at bat and on defense. But a week or so ago, when one of the Cubs' roving instructors was in town, I had a really good game. On Friday night, we lost, and I didn't have a great game, but when Steve McFarland, our manager, called me into his office after, I really didn't think about being sent down. I was more worried that something might be wrong in my family."

When he got the news that he was to head to the Boise airport Saturday morning to catch the 8 o'clock flight to Chicago, where he'd transfer to a plane heading to Lansing, he was shocked. "I could feel my

First-year player Joey Monahan was promoted to Lansing after appearing in 41 games for the Boise Hawks. A native of Georgia, Monahan has an unusual athletic lineage: his grandfather, Bernie "Boom Boom" Geoffrion, and great-grandfather, the late Howie Morenz, are members of the Hockey Hall of Fame.

heart beating. I rushed home, threw some stuff into a suitcase and made sure I was at the airport in plenty of time. I got here just after the team had started stretching exercises. I looked at the lineup taped up on the dugout wall to see who I knew and found that I'd be starting the game at short."

While being promoted to Lansing was an important step in Monahan's career, it wasn't, as it also wasn't to Burlington's Barry Armitage, a step in the realization of boyhood dreams and fantasies. When asked what player he had pretended to be when he was a child, Monahan replied that baseball hadn't been that important to him then. "My family was really into hockey," he continued. To the remark that this seemed unusual for someone growing up in Marietta, Georgia, he explained: "My dad, grandfather, and great-grandfather all played professional hockey." And when he identified them, he revealed that he possessed a very distinguished hockey pedigree. His father, Hartland, had played 334 National Hockey League games over seven seasons, before retiring in 1981 and moving to Marietta where his wife's father and mother lived. Hartland's father-in-law was Bernie "Boom Boom" Geoffrion, a right winger on the great Montreal Canadiens' teams of the 1950s, a member of the Hockey Hall of Fame, and, from 1972 to 1975 coach of the Atlanta Flames, a National Hockey League expansion team. Geoffrion's father-in-law, in turn, was Howie Morenz, another Hall-of-Famer who had died in 1937 as a result of hockey-related injuries.

Although as a small boy Joey followed in the family tradition, opportunities to play hockey in northern Georgia were limited, and he spent an increasingly greater amount of time on basketball courts and baseball diamonds. In the latter sport, he had a role model at home in older brother Shane, who had attended Clemson University in the early 1990s and, in 1995, had been drafted by the Seattle Mariners in the second round. Although the older Monahan played only 78 games in the major leagues before retiring after the 2001 season, his example led Joey to focus on baseball. "When he went to college on a baseball scholarship, I was only 11 or 12," Joey remembered. "But I was impressed, and he encouraged me, when I was in high school, to think about college baseball. During high school, I began to realize that I had a shot at it." After his senior year, the Minnesota Twins drafted Joey in the 36th round, but he chose to accept a baseball scholarship at Liberty University, a small Virginia college that was a member of the very competitive Big South Conference.

During his junior year at college, pro teams began to notice the young infielder, and two or three scouts talked with him. "In fact," he said, "two called the day before the draft." On the big day, his friend watched proceedings on the Internet while he did chores and worked on his dad's car. "My friend got so nervous that he turned the computer off after the fifth round. Then, a little while later, Billy Swoope, the Cubs' Virginia scout, called. I had hoped to go somewhere in the first eight rounds and they'd picked me in the seventh. I signed as quickly as possible and headed to the Cubs' mini-camp in Mesa. Then we went to Boise for a week before the season began."

Like most collegians in their first year of professional baseball, Monahan had to make considerable adjustments which, unlike some players, he admitted had been difficult. "When I was in Boise, the travel really got to me at first. I wasn't used to the constant play and the long bus rides. At college, we might have a fairly long ride home after a game, but we didn't usually have to play again for a couple of days." The Hawks had opened the season with a five-game series in Salem, Oregon, made the 432-mile bus ride back home arriving a few hours before their home-opening series, and, the night they finished that five-game series headed for Vancouver, Canada, 605 miles to the northwest. "After the first week, I got sick; I wasn't getting enough sleep. But I learned to sleep on the bus." He was still adjusting to using wooden bats rather than the aluminum ones of college, and he found the pitching he was facing a real challenge: "In the pros they have a whole bullpen full of great arms; and they've all got control and movement."

It had been a whirlwind of activity for Joey Monahan since June 4, almost as dazzling as the whirlwind end-to-end rushes down the ice made by his hockey-playing family. But tonight and tomorrow he'd have time off, and, on Thursday, he wouldn't have to report to the park until two in the afternoon—nearly forty-eight hours away from the diamond and no bus rides in the middle. What was he planning to do with the "extended" vacation? "I think I'll do my laundry; it's sort of been piling up for the last few days."

As Monahan put on his warm-up shirt and headed down the tunnel toward the dugout, manager Julio Garcia held a brief conference with his coaches in the windowless, cramped room that served as an office for the three-man coaching staff. It was brief because of the early start of today's game. But in his 15 years of coaching and managing in minor-league baseball, he had become used to situations like this. "The money isn't great; but I love it," the 42-year-old Cuban-born resident of Industry, Texas, remarked. "After I'd finished playing," he continued, "I realized that the only thing I really knew was baseball. It had gotten into my blood, and I couldn't get it out. I wanted to stay in the game, maybe as a scout, but preferably on the field." Julio got a job at a four-year college so that he could acquire coaching experience. It worked, because in 1988, he joined the Texas Rangers as a bullpen coach. Then he worked in the Pittsburgh, Baltimore, and Tampa Bay organizations before joining the Cubs last year as Lugnuts' manager.

Like most managers, Garcia found that during his first season working in the minor leagues he learned as much as, if not more than, his players. "I learned from the people I taught. Seeing them made me remember what it was like when I started out. There were times when I struggled like some of them were struggling. It was a whole new experience for them, and a tough one. I had to help them deal with it and, at the same time, help them acquire the skills they needed to move on to the next level. The players dictate whether they'll move up to play in the majors; it's my job to help them." Unlike high Single-A ball, like the Florida State League, where some of last year's Lugnuts were playing this year, the Midwest League was a place where a lot of teaching and learning still went on. "In Daytona [home of the Cubs' Florida State League team], they've had three and sometimes four years of pro experience. Here some of the younger players don't yet realize it's a career, not a summer job or a summer college league. Unfortunately, some won't find out until it's too late!"

Garcia commented on the fluidity of the Lugnuts' roster so far this year. "Early in the season, the Cubs sent some of the younger players here to get experience. Then, after the June draft, they were sent down, back to the level that best helped them develop. We put them into the fire to see if they'll melt or glow." He explained that the Cubs' philosophy was to mix college players and younger kids on their teams. "The college kids are often on the fast track ; the younger players need a lot of instruction. You still have to be a father to some of them; many haven't had a father figure in their lives. You can help them to grow up off the field. Some need to be taught how to dress, how to show manners in the restaurant, and how to leave tips. When I was in the rookie leagues, some of the guys who'd grown up in poverty didn't even know about flushing toilets each time they used them."

A big part of the on-field learning experience, Garcia emphasized, was helping players turn mistakes into learning experiences. "When I was managing in Frederick, one of the old school guys told us that a manager had been known to deliberately let players make mistakes. As a result, he said, the next time the same situation came up, the player would know what to do." He viewed a player's time in the Midwest League as one of learning from mistakes. "Of course, we need to point out the mistakes as soon as we can—usually before the next day."

Another important aspect of his job was dealing with egos, or more precisely, helping players deal with their egos. "The Cubs' organization really backs us up here. Knowing you have that support, you can teach a kid about the importance of being a part of a team. Some of them try to mask their failures with a show of ego; they don't want anyone to know how much their failures have hurt them. For a lot, playing in a place like Lansing, with a beautiful park and big crowds, is like being in the major leagues. They get kids asking for autographs and young girls trying to flirt with them. It can go to their heads. You have to help them to help themselves, to see things in perspective. And occasionally, guys who signed for big money feel a bit swell-headed. You tell them that major leaguers have earned the right to be cocky; but minor leaguers still have a lot to learn. And I've found that they like and need discipline, even if they don't show it."

Garcia admitted that the bus trips were long and the weather in April was often terrible; but he put a positive spin on both. "I hope that those road trips help the kids learn about dealing with people they meet. And the Cubs like them playing in the cold and sleet. Lansing is like Wrigley Field during the first few weeks of the season; and, if they want to play there, this will get them used to it. It's all part of helping them move up; it's a great challenge and I really enjoy facing it." And he closed the conversation by repeating his opening observation: "The money's not great; but I love it."

Just before 11 o'clock, school buses began stopping briefly along Cedar Street to unload their excited young passengers and already slightly weary-looking adults. The adults imposed a temporary order on the milling groups and began to guide them toward the main entrance to the stadium, where the Big Lug and Ratchet, secure behind the closed wrought-iron gates, waved greetings. On the first base concourse, Cherie Hargitt, the director of retail sales, stood quietly in front of Nuts and Bolts, the Lugnut gift shop. She was enjoying a few moments of quiet before she unlocked the doors to the store and the day's patrons stormed in looking for items that were both appealing and within the range of their budgets.

Over the next three hours, Nuts and Bolts would be almost as busy as the concession stands as young patrons purchased items ranging from $3 (a dog tag stamped with the team logo) to $80 (a nylon windbreaker, also adorned with a logo). Merchandise purchased at the store and online represented an important source of revenue for the team, ranking fourth behind admissions, concessions, and advertising.

Cherie had been involved with the store since 1995 when, nearly a year before the team played its first game, the Lugnuts opened their retail outlet in the nearby Washington Square. "There was a lineup around the corner waiting for us to open up our first day. Within a week, you'd see people wearing Lugnuts' hats and T-shirts at the grocery store, at the movies, at the malls," she remembered. "After the major-league strike of 1994," she explained, "the sale of minor-league merchandise grew. People were disenchanted with the big leagues, and it was cool to wear stuff from the hometown team."

The Lugnuts' merchandising success depended a lot on the catchy logo and name. And, while the club had changed neither the name nor the basic design, as some clubs had in an effort to boost souvenir sales, it had tinkered. "This year, our hottest seller is the bar cap," she remarked, referring to one of 23 varieties of hats displayed in the store behind her. "It's white and has the word 'Nuts' in capitals; underneath in smaller print is Lansing." While the store would soon be as crowded as, if not more crowded than any other day of the season, it would probably not be the best sales day, she noted. That was because virtually none of the children would be at the game with parents and most likely would not have been given the cash needed to buy the big-ticket items. Key chains, minibats, card sets, and pennants would most likely go the quickest. "Our best customers are family groups. The moms and dads will get something for each child. Next are the people in the suites. They'll get some of the bigger items." Cherie also noted that the store did a small but steady year-round mail-order business. "We've had requests from as far away as Korea and Australia."

At this moment, she glanced at her watch and looked down the concourse. It was 11 o'clock; the gates had been opened; Ratchet and the Big Lug had ducked out of the way, and Cherie's potential customers surged through the gates. She unlocked the door, called "Get ready" to her four-person sales staff and took a position behind a glass-topped display counter containing autographed baseballs.

As game time approached, the most senior and junior members of the press box sat in the glass-enclosed work area quietly talking baseball. Mike Clark, a professor of kinestheology at Michigan State University, had been the Lugnuts' official scorekeeper since the team's opening game. Dawn Klemish, who would be 21 in less than a week, was a student at the university and a reporter for the school paper, *The State News*. For both, observing Lugnuts' games was both a gratifying fix for their love of the game and a continuous learning experience.

Mike, who had coached baseball for many years and written an instructional book about coaching the game, had quickly learned that keeping score involved learning new subtleties about the game. "In the very first home game in 1996, I made a simple mistake on what looked like a double play. When it failed, I gave an error to the first baseman. There were four of the Kansas City Royals roving instructors in attendance. And one of them gently reminded me that you can never assume a double play. I changed the play to a fielder's choice." That same night, Mike had missed a pitching substitution, and he admitted that this still occasionally happened. "But I pay a lot more close attention to who's on the mound at the beginning of each inning now."

During the 1996 season, the professor became the student as members of the coaching staff showed him ways of noting the nuances of the game at the professional level. "I learned about the differences between hard and easy plays and not to take my eyes off a play before it's completed. When I was a fan, I thought I watched games with a pretty experienced eye; but it's a lot different now. I watch like a coach; but I also keep an eye on the entire field so I can see an entire play develop. That's really important when you have to account for what happened to all the base runners, not just the batter. And you have to know which fielders handled the ball, no matter where they were on the field when they touched it." And the experience, Clark believed, has helped him when he coached younger players. "I realize now just how much concern and effort is put into teaching athletes to play at their best."

For Dawn Klemish, a communications major, writing about baseball was "the next best thing to playing." She'd become a fan at age four, when she used to sit with her dad, an amateur player, listening to Ernie Harwell's radio broadcasts of the Detroit Tigers, and when she began to play T-Ball. "The 1968 Tigers are my favorite team," she remarked enthusiastically, referring to the world championship club whose great achievement had occurred 13 years before she was born. She went on to explain that her dad talked about them all the time, that she'd watched TV programs and read books about the club, and she'd seen several members play at Old Timers' Games in Tiger Stadium.

A year ago, she'd decided on a career in sports journalism and for several months had performed copy-editing duties and written sports briefs. "One day, when the beat guy couldn't get to a game, I asked if I could cover it." When the game ended, she trooped down to the clubhouse with the other reporters, all of whom were male. She'd been warned what to expect as a woman reporter. "But I didn't expect it to be so bad. A couple of the players came out of the showers with nothing on and began gyrating, and the Dominican players pretended they didn't understand English." But Dawn's most embarrassing moment came when she approached a player who'd come into the room with a towel appropriately wrapped around him and asked if Brad Bouras, whom she wanted to interview for her game story, was still in the shower. "That's me," he said, and she stammered something about still only knowing the players by their numbers, not faces.

Undeterred by her first experience, Dawn studied the craft of talking to players. "That first game, I didn't know how to ask questions; so, on days when I didn't have a story to do, I learned by watching how experienced reporters interviewed. In a way, I tried to become a knowledgeable fan who wanted to find out why things happened. I began informally talking to players during batting practice, and they began to trust and respect me. The other day, I did a piece on a player who just found out he was going up to the Daytona Cubs. We had a really interesting conversation."

And where did she hope this would all lead? It turned out that Dawn wasn't that different from the promoted player she'd written about. "My dream is to be a beat writer for the Detroit Tigers. But there are lots of steps along the way and a lot of people who'd love that job. It will take time and a lot of hard work." And she turned to today's work, studying the game notes and players' averages, preparing for interviews she'd be conducting in just over three hours.

The game that Mike and Dawn watched intently, but to which nearly all the kids running around the park were oblivious, marked the end of the Lugnuts' three-game winning streak. The Bees, led by Odannys Ayala and Donnie Murphy, who each collected three hits, won 5–0. Monahan went 1 for 3; the Bees' Armitage came in in the bottom of the ninth and held the Lugnuts to one hit and a base on balls. As the overfed and over-tired day-campers headed to the school buses, Dawn and her colleagues headed to the clubhouse. On Michigan Avenue, Dean Day pulled his bus close to the sidewalk and stood by the door awaiting the players. "This won't take long," he commented. "They want to get home as soon as they can. Tomorrow's an off-day. So we should be out of here just after three. But," and he paused, "that means we'll hit the Chicago area just in time for rush hour. I hope they've got some new movies with them."

Postseason Postscript

The Lugnuts were unable to maintain their first-place position in the East Division. However, because of their overall record, they earned a wild-card berth in the playoffs. They advanced to the finals, defeating in-state rivals Michigan and West Michigan. However, Peoria defeated them three games to one to win the Midwest League championship. The club attracted 380,820 fans, a decline of close to 24,000 from 2001. However, their 5,770 per-game average was the third-best in the league. Dayton won the attendance championship for the third consecutive season, in spite of their per-

game average decreasing by 13 people. Joey Monahan appeared in 25 games for the Lugnuts, hitting .225 in 80 at-bats. The Burlington Bees' Barry Armitage finished with a 5 and 2 record. He posted a 2.04 earned run average and was credited with 10 saves, tops on his team. It is not known whether Dean Day's clean-up activities inspired the Bees to be tidier on the bus.

7—Scrappers Training to Become Indians: Mahoning Valley of the New York–Pennsylvania League

In 1990, the Pittsfield Mets drew 101,000 fans to Wahconah Park, becoming the first team in the 33-year-history of the New York–Pennsylvania League— which had been a short-season Single-A circuit since 1967— to reach six figures. The Mets played in a park that had been built in 1919, before the introduction of lights, and frequently had to interrupt games because the sun setting directly beyond center field blinded batters. Pittsfield would never again match this attendance. In fact, it would not happen again in the league for four more seasons. However, between 1994 and 2001, the mark would be reached and greatly exceeded 39 times.

That was because nine of the league's franchises had moved to new cities and another into a new ball park. In 1990, the New York–Penn League generally conformed to most fans' images of what low-level professional baseball was like. Nine cities had populations of under 50,000; eight clubs occupied parks that had been constructed before World War II. In 1994, the first of the series of shifts that radically altered the league occurred. The Glens Falls Redbirds became the New Jersey Cardinals and the Niagara Falls Rapids became the Hudson Valley Renegades. Although their parks, both new, were located in relatively rural areas, both new teams were within an hour's drive of New York's expanding suburbs. The Cardinals attracted 156,000 and the Renegades 138,000. No doubt many of the people came into the country during August because the major leagues had gone on strike in early August.

A year later, the city of Erie, which had lost its franchise because of a totally inadequate facility, acquired a new club, which, playing in a brand new downtown park, broke the record set by New Jersey. In 1995, the Sea-

Wolves attracted 181,000 people and over the next two seasons broke their own records. The pattern continued: Elmira moved to Lowell; the Waterton, New York, Indians became the Staten Island Yankees; and the St. Catharines Stompers became the Brooklyn Cyclones. The Cyclones, in a market of 2.3 million, nearly 200 times that of the league's smallest city, Oneonta, New York, played before 289,000 people in 2001, their first season in their Coney Island stadium. In 2002, two more clubs moved. Pittsfield, whose 2001 attendance was just half of what it had been a dozen years earlier, moved to the Albany-Colonie-Troy, New York area, where the team became the Tri-City ValleyCats. The Utica Blue Sox were purchased by Baltimore Oriole great Cal Ripken, who moved them to his hometown of Aberdeen, Maryland, and named them the IronBirds.

Erie's success, paradoxically, resulted in its franchise being moved. Palisades Baseball, the ownership group, used its outstanding record to land an expansion team for Erie in the Double A–Eastern League. In 1999, the SeaWolves moved just over 100 miles south to Mahoning Valley, Ohio, where the franchise, named the Scrappers, promptly broke the Erie attendance record and then, a year later, its own. The move to Mahoning Valley not only benefited the fans and the bank accounts of the owners, but also the Cleveland Indians, who were delighted to have their best first- and second-year prospects playing only an hour away from Jacobs Field. The Indians, with the Scrappers and a Double-A team in Akron and a Triple-A one in Buffalo could save travel time for their roving coaches and increase instructional time for their young recruits.

Thursday, August 8

Cafaro Field is located behind Eastwood Mall, in Niles, Ohio, a part of the eastern Ohio–western Pennsylvania rust belt. After taking a winding road that passes by a Regal Cinemas complex, Sears, and Chuck E. Cheese's, fans drive into a huge chain-link-fenced parking lot and enter the four-year-old home of the Mahoning Valley Scrappers. They have no choice but to pay the $2 parking fee. In the mall parking lots, prominently displayed signs announce that spaces are for shoppers only and that the area is regularly patrolled. Both the park and the mall were built by Cafaro developments, and the parking fee makes both the stadium and mall tenants happy. The Scrappers have a good revenue stream, the mall has lots of space for its customers. The entire complex was designed as a family destination center: in one location, people could shop, dine, and watch either baseball or movies.

Scrappers' officials expected a good Thursday night crowd. It was

Located next to a major mall, Mahoning Valley's Cafaro Field is one of 10 New York–Pennsylvania League parks built since 1994. Once a league of small towns, the New York–Penn has moved into increasingly larger markets, including Brooklyn and Staten Island, New York.

Buck Night, with admissions and regular sodas going for half the price it took to park a car. The ball team had won eight of its last 10 games to pull within two games of the Pinckney Division-leading Auburn Doubledays and were tied with the Staten Island Yankees for a wild-card berth in the New York–Pennsylvania League playoffs. And it was, in the words of an old song, "a beautiful day for a ballgame." Early evening temperatures were expected to be in the low to middle 70s; there would be plenty of sun and a slight breeze. Nearly three hours before the game, cars regularly stopped in front of the advanced sales window, and the occupants got out to buy tickets.

At 4:30 P.M., the Dufour Stages bus pulled up behind the right field fence and the travel-weary members of the Tri-City ValleyCats headed to the visitors' clubhouse. They had spent a lot of time on their "iron lung" since Monday. For two days, they had made the 170-mile round-trip commute from Troy to Oneonta to play against the Tigers. On Wednesday, they'd made the trip one way and, after their game, had boarded the bus for the 428-mile, eight-hour ride to eastern Ohio. They'd had some sleep at the hotel, but were still bleary-eyed. On Saturday night, after their final game of the series with the Scrappers, they'd return 407 miles home for a

Sunday evening game. In contrast, Mahoning Valley had only traveled 137 miles after their Wednesday afternoon contest against the Jamestown Jammers and had enjoyed almost an entire evening of rest, recuperation, and recreation.

The Scrappers' trip was their shortest of the season. In late June, they'd traveled 411 miles to Brooklyn and in mid–July, 410 miles to Staten Island. Had the schedule makers been able to place the two series back to back, they'd have saved Mahoning Valley over 800 miles of travel. Brooklyn and Staten Island were listed in the league's mileage chart as being only 10 miles apart. In just over a week, the Scrappers would be making the league's longest trip: 604 miles to Lowell, Massachusetts. At least after that journey, they'd have a day off—one of three scheduled during the 76-game season. Although the young men sometimes grumbled about the time spent on the buses, farm directors of major-league teams considered the grueling travel an important element in the education of young professionals. Not only did it help develop a camaraderie among athletes who had only recently met each other, but also it introduced them to the rigors of professional life that were so different from what they'd experienced in college and high school.

Shortly after the gates opened, a fan stood on the concourse studying the roster sheets included in his program. "Boy," he remarked, "these guys are sure young; and look, there's a player named Peavey on both teams. I'll bet they're brothers." Both of his observations were correct. The players were young, and the Peaveys were brothers. The ages on the two teams ranged from 18 to 25; the majority were 22 (22 players) and 23 (13). A large number had played college ball, a characteristic of short-season Single-A ball as opposed to rookie league ball, where there were many recent high school graduates and Hispanic teenagers. Farm club directors generally considered that, with at least three more years experience, college draft picks could begin their professional careers at a more advanced level. Each of the 25 players from both teams who had been drafted in 2002 had come from university baseball programs.

At 7:00 P.M., during the presentation of the visiting team lineup, PA announcer Ed Byers announced that Tri-City's third baseman Patrick Peavey was the Buffalo Wild Wings strike-out batter. Should Peavey be rung up, all patrons could take their ticket coupons to one of four area locations to pick up their snack—but only tonight. Peavey obliged the fans, taking a third called strike to end the first inning. When he came to bat again in the fourth, the huge center field scoreboard carried the message: "Pat Peavey: Thanks for the Wings." He went one-for-four for during the evening. His brother, Billy, playing for the Scrappers, went hitless. Patrick later told reporters that, before the game began, his brother had cautioned "You'd better not strike out tonight." The elder sibling did not explain why, leaving his brother to discover only when he came to the plate in the first. Later that night, as Patrick and Billy enjoyed dinner with their parents, Pat and Bill (who had flown in from California to see their sons playing their first professional game against each other), the Scrappers' first baseman admitted that he'd arranged for his brother to be designated as the strikeout batter.

During the game, two press releases were distributed to media representatives. Both concerned promotions involving prominent Ohioans. The first stated that former Cleveland Browns' quarterback Bernie Kozar, who hadn't been able to make an appearance on the day when 1,000 bobbleheads with him in his football uniform were distributed, would be the guest of honor for Friday's game. The second involved Jim Traficant, a local politician, who had recently been expelled from Congress and convicted of bribery. "Former Congressman Traficant played a vital role in attracting the franchise to the Mahoning Valley and we feel that a Jim Traficant Night at Cafaro Field would show our sincere gratitude for his efforts," the release quoted general manager Andy Milovich as saying. "The past year has been very difficult for a lot of people in the community and it is our goal to have some light-hearted fun and show our appreciation for all that he has accomplished." The evening would include the appearance of a Jim Traficant look-alike, Traficant T-shirt prizes, and free admission to individuals wearing toupees (as did the congressman). A late addition to the Scrappers' promotions lineup, it represented the front office's ongoing efforts to enhance their patrons' game-day experiences.

At the end of the seventh inning, the evening's paid attendance was announced as 4,243. "I wonder," quipped a member of the press corps, "if those numbers include the three people in Loge 13." He was referring to the tree house in the back yard of a small residence beyond the right field wall. It was built by the resident so that he and his grandchildren could watch the games. The official figure brought the season's per-game average to 4,113. This was sixth-best in the 14-team league; but it was 600 a game less than last year. Should the team maintain this average for its 13 remaining home games, it would draw 30,000 fewer people than it had in 2001 and it would be the second consecutive year in which attendance had dropped. The Scrappers were experiencing a common minor-league phenomenon: a drop in attendance after the novelty of a new team and/or new stadium had worn off. Most minor-league officials accepted this drop-off as normal and, as the Scrappers had done, worked at maintaining the more realistic third- and fourth-year figures.

The game itself was quick, crisp, and clean. Scrappers' starter right-hander Brian Slocum, a rookie from Villanova University, scattered five hits over five innings and allowed one run to bring his season's record to three wins and no losses. The Scrappers scored a run in each of the first three innings and, after 2 hours and 18 minutes of play, emerged as 3–1 victors. The Auburn Doubledays also won; so Mahoning Valley remained two games behind the division leaders. Outside the clubhouse, Bill and Pat Peavey waited for their sons. Host families picked up the other Scrappers. The ValleyCats boarded their bus, exchanging comments on the visiting team hotel, reported to be one of the poorer in the league. "Hey," one player remarked, "I'm glad I'm on the second floor. If I was on the first, I'd be afraid of the roof caving in, there are so many cracks and stains on the plaster." "I hope the place is safe," another said. "When I opened the window, the pane nearly fell out of the frame." "I guess I'm lucky," a third smirked. "I got a renovated room. The TV remote works and there are pictures on the wall."

By 11 o'clock, the parking lot had emptied and the front-office staff had gone home. One person remained at work at Cafaro Field. George Brown, the clubhouse attendant moved around picking up soiled uniforms and towels and putting them in the heavy-duty washing machine. He gathered the batting-practice jerseys that he'd laundered during the game and hung them in the players' lockers. Then he put the dirty plates and bits of food from the post-game meal in large garbage bags and then picked up bits of tape, broken shoelaces, and gum wrappers. "I'll be here until at least two in the morning," the 17-year-old high school senior remarked. "I got here at noon and have been going non-stop ever since."

For George, who was batboy for the team during its first year in Mahoning Valley, Thursday had begun with his finishing folding yesterday's laundry, rubbing up 50 game balls for the evening's contest, and then performing a variety of odd chores. Just before three in the afternoon, he had headed to nearby downtown Niles to pick up food for the players' pregame meal: makings for peanut butter and jelly sandwiches, meat and cheese, fruit and vegetables, and flavored ices. After batting practice, he took food orders from the coaching staff and filled them at the stadium's concession stands. When the game was underway, he cleaned up the clubhouse, laundered the batting-practice tops, and set out the postgame meal.

"It's a fairly standard routine—clean, wash, get food; clean, wash, get food. But the players treat me well. It's hard work and long hours, and it's not for everyone. It would be great if I could do this at a higher level when I finish school. But right now it's a blast—outstanding!"

George Brown, Scrappers' clubhouse attendant, displays the tropical uniforms worn for each Friday's home game.

Friday, August 9

Although the Scrappers' players were billeted with host families in the Mahoning Valley region, they really considered the clubhouse their home. By 1:30 in the afternoon, three of them had already arrived there. Two watched a soap opera while they munched on sub sandwiches; another sat at a card table reading the sports pages of the local paper. George Brown came in from the back room carrying an armload of vivid green uniform tops and hung one in each locker. "Oh, no," groaned the newspaper reader as he watched the clubhouse attendant place one of the shirts, which sported a parrot where there was usually a hard-hatted bulldog, between his regular Scrappers' home jersey and a Cleveland Indians' T-shirt. "Are we wearing those things again? Why can't we just wear the usual ones?"

The three different tops symbolized the three different facets of the Mahoning Valley team. Although the players performed for a minor-league franchise called the Scrappers and run by Palisades Baseball, they were all under contract to the Cleveland Indians, on whose major-league team they all dreamed of playing. However, because Palisades was in the business of providing family entertainment, their contracts required that, to a certain extent, they cooperate with the non-baseball promotions staged

Cleveland Indians defense coordinator Johnny Goryl brings to his job 54 years of baseball experience as a minor- and major-league player, coach, and manager.

at Cafaro Field, and Friday nights were Jimmy Buffett nights. Fins to the Left, a Buffett tribute band, would play on the party deck for an hour and a half before the game; the front-office staff and many of the ushers, who usually wore plastic yellow hard-hats, would don tropical shirts, and the players would "wear those things again."

One person who wouldn't be wearing "those things" was Johnny Goryl, the defensive coordinator for the Cleveland Indians. He was in town for a few days to inspect the progress of the young players and would be wearing his Indians' practice attire. A native of Cumberland, Rhode Island, he had been in the game for over a half a century, and, by the time the Laureate of Margaritaville was beginning his musical career, Goryl's playing career had been over for almost a decade.

While some of the young players watched *Days of Our Lives* in the main clubhouse, the veteran Goryl sat in the coaches' office watching a videotape of the Scrappers' at-bats in recent games, replaying specific swings, often two or three times, and making brief notes. After studying the tape for close to half an hour, he turned off the set and headed to the playing field, where he leaned against the batting cage looking at some of the players he'd just seen on tape take extra batting practice. After each had stepped out of the cage, Goryl took him aside and talked briefly, sharing his observations and offering suggestions.

Half an hour later, he retired to the first base box seats where he discussed his career in baseball and the Indians' philosophy of player development. "The old Boston Braves signed me out of high school. It was a real thrill," he said, "because I'd grown up admiring their great pitchers Warren Spahn and Johnny Sain. They gave me a $250 signing bonus, which I used as the down-payment on a 1949 Ford Coupe, and a bus ticket for Bluefield, West Virginia, and told me to show up there. Things were a lot simpler then. The manager had complete charge of the players—he handled all the instruction. Sometimes I wonder if that wasn't the best way of doing things." Johnny Goryl worked up the ranks, being traded along the way to the Chicago Cubs' organization. He played briefly with the Cubs, between 1957 and 1959, and then, from 1962 to 1964, for the Minnesota Twins. He appeared in a total of 276 major league games, backing up such established stars as the Cubs' Ernie Banks and Alvin Dark and the Twins' Zoilo Versalles and Rich Rollins. As his career wound down, he turned his thoughts to coaching and, between 1967 and 1981, managed and coached Twins teams at both the minor- and major-league levels. During 1980, while he was coaching the Twins, he replaced long-time manager Gene Mauch. He, in turn, was replaced early the next season by Billy Gardner. In 1982, when they were such stuff as jokes are made of, he became a member of the Cleveland Indians' major-league coaching staff; and, since then, "I've been with them here and there, helping however I could."

Goryl stressed that learning was an ongoing process for both coaches and players. "When they're young, they're really anxious to learn; they want to know what they need to do to develop. At the major-league level, it's more difficult to teach because egos get in the way, particularly during the season. I learned that, to be effective, you have to meet with a player in private." When he worked with the younger players in the Indians' system, it was important to develop in them a professional attitude, both on and off the field. "The Indians have no flexibility regarding lack of professionalism," he stressed, adding that the coaches had to serve as role models as well as teachers. "If you set high standards and live by them, the players will, too." For the Indians, developing professionalism, unlike the focus in some major-league organizations, included winning, which often meant sacrificing personal goals for team ones. He gave an example: "Grounding out might be poor for your average. But in a tight game, it could advance a runner who could score a tying or winning run."

The Indians' development staff worked throughout the year. "We meet in January to set up our philosophy," he explained. "We have a plan for every player in the system. We want each one to develop his strengths and overcome his weaknesses. We come out of that meeting knowing what we want to accomplish with every club in the organization." At the end of spring training, the coordinators in the development staff met with the managers and coaches of all the teams to refine and articulate the season's objectives. "During the spring and summer, we'll pay four visits to each of our full-season clubs and two to the short-season ones. We'll watch the players for four or five days, evaluate the progress of each one since our last visit, and make follow-up suggestions to each manager." The coordinators met at the end of the season to assess the success of their development plan and again in late October to establish lists of which players the Indians wanted to protect at each level.

"We recognize that development is a gradual process. During the first month of a player's rookie year, we don't interfere with his mechanics. He's usually having enough of a challenge adapting to the new style of life in professional ball. For the younger kids it will be the first time away from home; the college kids need to adjust to the game-a-day routine. We give most players three years before deciding which ones don't have a future with us. It takes that long for us to assess their real potential and for them to begin to really develop. There's usually only one or two a year who get dropped before that. They're usually one-tool people who couldn't learn new skills."

The Indians' developmental philosophy had paid off. Sixteen members of the pre-season 40-man major-league roster, 40 percent of the list, had come through the Cleveland farm system. The success of the current rebuilding program would depend heavily on the development of those now in the system. As he prepared to return to the field to talk to some of the possible future Indians, Johnny noted that eleven Scrapper players had shown such promise that they would be attending the fall instructional camp in Winter Haven, Florida.

Not far from where Goryl had been sitting in the grandstand, general manager Andy Milovich had gathered several members of the Scrappers' off-field team: the game-day ushers, ticket takers, and concessions workers. "You are the people who can make or break this franchise," he told them, reminding them of the importance of customer service. "There may be invisible outside evaluators coming to the rest of our home games," he went on. He was emphasizing the fact that the attitude fans would take away from each game they attended would determine whether or not they would return. Success at the gate was not a given; it was a result of daily efforts by the staff. What went on in the stands was probably more important than what went on on the field.

A few minutes later, Milovich sat in his office talking on the phone. "I think it will be fun," he said to the caller. "We'd really like it if Jim's wife could join us. We really want to celebrate him." The call over, he explained that he'd been talking with the secretary of recently expelled congressman Jim Traficant. The special night at the ballpark had been Milovich's idea, one which he hoped would "help everyone in the area laugh and move on. It's meant to reflect Traficant's love of fun and a good joke; in that way it will be a tribute." He admitted that the event would generate considerable publicity, some of it national, for the team. "Some people may be a bit upset, but it's part of making coming to Cafaro Field family entertainment; not just a baseball game."

The 2002 season marked the 33-year-old South Bend, Indiana, native's eighth season with Palisades Baseball, the Scrappers' parent company. In 1995, he'd joined the staff of the Erie SeaWolves, a franchise that had just been relocated from Welland, Ontario, Canada. As the director of group sales, he'd helped the club establish a New York–Penn League attendance record and, after being promoted to general manager the following season, he'd again guided the club to attendance records: 187,000 and 196,000 in 1996 and 1997. When the Pennsylvania city received an expansion franchise in the Double-A Eastern League, the New-York Penn club moved to Mahoning Valley, with Milovich as the general manager. "Traficant was instrumental in our coming here," he explained. "He had

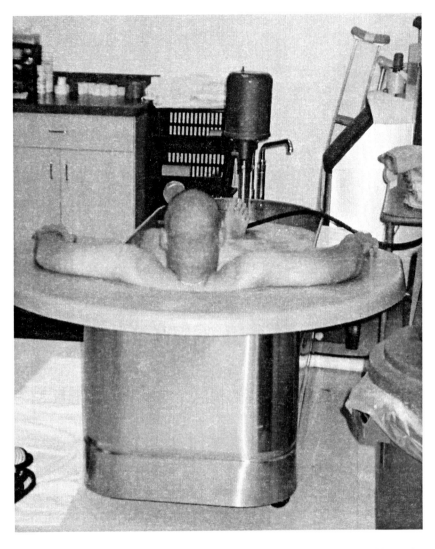

Marshall McDougall, a member of the Cleveland Indians Double-A affiliate the Akron Aeros, relaxes in the whirlpool. By having several of their farm clubs located close to each other, the Indians can easily and quickly send players on injury rehabilitation, as was McDougall, to a lower league to work back into playing shape.

contacted Bob Julian, the New York–Penn president, about obtaining a ball club for this area and learned that Erie would need to relocate after the 1998 season. He worked with the city of Niles and the Cafaro family on the building of a park suitable for pro ball."

Milovich explained the club's instant success. "I think that there were several elements that made us so popular. The people in this area love sports. The football Steelers and baseball Indians are hugely popular. In fact, being affiliated with the Indians has been very important." Two members of the Indians' pitching staff, Ryan Drese and C. C. Sabathia, played briefly with the Scrappers on their way to the major leagues, and, in 2000 shortstop John McDonald spent five days at Cafaro Park on a rehabilitation assignment. In addition to the Cleveland connection, the fact that the Scrappers had won their division championships in 1999 and 2000, advancing to the finals, increased interest. In their third season, the team finished a distant last in their division, and attendance dropped 25,000. "We also suffered from dreadful weather last year," Milovich added. "But I think it was a pretty good year, all things considered," he reasoned. "Our attendance was better than 10 other clubs in the league. Even if the baseball wasn't that good, we still provided lots of fun. It was affordable family entertainment."

Although, like most good general managers, Milovich kept a low profile around the stadium, his style of business was evident. When he'd been in Erie, the pregame ceremonies had begun with the wailing sound of a wolf coming from the loudspeakers followed by the announcer crying, "Let's have a howl of a good time." The fun at Cafaro park began with barking sounds introducing the song *Who Let the Dogs Out* and then the announcement of "Baseball with a bite." "We market aggressively and then work on providing a good atmosphere at the park," he explained.

However, to date this year, attendance had declined considerably— close to 800 fewer people were coming to each game than had last year. "This is our fourth year; and everyone says that the fourth, fifth, and sixth years after a team moves to a new city and a new park are the ones you really have to work very hard. Many people, when they heard we were coming to town, purchased three-year season ticket options. And studies prove that not all renew when the novelty has worn off. But we are working on creative marketing. Group sales will be important—if fact, we will have over 1,600 people in various groups coming on Saturday night. If we run a crisp, friendly operation and provide a good product, a lot of these individuals will come back, later this season or next year."

Milovich spoke in glowing terms about the New York–Penn League. "Ten years ago, people looked down on the league," he remarked. "I think that short-season baseball is the best-kept sports secret in America. However, in the places where it's played—like here—people love it. But we can't rest on our laurels. We have to keep working very hard to make it keep working." Like Jim Traficant Night—there were a lot of details to be worked out to make this creative and, some were saying, outrageous promotion work. But if it did, if people came out and then enjoyed themselves, it would be one element in the club's ongoing success.

Ever the promoter, Milovich expressed annoyance about only one thing—the tree house beyond the right field wall "When one of the Scrappers hits a home run, the old guy who built it has his grandkids light sparklers and wave them around. It's awesome. What bothers me is that it wasn't my idea. I could have got sponsors, and I'd have made comparisons between it and the roof seats on the apartment building outside Wrigley Field in Chicago. It would have been a kind of new twist to the knothole gangs of old."

After the visiting Tri-City ValleyCats finished batting practice, Patrick Peavey waved into the stands and then headed toward right field, stopping briefly to talk to brother Billy before going to the visitors' clubhouse. The recipient of his wave was his mother, Pat, and she watched her sons' brief encounter. "They're so close," she said later. "They always have been. It's a shame they couldn't have been drafted by the same team." She paused, then modified her statement: "They always competed against each other, even before they went to school, so I guess it's natural now that they should be competing in the professional leagues." Looking proudly at her sons, she recalled their early involvement in sports. After she and the boys' father, Bill, divorced, her father suggested that she get them into athletics to keep them healthy and involved. "By the time they were two and three, they were throwing the ball around. And they were very competitive. When they were just starting school, they developed a strikeout game that they'd play against each other for hours. And when they came home, they'd fight all the time with each other about what had happened in their game."

If the boys were constant competitors, they were also constant companions. Billy, who was just a year older, joined a baseball club, and Patrick, not yet eligible to play, became the batboy. After that they played on the same teams during the school year and in the summer until Billy left Brisbane, a small town just south of San Francisco, to attend the University of Southern California on a baseball scholarship. "The separation really strengthened their friendship," their mother remembered. "They weren't rivals on the same club or in the same league. They talked to each other on the phone nearly every night." A year later, Patrick headed to the University of Santa Clara. He'd received an academic scholarship and then made the college baseball team. Now that they were in college, the brothers revived their rivalry. "The two schools played an exhibition game, and Billy hit a home run. Patrick was playing third base and, as Billy rounded third, Patrick turned his back and looked at the outfield."

Billy was not drafted after his third year of college and so, when this year's draft took place, both brothers were eligible. It was a nerve-wracking day for their mother. "In the morning, I went to the jewelry store where I work. I was very nervous and everyone told me I looked really pale. We knew the draft would start at 10 o'clock California time and, after that, every time the phone rang, my heart almost stopped. In about an hour, Patrick called to say that Billy had been picked by Cleveland in the 11th round. We were really happy—and surprised because Billy hadn't expected to go until the second day. Then, on the second day, Patrick called again to say that he'd been picked in the 33rd round by Houston. I burst into tears, I was so happy." There wasn't any time for a family celebration as the brothers had to report immediately to their organizations.

Last night was the family's first chance to be together since the draft. The brothers, once again competitors, were playing to advance their professional careers. Beating each other's team wasn't just a game any more. "I was very nervous—I wanted them both to do well. But Billy's team was in playoff contention, so I wanted them to win. But Patrick had a hit. At dinner, we were all pretty tired, and Billy was quite down because he'd gone 0-for-4. Patrick teased him and said that it was because Billy had made him the strikeout batter. But I said to them both, 'You're really lucky. How many people ever get to follow their dreams?'"

As Pat Peavey was proudly talking about her family, a commotion arose on the concourse 50 feet away. People wearing Hawaiian shirts, Indians' jerseys, and Scrappers' caps, converged near one of the entrances. A few wore Cleveland Browns' jerseys. "I hope there hasn't been an accident," someone remarked. There hadn't: retired Browns' quarterback Bernie Kozar was slowly making his way toward the field where, in a few minutes, he would throw out the first pitch.

After the opening ceremonies had been completed, the ValleyCats came to bat. With a runner on second and two out, cleanup hitter Patrick Peavey walked to the plate and was announced, for the second evening in a row, as the Buffalo Flying Wings strikeout batter. And, for the second night in a row, he obliged the fans, striking out swinging. It was a portent of things to come for the visiting team. In the bottom of the inning the Scrappers sent nine men to the plate and, two walks, three singles, and a triple later, had a five-run lead. Billy Peavey drove in two of these with a single to left. Mahoning Valley added three each in the second and fourth innings and one in the sixth. Their 12–1 victory kept them in the Pinckney Division pennant race, two games behind Auburn, who also won. Tri-City sank to the basement of the four-team Stedler Division. "This game was a real nightmare," remarked official scorer Al Thorne. "In addition to seven pitching changes, there were nine defensive shifts. I'm glad I had the computerized score book; it could have been more confusing if I'd had to do everything by hand."

While Thorne reconciled his scorebook, Pat and Bill Peavey wandered out to the parking lot behind the clubhouses to wait for Patrick and Billy. The young athletes soon showed up and followed their parents to the car. It is not known whether, on their way to the restaurant, Pat and Bill stopped at Buffalo Wild Wings to redeem their ticket stubs for the snacks that their youngest son's strike out had made possible.

Saturday, August 10

Just after noon, over three hours before the scheduled departure from the motel to Cafaro Field, the ValleyCats' bus driver turned on his vehicle and opened the baggage compartment. Players wandered across the parking lot lugging suitcases and equipment bags and deposited them in the hold. A few headed out to the street and began walking to the ballpark, a mile away. Others climbed on the bus, where the air conditioning was on maximum cool. There they settled pillows against the windows, draped their legs over armrests and into the aisle, and began to read, play video games, or nap. The remainder of the team headed back into the motel where they crammed into the two rooms that had been held for the club past the noon checkout time. Tonight's starting pitcher, Mark Hamilton, was given one of the double beds; others sprawled on the remaining beds and on the floors, watching television or cat-napping until it was time to report for work.

They were engaging in one of the most boring rituals of professional baseball—killing time on getaway day. Relatively homeless, they could do little else but endure the three hours ahead. For the ValleyCats, it would be a long day and night. Should the game end by 10 o'clock, they'd be on the bus again by 11 and, then, after a short ride and brief stop at a fast-food restaurant, they'd start the eight-hour-plus trip back to Troy, New York. In four or five years, a few of them might be taking non-stop jet flights from one major-league city to another; they'd be staying in single rooms at five-star hotels; and there would be no early checkouts on getaway days. But in order to deserve those luxuries, these young men would have to make the major-league club, and that involved not only honing their athletic skills, but also learning how to survive the boredom of getaway days and the rigors of all-night bus travel.

While the ValleyCats waited at the motel or on the bus, the members of the Scrappers' front-office team had already begun preparations for the evening's game. At the edge of the parking lot, just behind first base, two people roped off an area half the size of a football field. Others rolled circular tables from a trailer, set them up in the enclosure, and surrounded them with chairs. Then they placed several large rectangular banquet tables on the grass. The area, along with the Bullpen Cafe just inside the park along the right field foul line, would be the site of a pre-game buffet. Close to 1,600 people who had bought new vehicles from the local Saturn dealership would be guests of the company. They'd enjoy as many hot dogs and hamburgers, and as much baked beans, potato salad, chicken, soda, and popcorn as they could ingest in the 90 minutes before the first pitch. And then, wearing the gift T-shirts decorated with the Saturn and Scrappers' logos and an America flag, they'd watch the game as guests of Saturn of Route 422.

The promotion was good business for the car dealership; it was even better business for the Scrappers, because group outings and picnics represented an important source of revenue. Before the season had begun, the club distributed a brochure entitled "DawgGone Fun!" that featured the team's hard-hatted, spiked-collared bulldog logo on the front. In addition to information about season tickets and mini-plan ticket purchases, it featured descriptions of available group outings. The advertising copy proclaimed: "Scrappers' games have always been a great place to get together with family [and] friends.... With our group outings, the Scrappers make it even better." About their picnics, the folder announced: "Take advantage of the ultimate group experience." This volume business was more cost-effective than selling individual tickets. In addition, a large number of the members of a group would purchase souvenirs and, during the game, drinks and snacks. Many would become repeat customers.

Jeff Meehan, one of the people setting up tables, was a Mahoning Valley resident, working for the Scrappers as an intern. Just as the players were beginning their careers on the field, he was beginning his in the front office. A student majoring in business and minoring in sports management at nearby Kent State University, he was one of nine interns on the staff, all of them working for very little or no money but gaining experience for resumes and university credit toward graduation. Nearly all minor-league clubs hired interns during the very busy spring and summer months, to the benefit of both parties. Over a decade ago, general manager Andy Milovich had performed a similar function for the South Bend Silver Hawks of the Midwest League.

Jeff Meehan's father had met Milovich and assistant general manager Dave Smith, both of whom had told him about the internship program and encouraged the father to send his son for an interview. The young man applied and worked in the concessions department during the summer of

Wearing a hard hat, Scrappy, the team mascot, projects the tough, determined look and attitude that is part of the franchise's marketing strategy.

2002, helping with inventory and with hiring and scheduling of game-day staff. "I enjoyed the job," he recalled as he took a breather from moving tables. "And I asked if I could come back in the winter to work in marketing as part of my university program." He did, becoming involved in planning and participating in off-season events. "I passed out candy for an Easter party the Scrappers held at the mall and even wore the Scrappy costume once."

He stayed on after having completed his course requirements, this time in sales, contacting businesses, churches, and community organizations to provide information about group outings. "I always liked sports, and this was a way of being involved. Working in the minor leagues is a lot of fun. I'm learning a lot and, no matter how tired I sometimes feel, coming here to the park doesn't seem like going to work." He plans to attend baseball's Winter Meetings to seek full-time employment. "Working for the Scrappers has really helped me; and I hope I've helped them, too."

At three o'clock the Peavey brothers arrived from the motel where they'd been staying with their parents, said good-bye to their mother and father, and entered their respective clubhouses. Billy's mother had said the previous night that he was the quieter of the two, and when he was asked to talk about his life as a ballplayer, his answers were relatively brief. He spoke about the same events his mother had, but his emphasis was different. About the boys' childhood, he reported: "We must have played together 20 hours a day. We were very competitive with each other, but in organized games each of us wanted the other to do well." It was, he agreed, difficult when the two went to college not to be able to hang around together all the time. His take on the home run he hit for U.S.C. against Patrick's Santa Clara team was that he had laughed when he'd passed his brother standing near third.

Draft days were as anxious a time for him as for his mother. "U.S.C. was in the playoffs, and so my mind was in two places. I was thinking about our upcoming games and also wondering whether I'd be picked in the draft this year or passed over again." After being ignored in 2001, he'd spent the summer in the Cape Cod League and had had a good season. This year the college season had also gone well; he had hit .361 with 15 homers. "As well," he added, "I've been able to finish my degree in economics." When he heard his name called in the 11th round, there were cheers, hugs, and phone calls, but a slight sadness. His brother, listening to the same internet broadcast 400 miles away, had not yet been selected. The U.S.C. playoffs ended on Saturday, June 8, with a loss to Stanford. Bill signed his contract with the Indians on Thursday, June 13, flew to Syracuse a few days late, and joined the Scrappers in time for their first league game, which was played in Auburn.

Coming into Saturday's game, Billy was hitting .272, but had only one home run. He'd appeared in 46 of the club's games. That number along with his 61 games at U.S.C, put him well over the 100 mark for the year. It was the longest season he'd played in so far, and he admitted that the greatest adjustment to professional ball was learning to handle the daily grind. "I've been really careful about my diet and getting plenty of rest—that's the key." He said that he treated the games against his brother as just some more games; but any observer could tell that he was glad to have his best friend on the same field with him again—even if it was in a different uniform.

As batting practice wound down for the Scrappers, some of the ValleyCats stood near the batting cage waiting their turn. Billy Peavey took his final cuts and, after circling the bases, strolled over to where brother Patrick waited, gave him a friendly punch on the shoulder and chatted briefly. As the two stood side-by-side, their differences became quickly apparent. The Scrapper roster listed Billy, the first baseman, at 6 feet 4 inches and 250 pounds; the ValleyCat roster reported that Patrick, the third baseman, was 6 feet 1 inch and 205 pounds. Patrick had the lean face and dark hair of his mother; Billy, the square jaw and sandy hair of his father. Patrick was more animated in their short conversation, gesturing and smiling, while Billy wore only a slight grin as he gave short, quiet responses to his brother. The two high-fived, and Billy headed to the clubhouse for his pregame meal while Patrick leaned on his bat watching the ValleyCat who had preceded him into the cage.

The ValleyCat third baseman laughed when reminded of his brother's nominating him as the strikeout batter. "I wasn't really surprised when I heard the announcement over the loudspeaker; I figured he'd probably suggested it." It was, he went on to explain, part of the competition between the two that had been going on for as long as he could remember. "When we played that strikeout game against the school wall, whoever won would rush home to be able to brag to Mom that he'd won. I didn't beat him very often, but that was okay because I looked up to him. But if he did something, I wanted to do it better. If he had a certain baseball card, I had to have it, too. Even when we were in university, we'd scrap with each other when we came home at Christmas. I tell Billy that, because he was bigger, he always took advantage of me."

Underlying the competitiveness, Patrick emphasized, was a tremendous closeness. The younger brother hadn't just become the batboy of the older brother's Little League team, he'd became the batboy so that he could be with his brother. The next year they had become teammates, and they'd played together on the same teams until Billy went to college. "It was a real shame he left the year before I did," Patrick remarked, "because in my senior year we had a great team; we were state champs and he missed out on it." The two called each other all the time, but they missed each other on more than the playing field. "We used to go to parties together, hang out at school. He's my best friend, and it seemed strange not to have him around."

Once Patrick attended college, their competitiveness took on a new edge—they'd never before been on different teams. They faced each other twice in exhibition games between their colleges. About the homer Billy got for U.S.C against the University of Santa Clara, Patrick had a humorous take. "I tell him he got lucky because he hit it over a short fence." And yes, his brother did smile as he rounded third. But no, Patrick didn't turn his back on Billy at that moment. "Mom always gets that wrong; I was just turning to remind the outfield that there were two away." As Billy's trick for the first two games of the Mahoning Valley Tri-City series proved, the rivalry continued now that both were in professional ball. These were not non-conference games, and each contributed all he could so that his club would defeat the other's. "But after the first two games, we spent a lot of time just talking baseball, just like old times, and offering suggestions to each other about our play." These weren't insider tips, just brothers and best friends sharing the sport as they had since their pre-school days.

By seven o'clock, the guests of Saturn of Route 422 had eaten all they could and turned their attention to the diamond. Patrick Peavey was not the strikeout batter, although he would strike out in the seventh inning. The Scrappers hit for two runs in the bottom of the first. Leadoff batter Ben Francisco, a fifth-round draft pick out of UCLA, led off with a single, adding a couple of points to his league-leading .407 average, then advanced to second on Jon Van Every's infield single. The two scored on Pat Osborn's double. Although the ValleyCats tied the contest in the top of the second, Van Every's sacrifice fly RBI gave the home team a one-run lead in the bottom of the fifth. Patrick Peavey singled and scored the tying run in the top of the sixth. But Mahoning Valley scored three in the bottom of the seventh to go ahead to stay. Van Every put the game out of reach with a two-RBI double down the right field line. The final score: 10 to 5 for Mahoning Valley. The win kept them in the race for the Pinckney Division title; the loss dropped Tri-City deeper into fourth place in the Stedler Division. The crowd of 4,869, most of them happy and a lot of them full, headed to the parking lots.

After the game, the area outside the clubhouses looked like parents' night after a Friday night high school game. Jim Francisco from Anaheim; Jim and Sue Haase of East Lake, Ohio; Pat and Pam Osborne of Bakersfield,

Jon Van Every, who, during the game, learned that he had been promoted to the
Indians' low Single-A team, the Columbus Red Stixx, autographs a baseball before
leaving the Scrappers' clubhouse.

California; and Florann Ramsey of Los Angeles had made the trip to Niles
to see, for the first time, their sons play professional baseball. They con-
gratulated each other on their sons' progress and compared notes on their
lives as baseball parents. Gradually the group broke up as the players
arrived and climbed in waiting cars to head to nearby restaurants to enjoy

parental generosity. Patrick Peavey said goodbye to his brother, mother, and father and boarded the idling ValleyCats' bus.

Soon the parking lot was empty of all but three vehicles. The first was Johnny Goryl's rental car; after he'd completed his notes, he'd be heading back to his motel—not the partially renovated one used by visiting teams. The second, much older and much less shiny and clean, belonged to George Brown and would probably be there for another few hours. The third, a late-model pickup, was the pride and joy of Jon Van Every, and where it would be parked after tonight had, just over an hour ago, become a problem for him.

"I was just ready to head to the on-deck circle in the bottom of the seventh when Chris [manager Chris Bando] called me over. He told me that I'd been called up to the Columbus Red Stixx of the South Atlantic League. I really didn't expect it, so I was surprised and excited. But there were two men on base and we only had a three-run lead. I really had to force myself to concentrate on the job I had to do. I guess I did, because I got a two-run double." There had been an injury on the Cleveland Indians' full-season low Single-A farm team, and they needed a quick replacement.

The move represented a triumph of sorts for Van Every. A native of the small central Mississippi city of Brandon, he'd attended Itawamba Community College, "a really little place that nobody outside the area has ever heard of," he noted. A member of the baseball team, he'd been selected by the Indians in the 29th round of the 2000 draft and then been declared a "draft-and-follow." That meant that Cleveland, who had until a week before the 2001 draft to sign him, could follow his progress as a player during the next season before deciding if they would sign him and, if so, for how much money. Jon joined the Scrappers for the 2001 season, bypassing the Indians' advanced rookie squad in Burlington, North Carolina. He had been enjoying a decent season and was leading the club in home runs, with six, when a shoulder injury had sidelined him for the final month of the season.

"I needed to see good pitching this year to get my average back up. So I'm glad I started here this year. The New York–Penn League has been a good preparation for the South Atlantic League because it's really loaded with pitchers. I'm glad the Indians had faith in me, and I think I can help them in Columbus. But I'll miss the guys on the team; I've made some really good friends. And, I'm not sure what to do about my truck. It won't be hard to pack for tomorrow, because I didn't bring a lot of stuff here. But I'll miss my truck. Maybe someone can drive it halfway for me, and I can meet them on an off-day."

At this point, Johnny Goryl stepped out of the coaches' office to offer his congratulations. "I knew they needed someone and I'm glad it was you—you've really been swinging the bat well." Then, George Brown brought two baseballs for him to sign. "I'm going to have the rest of the guys sign them later, but I want you on them," the clubhouse attendant explained. The young Mississippian obliged, finished packing his equipment bag, and headed to his truck. Tomorrow, he'd fly from Youngstown to Detroit and from there to Greensboro, North Carolina, where his new team would be playing. His ultimate destination lay only fifty miles to the west of where his truck was parked: Jacobs Field, home of the Cleveland Indians. But if he reached it, Jon Van Every would have traveled many thousands of miles, playing for clubs in Columbus, Georgia; Kinston, North Carolina; Akron, Ohio; and Buffalo, New York. For this Scrapper to become an Indian, it would take four or five years to reach a destination only an hour away on the freeway.

Postseason Postscript

The Scrappers ended the season in second place in the Pinckney Division, one game behind the Auburn Doubledays, and so did not make the playoffs. The ValleyCats remained in the cellar of the Stedler Division. Billy and Patrick Peavey finished with .279 and .236 averages respectively. Ben Francisco's average dropped over 50 points during the last month of the season. However, he still won the batting title, with a .349 average. The Scrappers attracted 158,000 to Cafaro Field, a decrease of 23,000 from 2001 and 213,000 fewer fans than attended the home games of the Brooklyn Cyclones, who established a short-season attendance record. In all, nine New York–Pennsylvania League teams drew over 100,000 people to their games. This included the Tri-City Valley-Cats, who attracted 108,000 spectators in the club's first season away from Pittsfield.

8—Moving Up, Moving On, Moving Out

By mid–September, the minor-league diamonds and the stands surrounding them were empty. The players had departed, and the fans had turned their attention to high school and college football games. But in the front offices beneath the grandstands, in league offices, and in the player development offices of the 30 major-league teams, minor-league baseball began its period of greatest change: the six months of fall and winter.

Two weeks after Labor Day, the National Association announced that 38,639,142 people had attended minor-league games during the 2002 season—a decline of 169,000 from the previous year, but still the third-highest total since World War II. Bad weather in the northeast, the midwest, and the western Canadian prairies contributed to the decline, as did the fact that attendance for the four lame-duck franchises—Calgary, Shreveport, Columbus, Georgia, and Macon—showed a decline of 192,000. The five clubs that moved into new stadiums during the season posted a combined increase of 720,000, while Aberdeen, Maryland, and Tri-City, New York, playing in new parks and new cities, attracted 340,000 between them. Sacramento and Memphis of the Pacific Coast League again led all clubs with 817,000 and 794,000 fans respectively; the Brooklyn Cyclones set a short-season record of 317,000.[1]

As the Calgary Cannons wound down their final Pacific Coast League season—in which 18 game of their home games were canceled because of bad weather or field conditions—and prepared to moved to Albuquerque, Mel Kowalchuk, who, after 21 seasons, had resigned as general manager of the Edmonton Trappers, prepared for the Cannons' arrival in the New Mexico city. As Albuquerque's new general manager, he oversaw the construction of a new stadium on the site of the recently demolished

(*Above and facing page*) After the 2000 season, the Albuquerque Dukes of the Pacific Coast League moved to Portland, Oregon. Albuquerque Sports Stadium, built in 1969, was torn down and construction of a new park begun on the same location. In 2003, it would become the home of the city's new Pacific Coast League team, the Isotopes.

Albuquerque Sports Stadium, home of the departed Dukes. As the $28 million park rose above the playing field, owner Ken Young announced that the club would be nicknamed the Isotopes. The choice made double business sense. First, the nickname Dukes belonged to the owners of the Portland Beavers, who had purchased it as part of the Albuquerque franchise that they'd moved to the Oregon city after the 2000 season. They weren't going to part with it unless they received a considerable fee. The name Isotopes was free. Moreover, it had been well-publicized on the hit television show *The Simpsons*. In one episode, Homer's favorite team, the Isotopes, were in danger of being sold and moved to Albuquerque. Although a few baseball purists complained, the name became wildly successful. Just before Christmas 2002, four months before the Isotopes' first home game, the club had sold $200,000 worth of hats, T-shirts, and other merchandise, all of it sporting the team's logo. In the last few weeks before the April 12, 2003, Opening Day, the demand for souvenirs and clothing was so high that suppliers had great difficulty in keeping up with orders.

The second highly publicized off-season franchise move took place in the Texas League. The Shreveport Swamp Dragons became the Frisco

RoughRiders. Although the move was not announced until the close of the 2001 season, rumors of its happening had been circulating since Hank Stickney's Mandalay Sports had purchased the team the year before. Stickney's organization had earlier bought and moved the California League team that became the Rancho Cucamonga Quakes. His group had also purchased the Rockford, Illinois, franchise in the Midwest League for the purpose of moving it to Dayton, Ohio. Interestingly, the new Shreveport owners changed the team's name from Captains to Swamp Dragons, perhaps to piggyback on the incredibly successful merchandising efforts of the Dayton Dragons. Before the 2002 season, the Shreveport front-office operation was slashed to two full-time employees. Fans in the Louisiana city responded to the at-first-rumored and then-stated move to Texas by not showing up in very large numbers. In 2001, Shreveport attendance dropped from 125,000 to 59,000, and then, in 2002, to 25,000.

However, greener pastures, both on the playing field and in the bank accounts awaited the franchise 185 miles west in the affluent north Dallas suburb of Frisco. The club would begin the 2003 season in a state-of-the-art 9,000-seat stadium built jointly by Mandalay and a group headed by Tom Hicks, owner of the Texas Rangers. In an article entitled "Double A ball never looked this expensive," the *Wichita Eagle* reported that season tickets to the RoughRiders ranged from $1,050 to $2,100.[2] With an average household income of $140,000, the area's residents and businesses were purchasing the tickets very quickly. The fact that the club would be affiliated with the nearby Rangers was cited as a secondary—although important—reason for the brisk sales.

In less-publicized moves, three of the five Georgia teams in the South Atlantic League moved north. The Atlanta Braves, owners of the Macon franchise, relocated the club in the northern Georgia town of Rome because Macon city officials wouldn't build a park to replace 73-year-old Luther Williams Field. Ohio resident Rita Murphy Cafagna purchased the Columbus Red Stixx and transferred the franchise to Eastlake, a suburb of Cleveland. The Indians would now have four of their farm teams within a three-hour drive of Jacobs Field. And, in a surprise move, the South Georgia Waves, who'd moved to Albany, Georgia, from Wilmington, North Carolina, just three weeks before the 2002 season, announced in mid-March that they would shift their operations to Golden Field, the Columbus park left vacant by the departure of the Red Stixx. In another move, the Pioneer League's Medicine Hat Blue Jays, after four consecutive seasons of averaging only 25,000 in attendance but still making a very small profit, moved to Helena, Montana, which had lost its Pioneer League team at the end of the 2000 season.

In September, important moves of another nature occurred. Major-league clubs moved 26 of their farm teams to different minor-league clubs. Such changes occur at the end of each even-numbered season as the big-league clubs seek minor-league cities that have better facilities or weather or that are closer to the major-league parent or to other teams in their farm system. Three interrelated affiliation shifts that were announced in the fall of 2002 were seen as having possible long-term implications. For the two previous years, the Rochester Red Wings of the International League had been expressing their displeasure about the quality of players sent them by their parent club, the Baltimore Orioles. While for most minor-league franchises the caliber of talent on the field does not appreciably affect customer satisfaction with the ballpark entertainment experience, in Rochester it does. Over the 41 years of the affiliation, such greats as Cal Ripken, Jr., Boog Powell, Jim Palmer, and Earl Weaver had worn Red Wing uniforms.

As the summer of 2002 wore on and it became apparent that Rochester was going to sever its relationship with the Orioles, it also became known that the Minnesota Twins wanted to move their Triple-A affiliate from Edmonton because of the extreme cold in which the Trappers' April home games were played, and that Ray Pecor, owner of the Ottawa Lynx, hoped to be able to move his struggling International League franchise to a better market in the northeast or middle–Atlantic states. A Baltimore-Ottawa relationship had great possibilities as a future relocation of the Lynx would place all of the Orioles' full-season affiliates within a few hours' drive of each other. And so Baltimore and Ottawa signed a deal. That left Minnesota with a warmer place to head to—Rochester. Edmonton and Montreal, the last teams without partners, were left with each other. One of the ironies of these interrelated moves occurred during the ceremonies marking Edmonton's 2003 home opener. During the festivities, the Pacific Coast League pennant and trophy that the Trappers had won in 2002 were displayed at home plate. However, no players and coaches were there to receive the fans' applause. Those who hadn't either moved up to the Twins or moved on to other clubs were now playing in Rochester.

As the franchise and affiliation moves were taking place, the players were also on the move. For many, this meant a return to their winter residences: either their home towns or, in increasing numbers, the areas around the training complexes of their major-league teams, where they could have access to supervised training facilities and could play golf to their hearts' content. For others, well over 1,500 minor leaguers, the fall meant moving to other ballparks to continue their development in the months before they reported to spring training.

On Sunday, September 1, the day major-league teams expanded their rosters from 25 to 40, 450 minor leaguers became big leaguers. During the final four weeks of the 2002 major-league season, 61 minor leaguers made their big-league debuts. One of these was Edmonton's Mike Ryan, who entered a game for the Minnesota Twins on September 20. Although he would hit only .091 in seven games, the experience marked a joyous conclusion to 19 consecutive months of playing baseball.

In late September, close to 900 promising first- and second-year players reported to major-league complexes in Florida and Arizona to become members of the Fall Instructional League, which provided intensive training designed to enhance and even accelerate their development. Among these were Billings' Chris Gruler, Victor Jumelles, and Walter Olmstead. At the same time, the top Double- and Triple-A prospects of each major league club, along with the occasional rookie major leaguer, joined the six-team Arizona Fall League, which has earned the appellation of ultimate baseball finishing school because nearly all of its players have graduated to either the National or American League. Included in this group were Edmonton's Brad Thomas, Lake Elsinore and Portland's Xander Nady, and El Paso's Chad Tracy.

And still another 500 players reported to winter leagues in the Dominican Republic, Mexico, Puerto Rico, and Venezuela (the Venezuelan League suspended operations early in the season because of civil unrest in the country). Although a large number of the players were athletes returning to their own countries, all the leagues permitted a limited number of imports—from five to nine—on each team.

As 2003's spring training neared its end, many players prepared to move up to higher levels. Nady returned to the roster of the San Diego Padres after a two-season absence; Edmonton's Michael Cuddyer and El Paso's Robby Hammock became members of the Minnesota Twins and Arizona Diamondbacks respectively. Billings's Chris Gruler, Onix Mercado, and Victor Jumelles started their seasons at low Single-A Dayton. Mike Campo of Rancho Cucamonga was drafted from the Angels by the Athletics and assigned to Midland of the Double-A Texas League. El Paso's Chris Cervantes, Mike Gosling, and Tracy reported to Triple-A Tucson, Burlington's Barry Armitage to high Single-A Wilmington, Mahoning Valley's Billy Peavey to high Single-A Kinston, and his brother, Tri-City's Pat, to low Single-A Lexington. Jon Van Every remained in the low Single-A South Atlantic League, although the team had moved to Eastlake, Ohio. Walter Olmstead, Troy Cairns, and Joey Monahan returned to extended spring training, possibly to resume their careers in the short-season leagues.

The offseason was also a time of promotion or advancement for many minor league coaches and trainers. Edmonton's John Russell, named minor-league manager-of-the-year by *Baseball America*, left the Minnesota organization after eight years of managing to become third base coach of the Pittsburgh Pirates. He was rumored to be first in line should the Pirates' decide to replace incumbent manager Lloyd McClendon. El Paso's manager Chip Hale became the Diamondbacks' minor-league infield coordinator and Mark Davis, their major-league bullpen coach. Billings' trainer Steve Baumann, a rising star in the Cincinnati organization, jumped three rungs of the Reds' ladder and opened the season as trainer of Chattanooga of the Southern League.

But for some minor leaguers, April 2002 would prove to be the cruelest month. El Paso's Jack Santora, who for four seasons had made up for his diminutive stature through hustle and intensity, received his release in the final week of spring training. So, too, did Todd Shiyuk of Lake Elsinore. He had beaten cancer, but he couldn't beat the numbers game.

As April 3, 2003, the opening date of the minor-league season approached, the days lengthened and grew warmer. In more southerly cities, the grass turned greener and trees developed a pale lime sheen as leaves popped from their buds. In minor-league training camps and minor-league cities, fans, front-office officials, and players anticipated new beginnings. In the upcoming year, there would be new teams, new parks, new players, and new managers. And for the people in the stands, creative administrators would devise new contests and new entertainments. Because of these changes, but mainly because it was spring and opening day was fast approaching, fans, officials, and players would all have the feeling that they were about to experience a brand new ballgame.

Epilogue

That's a Wrap for the Trap:
Edmonton's triple-A baseball franchise
Has been sold and is heading to Texas.
—October 24, 2003

Almost half a century after reading the newspaper headlines announcing the collapse of the Victoria Tyees of the Western International League, I stared at headlines that announced that another minor-league team that had been the focus of many summer evenings would soon be no more. The Trappers of the Pacific Coast League had been sold to a group headed by Hall-of-Fame pitcher Nolan Ryan and would be moved to Round Rock, an affluent suburb of Austin, Texas. The 2004 season would be the final year that the best baseball outside of the major leagues would be played in Canada's northern-most and sixth-largest city.

To a very young teenaged boy, the news about the demise of the Tyees came as a surprise. I didn't know that minor-league baseball was entering what would be a 20-year depression, that my favorite team was one of many that couldn't survive in the face of television, air conditioning, and a transportation boom that made the lake or the seashore as easily accessible as the old downtown or fairgrounds ballpark. I wasn't surprised that the Trappers had been sold, just that it had happened so soon. Rumors had been circulating in baseball circles and in American sports pages that the Trappers were an endangered species, and the senior administrators of the Trappers vehemently denied the rumors (an action which, along with a manager's receiving a vote of confidence, indicates that change is imminent).

In the official press release announcing the sale, the Trappers emphasized its necessity. "Scheduling, air and cross-border travel and the Canadian

207

dollar were factors in the PCL being desirous of not having a Canadian team in the league." However, scheduling was difficult for all teams in the far-flung league; crossing the international border presented inconveniences rather than difficulties, and, during 2003, the value of the Canadian dollar increased by 25 percent. Conversations with baseball insiders left the impression that the league had not pressured the Edmonton Eskimos, the professional football team that owned the Trappers, to sell.

The Eskimos had purchased the club in 2000 for a price reported to be 6.5 million dollars Canadian ($4.3 million American at that time). The organization sold the team not quite four years later for $10.5 million American, an extremely healthy return on the initial investment. The sale was another example of the escalating value of minor league franchises over the last decade. Unlike Tyee fans who, in 1954, were casualties of a minor-league bust, the Edmonton Trapper fans of 2004 would be the victims of the minor-leagues' major boom.

Notes

Preface

1. These and other statistics in this preface are based on standings and attendance figures published in *The Encyclopedia of Minor League Baseball*, 2nd ed., edited by Lloyd Johnson and Miles Wolff (Durham, NC: Baseball America, 1997).

2. Lamb, David, *Stolen Season: a Journey Through America and Baseball's Minor Leagues* (New York: Random House, 1991).

3. Green, Ernest J., *The Diamonds of Dixie: Travels Through the Southern Minor Leagues* (Lanham, MD: Madison Books, 1995).

4. Stott, Jon C., *Leagues of Their Own: Independent Professional Baseball, 1993–2000* (Jefferson, NC: McFarland, 2001).

Introduction

1. The names of the leagues are only roughly indicative of the areas in which their teams played. For example, until 1993, when Ottawa joined the circuit, the International League hadn't had a non–U.S. team since Toronto departed after the 1967 season. When it absorbed teams from the American Association, the Pacific Coast League stretched from Vancouver, Canada, to Nashville, Tennessee, which was closer by nearly a thousand miles to the Atlantic than the Pacific. By the 2003 season, the South Atlantic League would stretch from southern Georgia into New Jersey and the Ohio shores of Lake Erie. The Texas, New York–Penn, and Carolina leagues extended beyond the states that gave them their names. Only in the California and Florida State Leagues did all the teams reside within the named states.

2. See "Minor League Baseball Regular Season Attendance Since World War II," www.minorleaguebaseball.com/pagetemplate/3col_gray_hdr.asp?pageid=844. Other attendance figures are drawn from Lloyd Johnson and Miles Wolff, eds., *The Encyclopedia of Minor League Baseball*, 2nd ed. (Durham, NC: Baseball America, 1997).

3. Many of these ideas have been summarized in Johnson and Wolff, *The Encyclopedia of Minor League Baseball*, 2nd ed. See also *Baseball America*, 18/4 (December 24, 2001), a 20th anniversary issue focusing on the last quarter of the 20th century.

4. Klinkowitz, Jerry, *Owning a Piece of the Minors* (Carbondale: Southern Illinois University Press, 1999), 14.

5. Lingo, Will, "Minor League Licensing Windfall Comes to an End," *Baseball America*, 18/4 (February 16, 1988), 24.

1—Minor League Baseball's Winter of Discontent

1. www.minorleaguebaseball.com/pagetemplate/3col_gray_hdr.asp?pageid=1614.
2. www.minorleaguebaseball.com/pagetemplate/3col_gray_hdr.asp?pageid=1614.
3. www.minorleaguebaseball.com/pagetemplate/3col_gray_hdr.asp?pageid=1611.
4. www.minorleaguebaseball.com/pagetemplate/3col_gray_hdr.asp?pageid=1614.

2—The Great White North

1. Panek, Richard, *Waterloo Diamonds: A Midwestern Town and Its Minor League Team* (New York: St. Martin's Press, 1995), 80.
2. *Baseball America* (May 14, 2001), 15.
3. *Edmonton Journal* (April 14, 2002), C 10.
4. www.minorleaguebaseball.com.
5. www.australianbaseballhistory.webcentral.com.

3—At the Epicenter of Baseball

1. "Magnitude 10," *Ontario Daily Bulletin*, April 4, 2002, 2.
2. "Quakes' 2002 Preview," *Inland Valley Times*, April 4, 2002, 1.
3. *Baseball America Prospect Handbook 2002* (Durham, NC: Baseball America, 2002), 378.
4. Geffner, Glenn, ed., *2002 San Diego Padres' Media Guide* (San Diego: San Diego Padres, 2002), 157.

4—Cincinnati's Kids Come to Billings

1. Breton, Marcos, and Jose Luis Villega, *Away Games: The Life and Times of a Latin Baseball Player* (New York: Simon and Schuster, 1999).

5—Down in a West Texas Town

1. Bill Knight, "Diablos Open 'Marquee' Homestand," *El Paso Times* (July 6, 2002), C1.
2. Bill Knight, "Diablos Fall Behind Early, Drop Game to Express," *El Paso Times* (July 9, 2002), C1.

6—Turning Diamonds into Lugnuts

1. Richard Panek, *Waterloo Diamonds* (), 15.
2. Panek, 16.
3. Panek, 167-8.
4. Panek, 172.
5. Frank Jossi, "Take Me out to the Ball Game: Going Bonkers Over Minor League Baseball," reprint from *Planning* (May 1998), [2].
6. Jossi, [3].
7. Prout, David and Seth Van-Hoven, eds. *2002 Lansing Lugnuts Information Guide* (Lansing, MI: Lansing Lugnuts, 2002), 74.

8—Moving Up, Moving On, Moving Out

1. For attendance figures see www.milb.com/pageblank/?id=347.
2. "Double-A ball never looked this expensive," *Wichita Eagle* (Sunday, August 25, 2002), www.kansas.com/mid/eagle/sports/3931533

Bibliography

Websites

www.australianbaseballhistory.webcentral.com
www.baseballamerica.com
www.minorleaguebaseball.com
www.oursportscentral.com

Periodical Articles

Baseball America. Biweekly from August 21, 1995 (volume 15, number 15) to March 17, 2003 (volume 23, number 6).
"Double-A Baseball Never Looked This Expensive." *Wichita Eagle* (Sunday, August 25, 2002). www.kansas.com/mid/eagle/sports/3931533.
Gallant, Colin. "Trappers Win Opener." *Edmonton Journal* (Sunday, April 14), C10.
Jossi, Frank. "Take Me Out to the Ball Game: Going Bonkers over Minor League Baseball." Reprint from *Planning* (May 1998).
Knight, Bill. "Diablos Fall Behind Early, Drop Game to Express." *El Paso Times* (July 9, 2002), C1.
_____. "Diablos Open 'Marquee' Homestand." *El Paso Times* (July 6, 2002), C1.
"Magnitude 10." *Ontario Daily Bulletin,* April 4, 2002.
"Quakes' 2002 Preview." *Inland Valley Times.* April 4, 2002.

Books

Acton, Jay, with Nick Bakalar. *Green Diamonds: The Pleasures and Profits of Investing in Minor League Baseball.* New York: Zebra Books, 1993.
Adams, Bruce, and Margaret Engel. *Fodor's Baseball Vacations.* 3rd ed. New York: Fodor's Travel Publications, 2002.
Adelson, Bruce, Rod Beaton, Bill Koenig, and Lisa Winston. *The Minor League Baseball Book.* New York: Macmillan, 1995.
Ballew, Bill. *Brave Dreams: A Season in the Atlanta Braves' Farm System.* Indianapolis: Masters Press, 1996.

Benson, Michael. *Ballparks of North America*. Jefferson, NC: McFarland, 1989.

Benson, Robert. *The Game: One Man, Nine Innings, a Love Affair with Baseball*. New York: Jeremy P. Tarcher/Putnam, 2001.

Blahnik, Judith, and Phillip S. Schultz. *Mud Hens and Mavericks: The New Illustrated Travel Guide to Minor League Baseball*. New York: Viking Studio, 1995.

Blake, Mike. *The Minor Leagues: A Celebration of the Little Show*. New York: Wynwood Press, 1991.

Bosco, Joseph. *The Boys Who Would Be Cubs: A Year in the Heart of Baseball's Minor Leagues*. New York: William Morrow, 1990.

Breton, Marcos, and Jose Luis Villegas. *Away Games: The Life and Times of a Latin Baseball Player*. New York: Simon & Schuster, 1999.

Callis, Jim, and Will Lingo, eds. *Baseball America Prospect Handbook 2002*. Durham, NC: Baseball America, 2002.

Chadwick, Bruce. *Baseball's Hometown Teams: The Story of the Minor Leagues*. New York: Abbeville Press, 1994.

Chance, Elbert. *The Blue Rocks Past and Present: Wilmington's Baseball Team 1940–1999*. Wilmington, DE: Cedar Tree Books, 2000.

Davis, Hank. *Small-Town Heroes: Images of Minor League Baseball*. Iowa City: University of Iowa Press, 1997.

Deal, David. *Prospects: A Portrait of Minor League Baseball*. Baltimore: Alter Communications: 2001.

Dobbins, Dick. *The Grand Minor League: An Oral History of the Old Pacific Coast League*. Emeryville, CA: Woodford Press, 1999.

Edwards, Christopher T. *Filling in the Seams: The Story of Trenton Thunder Baseball*. Moorestown, NJ: Middle Atlantic Press,1997.

Fireovid, Steve, and Mark Winegardner. *The 26th Man: One Minor League Pitcher's Pursuit of a Dream*. New York: Macmillan, 1991.

Geffner, Glenn, ed. *2002 San Diego Padres Media Guide*. San Diego: San Diego Padres, 2002.

Gmelch, George. *Inside Pitch: Life in Professional Baseball*. Washington: Smithsonian Institution Press, 2001.

_____, and J. J. Weiner. *In the Ballpark: The Working Lives of Baseball People*. Washington: Smithsonian Institution Press, 1998.

Green, Ernest J. *The Diamonds of Dixie: Travels Through the Southern Minor Leagues*. Lanham, MD: Madison Books, 1995.

Hemphill, Paul. *The Heart of the Game: The Education of a Minor-League Ballplayer*. New York: Simon & Schuster, 1996.

Holcomb, Steve. *It's Raining Rock Cats and Sea Dogs: A Fan's Guide to the AA Ballparks and Towns of the Eastern League*. Bowie, MD: Pax River Press, 1997.

Humber, William. *Diamonds of the North: A Concise History of Baseball in Canada*. Toronto: Oxford University Press, 1995.

Johnson, Arthur T. *Minor League Baseball and Local Economic Development*. Urbana: University of Illinois Press, 1993.

Kahn, Roger. *Good Enough to Dream*. Garden City, NY: Doubleday, 1985.

Klinkowitz, Jerry. *Owning a Piece of the Minors*. Carbondale: Southern Illinois University Press, 1999.

Lamb, David. *Stolen Season: A Journey Through America and Baseball's Minor Leagues*. New York: Random House, 1991.

Lazzaro, Sam. *More Than a Ballgame: An Inside Look at Minor League Baseball*. Blacksburg, VA: Pocahontas Press, 1997.

Lechner, Tammy. *In the Cal: Pastime Goes Primetime in California's Minor League*. Laguna Beach, CA: Still Productions, 1994.

Mandelaro, Jim, and Scott Pitoniak. *Silver Seasons: The Story of the Rochester Red Wings*. Syracuse: University of Syracuse Press, 1996.

Mandell, Brett H. *Minor Players, Major Dreams*. Lincoln: University of Nebraska Press, 1997.

National Association Agreement. St. Petersburg, FL: National Association of Professional Baseball Leagues: 1997.

Obojsky, Robert. *Bush League: A History of Minor League Baseball*. New York: Macmillan, 1975.

Okkonen, Marc. *Minor League Baseball Towns of Michigan: Adrian to Ypsilanti*. Grand Rapids, MI: Thunder Bay Press, 1997.

O'Neal, Bill. *The American Association: A Baseball History 1902–1991*. Austin, TX: Eakin Press, 1991.

_____. *The International League: A Baseball History 1884–1991*. Austin, TX: Eakin Press, 1992.

_____. *The Pacific Coast League: A Baseball History 1903–1988*. Austin, TX: Eakin Press, 1990.

_____. *The Southern League: Baseball in Dixie 1885–1994*. Austin, TX: Eakin Press, 1994.

_____. *The Texas League 1888–1987: A Century of Baseball*. Austin, TX: Eakin Press, 1987.

Panek, Richard. *Waterloo Diamonds: A Midwestern Town and Its Minor League Team*. New York: St. Martin's Press, 1995.

Pietrusza, David. *Minor Miracles: The Legend & Lore of Minor League Baseball*. South Bend, IN: Diamond Communications, 1995.

Quigel, James P., Jr., and Louis E. Hunsinger, Jr. *Gateway to the Majors: Williamsport and Minor League Baseball*. University Park: Pennsylvania State University Press, 2001.

Simpson, Alan, ed. *Baseball America Directory 2002*. Durham, NC: Baseball America, 2002.

_____. ed. *Baseball America's 1991 Almanac*. Durham, NC: American Sports Publishing, 1991. Also each succeeding almanac through the 2003 edition.

_____, and John Virshbo, eds. *Super Register 2002*. Durham, NC: Baseball America and SportsTicker, 2002.

Sullivan, Neil J. *The Minors: The Struggles and the Triumph of Baseball's Poor Relation from 1876 to the Present*. New York: St. Martin's Press, 1990.

Sumner, Jim L. *Separating the Men from the Boys: The First Half-Century of the Carolina League*. Winston-Salem, NC: John F. Blair, 1994.

Violanti, Anthony. *Miracle in Buffalo: How the Dream of Baseball Revived a City*. New York: St. Martin's Press, 1991.

Wolff, Miles, and Lloyd Johnson. *The Encyclopedia of Minor League Baseball*. 2nd ed. Durham, NC: Baseball America, 1997.

Wright, Branson. *Rookie Season: A Year with the West Michigan Whitecaps*. Grand Rapids, MI: William B. Eerdmans, 1995.

Index